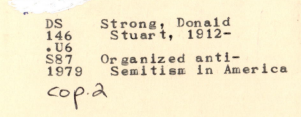

ORGANIZED ANTI-SEMITISM IN AMERICA

American Council On Public Affairs

Dedicated to the belief that the extensive diffusion of information is a profound responsibility of American democracy, the American Council on Public Affairs is designed to promote the spread of authoritative facts and significant opinions concerning contemporary social and economic problems.

It endeavors to contribute to public knowledge through the publication of books, studies and pamphlets, encouragement of adult education, stimulation of interest in non-fiction materials, initiation of research projects, organization of lectures and forums, arrangement of radio broadcasts, issuance of timely press releases, compilation of opinions on vital issues, and cooperation with other organizations.

The Council believes that the facts presented and opinions expressed under its sponsorship deserve careful attention and consideration. It is not, however, committed to these facts and opinions in any other way. Those associated with the Council necessarily represent different viewpoints on public questions.

ORGANIZED
ANTI-SEMITISM
IN AMERICA

The Rise of Group Prejudice
During the Decade 1930-40

DONALD S. STRONG, Ph.D.

GREENWOOD PRESS, PUBLISHERS
WESTPORT, CONNECTICUT

Library of Congress Cataloging in Publication Data

Strong, Donald Stuart, 1912-
    Organized anti-Semitism in America.

    Reprint of the ed. published by the American Council
on Public Affairs, Washington, D. C.
    Includes bibliographies.
    1. Antisemitism--United States. 2. Jews in the
United States--Politics and government. 3. United
States--Politics and government--1933-1945.
I. American Council on Public Affairs. II. Title.
DS146.U6S87 1979   301.45'19'24073   78-26198
ISBN 0-313-20883-2

Copyright, 1941, by the American Council on Public Affairs

This edition published in 1941 by the American Council on
Public Affairs, Washington, D.C.

Reprinted in 1979 by Greenwood Press, Inc.
51 Riverside Avenue, Westport, CT 06880

Printed in the United States of America

10 9 8 7 6 5 4 3 2 1

INTRODUCTION

By Clyde R. Miller *

When Adolph Hitler set out to become dictator of Germany and then of Europe, and finally, of the world, he began with a definite propaganda plan. This had for its immediate purpose the unification of Germany, and the disorganization of the Western democracies. This he accomplished by skillful utilization of psychological processes and propaganda techniques.

He appealed primarily to the processes of frustration, displacement, and anxiety. The Germans were frustrated—the natural result of a series of disasters: loss of the war; inflation; and then, the impact of devastating depression. To the astute propagandist frustrated people are made to order. Hitler, the most astute propagandist of modern times, gave the German people new goals for which they could pitch in and work—goals which to them seemed to provide a way out of their troubles. He set before them hopes and aspirations, in the seeking of which they could canalize their frustration in terms of aggressive action. Shrewdly, to the masses, he gave an outlet for their aggressiveness: destroy the Jews.

By the psychological process of displacement the Germans were eager to shift the blame for defeat, inflation, and depression upon some scapegoat. Historically, the Jews provided it. For many centuries they had been an "outside group," different from the great majority group of Christian Germans. It is in the nature of man to fear and suspect groups whose practices and rituals differ from their own. The Christian churches had done little to break down the basis for such fear and suspicion. Thus, Hitler found at his disposal in the small minority Jewish group a scapegoat which could be blamed for all of Germany's troubles. A small Catholic group, a small Masonic group, a small group of capitalists or bankers—psychologiaclly, *any* such group would have answered the same purpose. Indeed, Hitler made use of these other minority groups as scapegoats, but he achieved mass hatred most effectively by thus utilizing the Jewish minority. Centuries of "conditioning" made that end more easily obtainable, plus the fact that the Jews in Germany were such a small minority.

To win the "upper classes" and the dwindling middle class, Hitler found another scapegoat: the Communists. It is quite beside the point to say that in the original platform of the Nazi Party he included many

---

* Associate Professor of Education at Teachers College, Columbia University, and Secretary of the Institute for Propaganda Analysis.

i

Communist planks. Obviously, he did—purposefully, to get mass appeal—but he didn't label the planks "Communist". On the contrary, he made of Communism a "poison word" to win the classes—the business men, bankers, industrialists, the Protestant and Catholic churchmen, the statesmen, and the newspaper owners. These German leaders feared Communism. Many of them welcomed Hitler as a leader who would safeguard Germany against it. Thus Hitler united masses and classes by shrewdly associating "Jew" with "Communism". Next, he associated with both Jew and Communism the word democracy which he called "the foul and filthy avenue to Communism". Once in power, he destroyed labor unions, and by threat of concentration camp or death stopped all public and much private criticism of his acts. To some industrialists, churchmen, journalists, and political leaders, what he was doing was good—a necessary "defense mechanism against Communism". Quickly, after he came to power, in 1933, he won the support of such persons in France, England, and the United States.

One has only to survey the world events since 1933 to see how much support he won, how much help he received from the statesmen of France, England, and even the United States. Documented evidence of how Hitler was aided in his own country and in the Western democracies may be seen in abundance in summaries such as *The Spirit and Structure of German Fascism*, by Robert Brady; *The Nazi Dictatorship, Europe on the Eve*, and *Night Over Europe*, by Frederick Schuman; *Betrayal in Central Europe*, by G. E. R. Gedye; *Europe in Retreat*, by Vera M. Dean; *Ambassador Dodd's Diary*, and various of the bulletins issued since 1937 by the Institute for Propaganda Analysis.

Hitler used no secret devices or methods in his amazing accomplishments as a propagandist. The secret of his effectiveness lies in the astute utilization he made of the frustration of millions of people, of the anxiety of business, religious, and political leaders that there would be social upheaval. Once he had unified the masses and classes by giving them Jews, Communists, and democracy as scapegoats, he utilized the projection process to make them all work with missionary zeal for a type of world and national leadership which would forever safeguard against the evils of Judaism, Communism, and democracy. His task was made easier when the Communists propagandized for a "United Front", with "democracy" featured. Thus, in France, in England, and even in the United States, the *Fuehrerprinzip*, or leadership principle, obtained increasing backing. Hitler's simple pattern with its name calling, its use of the poison words—Jew, Communism,

INTRODUCTION

democracy—evoked automatic support for him from many in France, England, and the United States—as the same pattern had evoked the same response in Germany.

In America, too, in the Thirties, there were frustrations and anxiety; there were industrialists who feared social upheaval as an outcome of the depression. There were churchmen and politicians as well as less respectable agitators who seemed to see in the Hitler technique a sure-fire method to achieve power and prestige. America, since 1929, has had its share of frustration caused by depression and unemployment; and America has had its share of anxiety, particularly on the part of the well-to-do, that the masses, encouraged by the New Deal, would go "socialistic". Hence, there has been a missionary zeal on the part of some of the anxious rich to establish the leadership principle in the United States. They would keep the unemployed in their places, keep labor docile, prevent strikes, and emphasize in religion an authoritarianism to control education and labor and, at the same time, to transfer to the leadership principle the sanction of God.

As passages in Ambassador Dodd's Diary reveal, some of the most influential and respectable men in America, in the Thirties, were approving the leadership principle for America. One United States Senator was described by Dr. Dodd as a man who "talks like a National Socialist". Dr. Dodd, in his diary (p. 213), mentioned the Senator as citing his influence with Huey Long. Dr. Dodd quoted the unnamed Senator as saying, "We shall soon be shooting up people here, like Hitler does." [1]

For the most part, however, it was not respectable citizens who openly used the Hitler propaganda pattern in an attempt to bring Fascism to America. With the exception of Father Charles E. Coughlin, most of the American propagandists operating the Hitler pattern were curious individuals with curious backgrounds. Some had records of crime; nearly all were neurotic. But their very neuroses could make them effective propagandists. Financial support came from the masses. It came also from some individual contributors, both wealthy and "respectable".

Dr. Donald S. Strong has performed a service of value in these days of crisis by preparing this comprehensive study—a project which has had the encouragement of the American Council on Public Affairs. His findings will help prevent Fascism in America if they obtain immediate and wide attention. From his study it is clear that anti-semitic groups in the United States utilize Hitler's appeals to frustra-

---

[1] President Roosevelt, in the controversy over the Lease-Lend Bill, identified this unnamed Senator as Burton K. Wheeler—an identification approved later by William E. Dodd, Jr., who edited the Ambassador's diary.

iii

tration and anxiety; they seek to create a leadership which will be America's safeguard against the evils of Jew, Communism, democracy. The German-American Bund, one of the groups described in detail by Dr. Strong, has been part of the Nazi propaganda organization. Father Charles E. Coughlin, his magazine, *Social Justice,* and his organization, The Christian Front, while not technically a part of the Nazi propaganda machine, have followed the major outlines of Hitler's pattern.

A chief immediate danger—assuming that mass unemployment and discontent continue in America—would seem to be a united front of the Hitler-inspired, anti-semitic organizations. This front seems unlikely immediately for the reason that many of the anti-semitic leaders are getting their bread and butter out of the movement and do not wish to yield place or prestige to rivals. Another factor militating against united front is the fact that Father Coughlin, a Catholic priest and one of the ablest of all the preachers of anti-semitism, probably would experience difficulty in getting many Protestants to follow his political leadership.

It seems not unlikely that, with the United States committed to a victory over Hitler, anti-semitism for the time being will take a minor place in the propaganda plan of these dozens of organizations battening upon the discontent of the unemployed. New scapegoats, including aliens, Negroes, and, perhaps, the Catholic minority itself, may be found. But in the post-war days to come there may be a revival of anti-semitism. Whether the war against Hitler is won or lost, post-war conditions may be conditions of increased hardship and poverty. Again a scapegoat will be found. Psychologically, it matters little whether the scapegoat is alien, Negro, Jewish, Catholic, Socialist, or Communist. Post-war excesses will bear heavily upon one or more of these or other minority groups. To prevent post-war excesses, measures must be taken to prevent post-war depression and mass unemployment. And immediately educational measures should be taken to analyze the propagandas which can make great masses of people victims of hysteria. Dr. Strong's study is a timely contribution to the educational safeguard against Fascism.

The Hitler method will not work in America if economic democracy, political democracy, and education to help people recognize and analyze propaganda increase rapidly enough. The first means jobs; the second means full freedom for all adults to vote and to discuss the issues on which they vote; the third means many more educators who, like Dr. Strong, are committed to economic and political democracy.

CONTENTS

Preface

SEVERAL years ago I became intensely interested in the operations of anti-semitic organizations in the United States. Fortunately, my research duties at the University of Chicago, together with the excellent opportunities available in that city for first-hand scrutiny of anti-semitism, made it possible for me to give the matter a considerable amount of attention.

I should emphasize that my concern with the subject is based upon a profound belief in the capacity of democratic America to cope with its enemies and counter-currents and that I have striven for complete objectivity in presenting the facts here assembled. My personal origins cannot, of course, be considered an influence in choosing or developing the theme in question. In this connection I wish to add that the unbiased interest of the American Council on Public Affairs has been both encouraging and helpful.

My chief guide and critic has been Dr. Harold D. Lasswell, formerly of the University of Chicago and now associated with the William Alanson White Psychiatric Foundation of Washington, D. C. For penetrating criticism I am indebted to Dr. Harold F. Gosnell of the University of Chicago and Lewis E. Gleeck, now with the American Consular Service in Canada.

I followed the standard practice among scholars and exploited my wife for help in typing, revising, and other tedious jobs. She was most helpful in encouraging me to dispense, whenever possible, with ponderous academic jargon and to express my ideas in simpler terms.

DONALD S. STRONG

Department of Government
The University of Texas
Austin, Texas

CHAPTER I

Anti-Semitism Throughout the World

THIS STUDY is an effort to throw some light on the growth of fascism in the United States. Two difficulties confront the person who attempts to inquire into this subject. First, the growth of fascism in the United States is too broad a subject for any one study to handle adequately. Secondly, the term *fascism* is vague and unsatisfactory. It has been used so extensively as a polemical term and it has so many different connotations to so many groups that it is hardly suitable for use in this study. The first difficulty may be solved by confining oneself arbitrarily to one phase of the subject that is loosely called *fascism*—to a phase that would come within almost anyone's definition of *fascism*. The second difficulty may be met by showing how that which is called *fascism* fits in a general way into the framework of concepts that are developed in this study.

The special phase of fascism with which this study deals is the host of anti-semitic organizations that have developed in the United States since 1933. Although organizations of this type—particularly such highly publicized groups as the German-American Bund and the Silver Shirts—have been discussed in hundreds of newspaper and magazine articles, to date they have not been subjected to any comprehensive or systematic examination. The purpose of this study is to provide such a thoroughgoing examination and simultaneously to orient these organizations in the broad sweep of world political movements. In connection with the latter point, it is pertinent to note here that the ideology spread by anti-semitic groups in the United States is the same as that which accompanied certain political developments in Russia before World War I, in Poland and Hungary shortly after that war, and more recently in Nazi Germany and Fascist Italy.

What is the significance of anti-semitic organizations in the United States? What is the relation of these groups to what is generally termed *fascism* in the United States. In order to be able to answer these questions adequately, it is necessary to present them in language better adapted to a precise examination of the subject.

At the outset we must note that within any society there exists what may be termed roughly the *ruling class* or, more precisely, the *élite.* The élite consists of those persons who get the most of a given social value—for example, income or deference. An élite justifies its ascendency by an ideology, i.e., a set of ideas and symbols by which it endeavors to rationalize its ascendency and to win the loyalty of the masses to that order of society.[1] Essentially, the ideology involved depends upon non-rational acceptance. Loyalty to it means that one accepts certain beliefs, loves certain heroes, cheers at the sight of such symbols as flags, thrills at the singing of certain songs, and gives deference to the proper persons. The stability of any social order depends to a large degree on the acceptance of the ideology upon which the ascendency of the élite rests.[2]

Within any society there usually circulate other sets of symbols or counter-ideologies—other sets of ideas justifying a different order of society. These competing ideologies point out the weaknesses of the present social order and demand more or less fundamental changes in the social practice. If the demands are for fundamental changes in the social practice, the ideology is *revolutionary.* Demands for less sweeping changes in the social practice characterize a *reform* ideology. *Radical* demands are those for the accomplishment of these changes by drastic methods—i.e., methods that would be counter to the morés under ordinary circumstances. *Moderate* demands ask for change by methods within the morés. A *radical revolutionary* ideology is one that demands fundamental changes in the social practice to be accomplished by drastic methods. If the ideology demands changes in all countries of the world, it is a *world radical revolutionary* ideology. Obviously the most important world radical revolutionary ideology at present is the Communist ideology emanating from Moscow. It points out the weaknesses of the present capitalistic society and demands that fundamental changes be made in the social practice and that they be accomplished by drastic methods. The élite of all occidental countries except Russia today justify their ascendency by variations of what may be called capitalistic, bourgeois, or French revolutionary ideology. The ideologies of the French and Russian revolutions are the two great competing ideologies of our time. Variations of the former justify the social structure as it has existed in western Europe and America; the latter attempts to justify the emergence of a new élite to replace those justifying their ascendency by the older ideology. Hence, significant observations about any political movement today must orient it with relation to these two great revolutions and their ideologies.

Our immediate problem is simply to orient anti-semitic groups the world over within the pattern of political changes between the two revolutions. We can do this more readily if we first note that whenever a world radical revolutionary ideology assumes threatening proportions any place in the world, there develops in all countries a defensive reaction against it. This reaction may simply take the form of a reactivation of the ideology that justifies the present order. The old ideology may simply be reasserted more loudly and more frequently. Any group that opposes the world radical revolutionary ideology may be designated as anti-world radical revolutionary in its ideology. Usually the defense takes place in the name of the national symbol and the world radical revolution is pictured as foreign. Occasionally the defense against the world radical revolutionary ideology takes the form of a national radical revolutionary ideology which demands that within the nation drastic measures be taken against those persons identified with the world radical revolutionary symbol and that fundamental changes be made in the existing governmental practices so that the world radical revolutionary threat will be definitely suppressed. Italian Fascism is an example of a national radical revolutionary movement. It was *national* in that the demands for change were limited to Italy. It was *radical* in that it demanded drastic methods—not the ordinary democratic procedures. It was *revolutionary* in that it demanded fundamental changes in the existing governmental practices, namely the replacement of the parliamentary democracy with a dictatorship. One of the avowed purposes of this movement was the crushing of the threat of a world radical revolutionary movement and those groups identified with it.

Similar examples of national radical revolutionary movements are to be found in pre-revolutionary Russia, post-war Poland and Hungary, German National Socialism, the British Union of Fascists, and the *Croix de Feu* of France. Whether the American anti-revolutionary, anti-semitic groups may be properly described as national radical revolutionary groups is one of the questions this study seeks to answer. The relation between anti-world radical revolutionary and national radical revolutionary ideologies may not yet be clear. The latter is a specialized type of the former. Any opposition to a world radical revolutionary ideology takes the form of an anti-world radical revolutionary ideology. A national radical revolutionary movement is one form the opposition may take.

A few other points about national radical revolutionary movements are worth noting. Usually, these movements take place in the name of the national symbol and are accompanied by an intense, exaggerated nationalism. In certain instances, they need not be inaugurated by

[3]

the élite; indeed in their less developed forms they usually get little or no support from the élite.

As used here, the term *national radical revolution* is roughly equivalent to the popular term *fascism;* however, the two terms are by no means synonymous. *Fascism* has for many people a large number of implications that cannot correctly be attached to a *national radical revolution;* moreover, we are applying the latter term to several movements that many persons would hesitate to call *fascist.*

Anti-semitic ideology is merely a variation of anti-world radical revolutionary ideology and similarly a variation of the national radical revolutionary ideology. So-called *anti-semitic* ideology is really anti-revolutionary, anti-semitic ideology. The Jew and the revolutionary are closely identified as one and the same thing. As a political ideology, anti-semitism without an anti-revolutionary aspect is so rare as to be almost unknown.[3] That anti-revolutionary and anti-semitic sentiments should be grouped together in one ideology is not surprising. Let us recall that opposition to revolutionary movements always occurs in the name of an aroused nationalism.

Any intensively nationalistic movement is against the alien. It tends to suppress differences and to force all citizens into the standardized nationalistic mould. Any minority is looked upon with suspicion. The Jew is everywhere a national minority—the perpetual alien. Hence, he is an eligible target for any aroused nationalism. Revolutionary ideas can, of course, be conveniently identified with the Jews. Revolutionary ideas are held to be alien; hence, these alien ideas must be disseminated by the alien people in our midst, the Jews. Thus arises the identification of Jews with the revolutionary ideology. One discredits the revolutionary ideology by pinning the Jewish label on it.[4]

Now let us turn to an examination of this anti-revolutionary, anti-semitic ideology in action outside of the United States. Our purpose is to make abundantly clear that it is not an isolated American phenomenon but that, on the contrary, anti-revolutionary, anti-semitic ideology flourishes wherever social and political conditions are favorable to it. An examination of its operation in other countries will make more clear what these conditions are and enable us better to understand the significance of the movement in the United States. However, before proceeding it is necessary to explain the shift in terminology from the cumbersome expression *anti-world radical revolutionary* to the briefer *anti-revolutionary.* The term *revolutionary* is more inclusive than *radical.* *Revolutionary* indicates simply a demand for fundamental changes in the social practice; it does not specify what means are to be used. Hence, the European Social Democratic parties would, historically speaking, fall within the term *revolutionary* since they have believed in a fundamental change in the social practice—the abandonment of capitalism—although they have not demanded the use of drastic means which would make them *radical revolutionaries.* *Anti-revolutionary*, then, is the term we wish to use. These movements—which can be best described as anti-revolutionary and anti-semitic—are opposed to all groups which believe in any fundamental changes in the social practice, even though it is to be achieved peaceably. They make no fine distinctions in selecting their opponents. In fact, reformist groups whose beliefs are merely suggestive of the beliefs of the revolutionaries are usually attacked just as vigorously as the revolutionaries themselves by the anti-revolutionary, anti-semitic groups.

Before turning to the earliest instances of anti-revolutionary, anti-semitic ideology, let us remember that we are interested in anti-semitism only when it is associated with an anti-revolutionary ideology. Anti-semitism has existed throughout Christian civilization. For the last two thousand years Jews have been dispossessed, tortured, and murdered on religious and other justifications. However, we are not interested in anti-semitism as such.[5] If a Jew is killed merely because he is a Jew, that is not pertinent to this study. However, if he is killed on the ground that he and all other Jews are revolutionists bent upon changing the present social order, his fate comes within the scope of our inquiry. This distinction makes it a little difficult to state just when the anti-revolutionary, anti-semitic ideology first appeared. Pogroms against the Jews were not infrequent in nineteenth century Russia. In 1882, 1902, and 1903, for instance, extensive pogroms broke out in that country. However, it was in 1905 that anti-semitism was used as an instrument to repress revolutionary ideology. Only after the revolution of that year was a clear-cut effort made to discredit a revolutionary movement by pinning the Jew label on it. Extracts from the pamphlets circulated at that time plainly show the effort to stigmatize the liberal revolution as Jewish:

> The cry of "Down with the autocracy!" comes from the bloodsuckers who are commonly known as Jews. . . . Beware of the Jews! They are the root of all evil, the sole cause of our misfortunes. The glorious moment is already approaching when there will be an end of all Jews in Russia. Down with the traitors! Down with constitutions!

That the revolutionary ideology with which the Jews were held to be associated was a demand for the change from a feudal, autocratic state to a bourgeoise, liberal state makes no difference. Such a demand would be within our definition of *revolutionary*. Much more important for our purposes is to note that this anti-semitic, anti-revolutionary activity was initiated by the government. The Russian élite initiated this new ideology, or this variation of an old ideology, to ward off a threat to their ascendency. Much of the literature was "produced in the printing-office of the police department and financed from the Tsar's so-called privy purse."[6] The Russian élite did not join the powerful anti-revolutionary, anti-semitic movement which had been developing among the lower classes for years while they had been ignoring it; operating through the government, the élite *facilitated* the movement by instigating brutal pogroms. Here was one of the first instances of the anti-revolutionary, anti-semitic ideology being used to quell a threat to the ascendency of the élite.

Once started, this ideology continued in Russia. It played its most significant role in the years 1917-1920. The counter-revolutionaries quickly realized the potentialities of anti-semitism in rousing sentiment against the Kerensky government and, later, the Bolsheviks. The revolution was blamed on the Jews. At this time the *Protocols of the Elders of Zion*[7] became very prominent as a factor in agitation against the Jews. Here again this ideology led to violence. White Guard generals deliberately handed Jewish communities over to their troops for butchery.

Recent anti-semitism in Poland was not closely tied up with anti-revolutionary ideology. Hence, it is not so significant for our purposes as the brief wave of the anti-revolutionary, anti-semitic ideology that struck Poland after World War I. The anti-semitic policy of White Russia spread to Poland. Here, too, the Jew became identified with Bolshevism. The conflict with the Soviet forces in 1919 stimulated the hatred for Jews and led to the pogroms against the Polish Jews.

The appearance of this ideology in post-war Hungary is of interest because, before World War I, anti-semitism was almost unknown there. Hungarian Jews not only were thoroughly Magyarized but were zealous pioneers in developing the national consciousness and culture of Hungary.[8] It was during the crushing of the short-lived Soviet regime that the anti-revolutionary, anti-semitic ideology made its appearance.[9] Here, as in post-war Russia, the ideology was not used as a means of élite defense; instead an old élite, temporarily dislodged, employed it as a means of discrediting the new revolutionary élite and justifying its own return to power. Thus, in the name of this anti-revolutionary, anti-semitic ideology, the White Terror was directed not only against the Bolsheviks in general and the few Jewish Bolsheviks but against all the half million Jews in Hungary. The speedy association of Jews and Bolsheviks in the ideology came about partly from the spread of the ideology from the White Russians and partly from the fact that Bela Kun and several other leaders of the revolution actually were Jews. Anti-semitism had another use in addition to bolstering the position of the élite. Defeat in the war and territorial dismemberment by the post-war treaties heaped tremendous humiliation on Hungarian nationalism. Too weak to direct the bitterness produced by these misfortunes toward an alien nation, Hungary found the Jews an excellent scapegoat for her national humiliation.

Germany is, of course, the country most closely associated with the anti-revolutionary, anti-semitic ideology and the chief distributing center of it at the present time. The study of the rise of this ideology in Germany gives one a better picture of its rise throughout the world.[10]

The German experience differs from that of Russia, Hungary, and Poland in that the revolutionary menace to the existing social order was never so real. In Russia, the Bolsheviks seized the government. In Hungary, the Soviet regime managed to control the country for several months. In Poland, the Red Army invasion was ominous. In Germany, although a short-lived Soviet regime actually did hold power in Munich and although the Communist and Social Democratic parties gained tremendous popular support, the menace to the ascendency of the élite was never comparable to the post-war experiences of Russia, Hungary, or Poland.

In addition to the "revolutionary threat," a factor that led to the Nazis' rise to power in Germany was the profound economic distress from which Germany suffered ever since 1918. True, Germany enjoyed a brief period of relative prosperity from 1925 to 1929, but she never enjoyed the degree of prosperity that the victor nations did in the post-war years. Since economic insecurity is fertile soil for new ideologies, whether they attack or uphold the existing social order, it is small wonder that a large percentage of the German population became associated with the revolutionary parties. The more menacing the revolutionary movement became, the stronger the Nazis grew, ever professing to be defenders of the existing social order against revolutionary chaos. Simultaneously, the anti-semitic part of Nazi ideology attracted many Germans who felt the pinch of economic deprivation. The Jew could be readily blamed for the depression; he made a fine target for the aggressions generated by economic deprivation.

The comments applied to Hungary regarding the anti-revolutionary, anti-semitic ideology in relation to national humiliation from military defeat apply equally here. Defeat, dismemberment, disarmament, and the stigma of sole war guilt were profoundly humiliating to the national pride of Germany, but this very humiliation stimulated a more intense wave of nationalism. Defeat gave Germany an intense feeling of inferiority—an inferiority complex on a national scale—and led to a violent over-compensation against it in the form of extreme nationalism. Moreover, since Germany was disarmed and encircled by armed neighbors, bitterness could not be discharged against the foreigner beyond the frontier. Thus, the "foreigner" within Germany, the Jew, became the target of the awakened nationalism. Therefore, it was the Jew that caused Germany to lose the war; it was the Jew that produced Germany's national humiliation.

Anti-semitism was readily accepted in Germany because the nation had a long tradition of anti-semitism. This situation stands in marked contrast to that of the United States and England, where anti-semitism has not appeared until quite recently. Without attempting to trace the origin and history of anti-semitism in Germany, it can be noted that anti-semitism had become a politically significant ideology by 1870 and that it was a doctrine about which books were being written at that time. In 1871, Professor August Rohling, a theologian, had published *Der Talmudjude,* which represented Judaism as a devilish doctrine; this book circulated by the hundred thousand. In connection with the *Kulturkampf,* the Catholic Church launched a campaign of anti-semitism, blaming the church's troubles on the Jews. In 1878, Adolf Stocker, the Court preacher, founded the anti-semitic Christian Social Labor Party. In 1887, Otto Bockel drew up his *Antisemitenkatechismus,* a handbook for anti-semitic agitators, which went through many editions. Although this early German anti-semitism was not yet combined with an anti-revolutionary ideology, the point to be emphasized is that political anti-semitism had been well rooted in German culture for half a century when the National Socialists appeared on the scene with their anti-revolutionary, anti-semitic ideology.[11]

In the German situation another feature of interest is the fact that the Nazis started as a middle-class movement. All writers on the German situation emphasize the fact that it was middle-class rather than proletarian. The German proletariat was attracted to a large extent by the two Marxist parties, the Social Democrats and the Communists. The middle classes, on the other hand—especially the lower middle classes—were drawn to the Nazis.[12] At first, the upper classes considered the Nazis a bit vulgar and tended to support the German People's Party and the Nationalists.[13] As the Nazis gained in strength, however, they drew members heavily from the upper classes. But from the standpoint of origin and of mass support the National Socialist Party is essentially a middle-class party.

Although the bulk of the party's early membership was middle-class, a large proportion of its finances came from the wealthy. As it grew stronger, contributions from the industrialists became more and more generous. The contributions should occasion no surprise. The National Socialists were one of several German parties with an anti-revolutionary program. Uneasy over the growth of revolutionary ideology, the wealthy backed the Nazis and all other groups that did not challenge their position as the economic élite. As the Nazis emerged as a continually more powerful champion against revolutionary propaganda, they began to draw increased support from those who had the most to lose from the growth of revolutionary sentiment.

These comments on the anti-revolutionary nature of the Nazi party do not tell the whole story. The National Socialists became anti-revolutionary in the course of their development. In the early stages they were revolutionary; for a time the word *Socialist* in the party name really meant something. The party's original twenty-five point program, drawn up in 1920, called for the abolition of interest, the creation of state ownership of trusts, state sharing in the profits of large industries, and the abolition of department stores. Only after a period of years and after considerable internal strife in the party was it definitely settled that the revolutionary planks should never be carried into practice.

The rise in Italy of an anti-revolutionary movement, Italian Fascism, is another subject worth analysis. Despite the absence until recently of anti-semitism, Italian Fascism is essentially similar to all the other movements we have noted and it particularly resembles German National Socialism. Like that movement, it rallies its followers in the name of the national symbol against an alleged menace of revolution. The minor role of anti-semitism in Italian Fascism is due only to the fact that there are too few Jews in Italy to make them a sizeable target. Only about one tenth of one percent of the Italian population is Jewish; in Germany, the Jews make up nearly one percent. Although in both Germany and Italy the existing social practices have been defended by the development of an anti-revolutionary movement, the Italian Fascists have not attempted until recently to seek out and berate the Jewish conspiracy.[14]

Now let us note the several points at which the rise of Italian Fascism parallels that of National Socialism.[15] In the first place, Italian Fascism was a reaction against what was considered a menacing growth of revolutionary sentiment. The elections of 1919 returned to the Chamber of Deputies 156 Socialists and 100 members of the *Popolari* Party, a Catholic party with revolutionary leanings. A Bolshevik wing of the

Socialist Party engaged in some direct action; agrarian labor was militant and in some cases resorted to violent tactics. A wave of strikes reached its high point in the autumn of 1920, when strikers in the Turin metal works seized plants, remained in them, and attempted to operate them. Thus, groups identified with revolutionary symbols showed a high degree of militancy. Whether these groups ever intended to seize power or ever came near having an opportunity to do so is most doubtful. At any rate, the significant point is that the increase of revolutionary strength was such as to make the élite insecure and to start among the threatened middle classes a violent reaction against the revolutionary symbols. The upper and middle classes became frightened and willing to support any definitely anti-revolutionary movement.

Another point of similarity to the German experience is that Italian Fascism also grew out of economic stress. The end of the war brought industrial depression to Italy. This economic insecurity swelled the ranks of the revolutionary parties and led to the growth of the Fascist reaction against them. But depressions increase the size of all parties other than those in power and many Italians expressed their discontent with economic conditions by joining the Fascists. As in the case of Germany, national humiliation accounts for the intensely nationalistic character of this movement. Though Italy was one of the victors in the war, she had been treated at the peace conference like a second-rate power. She secured only a few increases of territory; France and Great Britain took the lion's share. Injured Italian pride expressed itself in the form of over-compensation—in exaggerated nationalism. Such an atmosphere was unfavorable to revolutionary movements that talk in terms of world unity on a class basis and devalue nationalism. Conversely, Italians, smarting from the lack of recognition their country received at the peace conference, responded quite readily to nationalistic Fascists.

Italian Fascism resembles German National Socialism in that both are middle-class movements. Middle class Italians made up the squads that smashed the trade union and Socialist Party headquarters and generally destroyed the organization of the proletariat. As in Germany, wealthy groups gave financial backing to the movement. Their ascendancy in society had been challenged by the wave of revolutionary sentiment and they were altogether willing to contribute to a movement that would make their position more secure.

A final point of similarity is the fact that Italian Fascism originally was a revolutionary movement. It is, of course, significant that Mussolini was a Socialist leader before the first World War. But it is even more significant that when he made his unsuccessful campaign for a seat in the Chamber in 1919 (after he had turned Fascist), he ran on a platform that among other things called for the confiscation of non-productive capital. The leader, who became the defender of the social order, started out as one of its mortal enemies.

The two great European democracies, Great Britain and France, have also had groups disseminating anti-revolutionary, anti-semitic ideologies. In England the chief group has been the British Union of Fascists, headed by Sir Oswald Mosley, a former Labor M.P., who is now involuntarily spending his time with the British authorities.[16] At the outset it should be noted that there have not been present in England two factors that have been invariably associated with the rise of anti-semitic ideology in all the other countries discussed so far. The two factors are national humiliation and a threat of revolution. England, a victor in the first World War, has as yet suffered no diplomatic defeat significant enough to produce national humiliation. Moreover, there has been no threatening growth of revolutionary ideology. The Conservative Party has been firmly in the saddle since 1931. The Labor Party, with its reformist program, is not a revolutionary party in the sense we are using the term. The only genuinely revolutionary groups in England—the Independent Labor Party and the Communists —have, of course, been insignificant.

The propaganda of the British Fascists has been very similar to that of Hitler. It has been intensely anti-semitic, emphasizing that aspect perhaps even more than its anti-revolutionary aspect. Mosley has made no effort to conceal his admiration for the German and Italian dictatorships. He has been photographed with Mussolini, and he has openly exchanged greetings with Julius Streicher, Germany's leading Jew-baiter. Despite his admiration for these foreign systems he has preached an intense nationalism and advocated a "strong" policy with respect to retention and government of the British Empire. Moreover, he has advocated the corporate state on the Italian model although he has gone into no details as to its structure.

The most significant fact about Mosley's group is its failure. It has never had a large following; it has never elected a member to Parliament; and since 1935 it has steadily declined in importance. Its failure is to be explained largely in terms of the absence of the two previously mentioned factors—national humiliation and a significant growth of revolutionary sentiment. A third factor that has made England barren soil for Mosley's ideology is the absence of an anti-semitic tradition. Contrast this situation with Germany, where anti-semitism as a political doctrine was half a century old when Hitler began his agitation. That the absence of a revolutionary menace contributed to Mosley's lack of success is clearly evident. The ideology he has circulated arose in continental Europe in situations where there was a significant amount of revolutionary sentiment, sometimes enough to make it seem that the social order was threatened. However, England has not been endangered by a revolutionary menace. Had Mosley endeavored to introduce his ideology during one of the Labor governments, he might have secured more followers. But with the Conservative Party firmly in power and the Labor Party offering no revolutionary challenge, the British Union of Fascists could hardly convince many Englishmen that revolution was just around the corner. In short, British Fascists found themselves in a more difficult position than their American counterparts. In America the New Deal was inaugurating a program of reform which could be interpreted to the politically unsophisticated as revolutionary; in England, such interpretation of the actions of the government was patently absurd.

Until its humiliating defeat in the summer of 1940, France had no important group disseminating anti-revolutionary, anti-semitic ideology. It has, of course, had several incipient national radical revolutionary movements in the *Croix de Feu* and the less well known *Jeunesses Patriotes* and the *Solidarite Francaise*.[17] Though none of these groups have been openly anti-semitic, they have all been intensely anti-revolutionary and nationalistic. Their anti-revolutionary propaganda, in common with that of all the groups examined so far, has tried to give the impression that the social order is in such immediate peril that the older conservative parties are of no value, that only their militant brand of opposition to revolution can save the state. It should be noted that violence has evidently been in the minds of those rank-and-file members of the *Croix de Feu* who have advocated a *coup d'etat* and that leader de la Rocque has on a number of occasions talked of the need for "drastic measures."

The organization of the *Croix de Feu* on the basis of a private army and its disciplinary characteristics have a good deal in common with Hitler's Storm Troops. The other French groups are organized on similar lines. All three groups appeal to a middle-class clientele. The nature of their anti-revolutionary ideology has shown no originality. It holds that the revolutionaries under democracy have been able to corrupt France and that they must be thrown out and France purified. Whether democracy should be preserved has not been mentioned. A mildly leftist government which was connected with the Stavisky scandal was an early target of anti-revolutionary sentiments. Disturbed economic conditions which the government did little to ameliorate later served to encourage these sentiments. A heyday was reached in 1934 and 1935. After that the strong leftist government of the Popular Front, alarmed at the growth of anti-revolutionary movements, took vigorous measures against them and they declined into obscurity. However, it is important to note that this anti-revolutionary ideology has shown signs of a revival—this time with an anti-semitic tinge. France in the Spring of 1941 fulfills so many of the conditions necessary for the spread of an anti-revolutionary, anti-semitic ideology that it is quite probably that a strong movement of this nature will develop out of the trends which have already become evident. Some scapegoat will have to be found to explain France's military collapse and the acute economic deprivations that are sweeping over the country. The Popular Front government, headed by the Jew, Leon Blum, and supported by the Socialist and Communist parties, seem to provide a simple explanation for France's misfortunes.

* * *

Surveying the anti-revolutionary, anti-semitic movements in the seven countries we have examined, we can say that there are three conditions that stimulate their growth. These conditions are: a revolutionary movement, national humiliation, and widespread economic insecurity. In Germany, Italy, and Hungary all three of these factors have been present. In England and France, where the movement has to date been insignificant, one or more of the factors have been absent. In the other countries, these factors have existed to varying degrees. Regardless of country, however, all of the national radical revolutionary movements surveyed are militant defenders of the existing social practices and of the existing economic élite. They are militant defenders in the sense that there is always at least a suggestion that the defense against groups identified with the revolutionary ideology may require violence or drastic measures.

CHAPTER II

Anti-Semitism in the United States

THE MAJOR purpose of the foregoing analysis is to show that the anti-revolutionary, anti-semitic ideology that has recently appeared in the United States is not a unique phenomenon. Far from being distinctly American, the ideology may appear in any country under certain conditions. The America of 1933-1940 has had several of these conditions: a severe depression and, in the opinion of some persons, a serious growth of revolutionary ideology.

In dealing with the latter aspect, it should be noted that the growth of genuine revolutionary sentiment in the United States has, of course, been slight. True, the revolutionary parties have been attracting somewhat more attention than usual. True, the reformist policies of the New Deal have appeared comparatively "revolutionary". But there has been no sign of any genuine revolutionary movement of significant proportions.[1] This, however, may be beside the point. The important fact is that some Americans, believing that a revolutionary movement has been growing, have been alarmed. This fear and, of course, economic privation, are the motivating factors in the appearance of 121 anti-revolutionary, anti-semitic organizations during the years 1933-1940.

When these organizations first began to make their appearance, their ideology was not entirely new. Anti-semitism in the United States may be considered as a phase of the anti-alien sentiment that has periodically manifested itself. The Jew is the perpetual alien. Since he is frequently identified as a member of a separate group, he is invariably a victim of any anti-alien movement.

The first anti-alien movement in the United States occurred during the administration of John Adams and resulted in the passage of the Alien and Sedition Acts. Another such movement flourished in the 1850's in the form of the Know-Nothing or American Party, a secret political organization aimed chiefly against the Irish Catholic immigrants who had become supporters of the Democratic Party. A third movement, sponsored by the American Protective Association during the years 1887-1894, was also directed against Catholic immigrants. The great wave of immigration that began in the 1890's brought many

Jews to American shores and resulted in an anti-alien movement which manifested itself in the restrictive immigration laws of 1921 and 1924 and in the widespread circulation of the Nordic race superiority theories propounded by such writers as Lothrop Stoddard and Madison Grant. Although anti-alien sentiment was not always specifically anti-Jewish, the Jew was invariably marked, along with Southern and Eastern Europeans, as a less desirable type of immigrant.[2]

Anti-semitism in its political form first appeared in the United States at the end of the World War. Previously, anti-semitism had expressed itself primarily in terms of social discrimination. At the time of the three earlier waves of anti-alien feeling there were too few Jews in the United States to attract serious attention. Between 1881 and the outbreak of the World War, however, some 2,000,000 European Jews entered the country. And when the fourth wave of anti-alien feeling broke in 1919, the Jewish population was large enough to make a sizeable target. The introduction of immigration quotas and the vaunting of Nordic racial superiority were not the only expressions of anti-semitism. As part of the post-war "Red Scare" large quantities of anti-semitic literature entered into circulation. This literature indicated the first effort in the United States to identify revolutionary ideology with the Jews. The Fellowship Forum and other groups distributed widely copies of the forged *Protocols of the Elders of Zion* and similar propaganda. In May, 1920, Henry Ford began an anti-semitic campaign in his *Dearborn Independent*, continuing it until January, 1922. The Ku Klux Klan, which began to grow rapidly at this time, was, of course, frankly anti-semitic.[3]

Most of the prejudice of this period may be explained by the effects of the post-war depression, the rise of labor, and aroused nationalism. Moreover, the power of the Bolsheviks in Russia made the bogey of revolution seem highly realistic. And since the war had made minority groups suspect, it was not difficult to generate anti-Jewish feeling. Though the high point of prejudice was reached during 1920-1922, anti-semitic sentiment continued for several years thereafter. In 1924, Ford revived his anti-semitic campaign in the *Dearborn Independent* and kept it going for a year. But with the Klan's decline into insignificance by 1927, organized anti-semitism virtually disappeared.

In 1933, anti-semitism reappeared on the American scene—this time boldly and blatantly. The causal conditions were the depression, a slight growth of revolutionary sentiment, the initiation of New Deal reforms, and the successful rise to power of the rabidly anti-semitic Nazis in Germany.

To understand precisely how and why anti-semitism has circulated in

America since 1933, it is necessary to examine the character of the proponent organizations. What are the personality types, occupations, and affiliations of the leaders? What is the class status, religion, and geographical distribution of the membership? How are funds raised? What sort of propaganda is issued and through what channels? To what extent do the groups cooperate? What objectives have they in common? These are the key questions to be answered.

Instead of attempting to cover with equal detail all of the 121 anti-semitic organizations that have arisen during the years 1933-1940, the following chapters deal primarily with eleven groups that may be considered the most typical and the most significant. The selection of the eleven groups is based upon an analysis of the entire field and the views of several competent authorities. A thorough knowledge of these groups will make it possible to examine the remaining 110 and will enable the formulation of some reasonably valid conclusions concerning the movement as a whole. The eleven organizations are:

German-American Bund
Silver Shirts
National Union for Social Justice
Defenders of the Christian Faith
Edmondson Economic Service
American Vigilant Intelligence Federation
Industrial Defense Association
James True Associates
American Christian Defenders
Order of '76
Paul Reveres

The term "organization" is used here rather loosely. A few of the groups consist only of a leader, a letterhead, and a mailing list. An organization in the sense of membership, dues, meetings, and elected officers does not always exist. However, a rigid definition of the term "organization" is inadvisable since some of the groups are important just because they are not everything they seem to be.

A word concerning the problems peculiar to this subject. It is by no means a simple matter to obtain information detailing the geographical distribution and the exact number of copies of each kind of propaganda literature published, the exact fluctuations in membership from year to year, complete annual financial statements, etc. The groups covered in this study do not bother to keep complete records and those they do keep are not open for public inspection. In fact, a distinguishing feature of several of the organizations is a romantic secrecy. Moreover, the officers of these organizations freely suspect any investigator of being a "Jewish Red". The only way to get accurate and comprehensive data under these circumstances is through the employment of private detectives with experience in espionage. Since such an investigating method is out of the question, this study will necessarily have some gaps. Although precision and completeness has not been possible in all cases, an effort has been made to use as rigorous a technique of analysis as the nature of the material will permit.

So far nothing has been said concerning the number or importance of Jews or revolutionary groups in the United States. A brief statement of the most significant facts may clarify the complex background of this study. In 1937 the total number of Jews in the United States was 4,770,647.[4] Since the number of Jewish immigrants in the last few years has been small (as the subsequent figures indicate), this is a good approximation of the total American Jewish population today. More Jews live in the United States than in any other country in the world; Poland and Russia have been second and third respectively. Although American Jews constitute approximately 25 percent of the world's Jewry, they represent only 3.69 percent of the total American population.[5] The vast majority of American Jews reside in the great metropolitan areas of the country; about 69 percent live in the 11 largest cities:[6] New York, Chicago, Boston, Cleveland, Philadelphia, Detroit, Los Angeles, Baltimore, Pittsburgh, St. Louis, and Newark—42 percent in New York City alone.[7] This concentration in the largest cities is further illustrated by the fact that the average density of Jewish population in cities of more than 100,000 inhabitants is 11.11 percent, whereas in cities of 25,000 to 100,000 it is only 3.11 percent.[8] In smaller urban centers and in the unincorporated rural areas the percentages are 1.61 and 0.15 respectively.[9] These population densities naturally suggest that the greatest percentage of Jews will be found in those Northeastern states where the large cities are located. Such is the case: 78 percent reside in the states of New York, Pennsylvania, Illinois, Massachusetts, Ohio, and New Jersey.

About 3,500,000 of the 4,228,000 American Jews are of East European birth or descent.[10] These Jews are comparatively recent arrivals, having entered this country between 1881 and 1924. Although the story of Jewish immigration began with the landing of 23 Spanish and Portuguese Jews at New Amsterdam in 1654, as late as 1880 the Jews numbered no more than 250,000, about one-half of one percent of the total population.[11] From 1881 through 1936 the total net increase in the Jewish population was about 2,350,000.[12] About 70 percent came from Russia, 25 percent from Austria-Hungary and Roumania.[13] This huge exodus of Jews from Eastern Europe resulted chiefly from the brutal anti-semitic policy of the Russian Czarist government. In eight years of the period, Jews entered America at the rate of over 100,000 a year.[14] Quota revisions and restrictions in 1921 and 1924 cut Jewish immigration to a trickle, and after 1931 a severer application of the "likely to become a public charge" provision of the immigration law, further thinned the trickle. As a result, during the years 1931-1936 inclusive, only 26,042 Jews entered the country—an average of about 4,000 per year.[15]

American Jewry has played a significant role in the political and economic life of the nation. More than fifty Jews have served in Congress since the founding of the nation; of these, six have been Senators. Nineteen have been in the diplomatic service with the rank of Ambassador or Minister.[16] Three have served as Associate Justices of the United States Supreme Court. Nearly 200 have served as delegates to the Democratic National Conventions, and 176 as delegates to the Republican National Conventions. Every convention post except temporary and permanent chairman has been held at some time by a Jew.[17] Eight Jews have been governors of states, Lehman of New York and Horner of Illinois being the most widely known.[18] Maurice Maschke, for many years the undisputed Republican leader of Cleveland, and Sam Koenig, the Republican chief of New York County, were Jews. In addition, Jews have served in state legislatures, Federal courts, Cabinet posts, and in many administrative offices in Washington. Jews have been particularly prominent in the politics of New York, city and state, where they have obtained numerous elective and appointive positions and where no party slate is considered well balanced without its quota of Jewish candidates.

The majority of Jews, like the majority of non-Jews, occupy humble positions as employees; only a few exercise control or ownership.[19] In commercial banking, Jewish firms are of little importance, but in the field of investment banking they occupy a prominent though not dominant role. Among the larger Jewish investment banking houses are Kuhn, Loeb, and Company, Lehman Brothers, and J. and W. Seligman. In the heavy industries Jews play a very minor role, with two exceptions: the scrap iron business and the Guggenheim copper interests. In the light industries, the Jews, though somewhat prominent, are confined to narrow sectors. The near monopoly enjoyed by Jews in the manufacturing of men's and women's clothing is traditional, and about half of the alcoholic liquor distillers are Jewish. In the silk, wool, and tobacco trades, Jews are usually not the manufacturers but the jobbers. Jews have been particularly active in the retailing, newspaper, broadcasting, theatrical, and motion picture fields.

The majority of New York's large department stores and a few of the national chain department and apparel stores are owned or controlled by Jews. The Ochs interests, J. David Stern, Paul Block, and Emanuel P. Adler own a number of important newspapers, the total circulation of which is 1,368,000. (Non-Jews own newspaper chains with much larger circulations: Hearst, 5,500,000; Patterson-McCormick, 2,332,000; and Scripps-Howard, 1,794,000.) Executives of Jewish descent direct the two large radio chains, the National Broadcasting Company and Columbia Broadcasting System. In the theatre, slightly more than 50 percent of the producers are Jewish. In the motion picture industry, although much more than 50 percent of the producers are Jewish, their control is not monopolistic. Perhaps a summary measure of Jewish influence in American industry may be obtained by examining the 80,000 names listed in Poor's *Register of Directors*. Only 4.7 percent appear to be Jewish. Any error in this percent owing to the possession by Jews of names common to other peoples would probably be approximately balanced by the inclusion of non-Jews with "Jewish-sounding" names.

The role of Jewry in the medical and legal professions is noteworthy. The Jew as a group has contributed a larger proportion of physicians and lawyers than any other group. Nevertheless, it is doubtful that the Jews' influence in these professions is in proportion to their number. Jews do not usually obtain the most desirable legal positions, nor are they represented, in proportion to their professional numbers, on hospital medical boards.

This survey of the role of Jews in American political and economic life is incomplete in one vital respect. It omits those sectors where Jewish participation is too small to be easily discernible.

*   *   *

Since this study is concerned with anti-revolutionary, anti-semitic groups, it is advisable not only to survey the place of Jews in American life but also to analyze the importance of revolutionary parties in the United States. A revolutionary party has been defined as one which demands fundamental changes in social practices.[20] Only two parties large enough to deserve attention fall within this definition—the Socialist and the Communist parties. These two parties differ from each other chiefly in that the Communists believe in the necessity of using radical methods in achieving their goal, whereas the Socialists believe in the possibility of realizing the same fundamental changes by gradual means. Our chief interest is in the number of persons affiliated or in sympathy with each of these parties. Estimates can be based on the number of votes received by the Presidential candidates of the parties, for the Presidential vote presumably includes not only the dues-paying party members but also party sympathizers. The data given in the accompanying table indicate the percentage of the total Presidential vote received by revolutionary party candidates. For the Socialist Party the figures go back to 1900; for the Communist Party, to 1924.

Table 1

PERCENTAGE OF PRESIDENTIAL VOTES RECEIVED BY REVOLUTIONARY CANDIDATES

Election Year	Socialist Vote	Communist Vote	Total
1900.................	0.68	....	0.68
1904.................	2.96	....	2.96
1908.................	2.85	....	2.85
1912.................	5.96	....	5.96
1916.................	3.15	....	3.15
1920.................	3.45	....	3.45
1924.................	....[1]	0.12[2]	0.12
1928.................	0.73	0.13	0.86
1932.................	2.22	0.26	2.48
1936.................	0.41	0.17	0.58

[1] The Socialist Party did not run a candidate in 1924 but instead supported Senator LaFollette.
[2] The Communist Party ran its first Presidential candidate in 1924, three years after it was organized.

Table I brings out two significant facts: first, the strength of revolutionary parties in this country is exceedingly small; second, the revolutionary parties show no increase in strength over the years. The second fact is particularly significant because some persons contend that although revolutionary parties are small at present they are steadily increasing in strength and will some day be a formidable menace. The table not only disproves this contention, but shows that revolutionary parties have been declining in strength. The period 1904-1920 was the golden age of revolutionary parties in the United States. In 4 of the 5 presidential elections of this period the Socialist party consistently polled about 3 percent of the votes, and in one election received nearly 6 percent. Since then the combined vote of the two revolutionary parties has only once (1932) approached the 3 percent mark; in the other recent elections, they did not get even 1 percent of the Presidential vote.

CHAPTER III

The German-American Bund

THE GERMAN-AMERICAN BUND (*Amerika-Deutscher Volks-bund*), known originally as the Friends of the New Germany, is the best known and most widely-publicized of the anti-revolutionary, anti-semitic groups. It has been the subject of numerous newspaper and magazine articles and its activities have been investigated and aired by two Congressional bodies, the McCormack and Dies Committees.[1]

The Friends of the New Germany was organized at a convention in Chicago on June 30, 1932.[2] Although new, this group was an outgrowth of other organizations advocating Nazi principles. In the United States the first German society with Nazi sympathies was a Chicago organization formed in October 1924 and called Teutonia.[3] It never prospered in membership, and in 1932, just before it dissolved, it could count 50 members in Chicago, and a dozen more in an allied group in Detroit. Many of these members had been active in "fighting communism" in Germany in the years immediately following the World War.[4] Teutonia's importance lies in the fact that its ranks included many men who later became the leaders of the Friends of the New Germany.

Early in 1932, locals of the National Socialist German Labor Party began to spring up in the United States. By April of the same year, a local had appeared in New York City, another in Chicago (supplanting Teutonia), and yet another in Detroit.[5] By March 1933 four more locals had sprouted in Cincinnati, Los Angeles, San Francisco, and Hudson County (N. J.).[6] These groups were very definitely branches of the Nazi Party of Germany and they took orders from it. When in April, 1933, Rudolf Hess, then assistant Fuhrer of the Nazi Party, ordered them to dissolve, they obeyed promptly.[7] Two months later, men who had been active leaders of the Nazi locals held a convention in Chicago and created the Friends of the New Germany. Presumably, former Nazi Party members constituted much of the charter membership of the Friends.

Another group that preceded the Friends of the New Germany and was later absorbed by it, was the Friends of Germany. Despite the similarity of name, these were two separate organizations. The Friends of Germany was organized in the spring of 1933, only a few months earlier than the Friends of New Germany. The Friends of Germany had a membership of American citizens and its purpose was apparently to provide a channel through which American citizens, who were barred from membership in the Nazi Party, might express their sympathy for Nazi Germany. Its organizer was an American citizen, a Colonel Emerson.[8] His office, which served as the headquarters and meeting place, was in Room 131, 17 Battery Place, New York City. On the same floor was the office of the German Consul-General of New York. The proximity of the two offices suggests that perhaps the Friends of Germany had not sprung up spontaneously and that although the leadership and membership of the group were American the real impetus was definitely German.

The Friends of Germany was not a large group, but it was influential in distributing propaganda throughout the country. The organization conscientiously carried out the following promise contained in its letter soliciting members: "we shall send you as occasion arises, free of cost, authentic information about the latest events in Germany". For about a year, the Friends of Germany and the Friends of the New Germany worked in the same fields without any conflict. Then, in May of 1934, the Friends of Germany quietly retired after suggesting to its members that they join the Friends of the New Germany. The final letter sent to its membership read in part:

> In recognition of the fulfillment of the major aims of this Society, the executive board of the Friends of Germany at its last meeting concluded that the mission of our Society is virtually accomplished.
>
> Accordingly the board accepted the offered resignations of the chairman, treasurer, and secretary . . . so it was resolved to cease further activities in the name of the Friends of Germany.
>
> In view of the circumstance that our Society shortly after its inception was followed by another organization, known as the League of the Friends of the New Germany (*Bund der Freunde des Neuen Deutschland*), some of the aims of which may appeal to those of our former members who might welcome another outlet for betokening their goodwill to Germany, we submit to your consideration the enclosed printed statement from that Society, in which the two undersigned already enjoy membership.
>
> After consultation between the officers of that Society and ours it was agreed that former members of our Friends of Germany, who had sent us one dollar, would be absolved of paying the customary initiation fee of one dollar to the *Bund der Freunde des Neuen Deutschsland*, in case they join the Bund.

These, then, were the two predecessors of the Friends of the New

Germany—the Nazi Party locals and the Friends of Germany.[9] In 1934, a year after its founding, the Friends of the New Germany had nearly 5,000 members. Considerable publicity and internal struggles for leadership accompanied its subsequent growth. At a convention in Buffalo on March 29, 1936, it changed its name to the German-American Bund.

LEADERSHIP

Since Bund leaders run the organization dictatorially, information about their backgrounds, prejudices, and techniques is extremely important. The first Bund leader was Heinz Spanknoebel, a young German photo-engraver, who entered the United States under the false assertion that he was a clergyman. In a letter to Walter Kappe, an important Bund member, he had asseverated that he was entitled to his post by virtue of "full authorizations from the Supreme Party Office [in Germany] as well as from the Ministry of Propaganda."[10] Fritz Gissibl, formerly prominent in Teutonia, was second in command. Rivalry arose between Spanknoebel on the one hand and Gissibl and Kappe on the other. Then, in the fall of 1933, a Federal warrant was issued for the arrest of Spanknoebel on the grounds that he was acting as an agent for Germany without being an accredited attaché of the German diplomatic or consular service and that he had failed to notify the State Department of his activities. When a Grand Jury in New York City indicted him in November 1933 he suddenly disappeared.[11] His office was promptly taken by Fritz Gissibl, a 31-year-old German citizen and a resident of the United States since 1923. For a brief period Gissibl lived in Chicago, working as a pressman for the *Chicago Daily News*. In 1926 he joined the Teutonia and became a very active member. When the magazine *Today* announced in late March 1934 that it would run a series of articles exposing the Nazis in America, Gissibl hastily resigned from office. His successor was Reinhold Walter, an American citizen. Although born in Germany, Walter had spent 28 of his 50 years in the United States and had been a naturalized citizen for 17 years. Presumably, his citizenship was to give the Bund a truly American character. Walter, however, was merely a figurehead, as he himself admitted to the McCormack Committee.[12] Gissibl remained the real power in the Bund and even continued to draw a regular salary.[18] Nevertheless Walter was not always willing to be a "yes" man, for on one occasion he called the police in an effort to expel Gissibl and his cohorts. In July 1934 Gissibl ousted Walter and appointed Herbert Schnuch, a naturalized citizen with a college degree, and a former president of Teutonia. At this time the two most influential men in the organization, though neither held office, were Gissibl and Kappe, both aliens.[14] Kappe, also a former president of Teutonia, was the editor of the organization's newspaper, the *Deutsches Zeitung* (subsequently called the *Deutscher Beobachter*). In the nominal regime of Schnuch, internal warfare lasting eight months broke out.

> Dr. Herbert Schnuch, the national leader of the Friends of New Germany, had named Anton Haegele as assistant national leader. These two men were working together harmoniously, until in the latter part of December, 1934, Haegele and a group of his adherents, by a *putsch*, took possession of the offices and the physical effects of the New York headquarters of the Friends of the New Germany including control of the official organ, the *Deutscher Beobachter*. From then on a ferocious internal strife raged. . . .[15]

Schnuch dragged the fight into court in an unsuccessful effort to win the return of the *Beobachter* and headquarters. Charges and counter-charges were hurled back and forth. Virtually all the charges Haegele made against Schnuch—terrorism, misappropriation of funds, and the like—Schnuch made against Haegele. By the fall of 1935, Haegele apparently realized that he could not hope to gain control of the organization, for he retired from it and with his adherents formed a new group, the *Bund des Amerikan National Socialists* or the American National Socialist League. This group soon passed quietly out of existence.

On December 1, 1935, Fritz J. Kuhn became head of the Friends of the New Germany.[16] Kuhn, born in Munich in 1895, has had a colorful past. Throughout the four years of the World War he served with the German Army and saw service on four different fronts—French, Italian, Serbian, and Roumanian.[17] After the war, he studied chemistry in Munich and participated in the troubled politics of post-war Germany. In 1919 he was a member of the *Epp Freikorps* and in 1921 he was active in the *Oberland Freikorps*.[18]

In 1923, Kuhn left Germany and went to Mexico. Exactly why he left his native land is not entirely clear. When questioned before the Dies Committee on this point, he answered:

> Because the revolution was going on; inflation was there. Every second man was out of work. I lost my job. I had a very good job with one of the greatest chemical concerns. We were thrown out by the French Army of Occupation. A colored regiment came in. A woman was not safe any more there. I had to take my wife away, because they attacked right and left. There was not any work in Germany at all. Every second one was out of work. And if a man had a job he got a salary he could not live on. I had to go somewhere.[19]

Though this statement offered some insight into the economic con-

ditions out of which Naziism arose and which evidently made Kuhn
sympathetic with the movement, Kuhn's reasons for leaving Germany
did not jibe with the testimony presented by other witnesses. Gerhard
Segar, publisher of a German language newspaper in New York City,
told the Dies Committee:

> In 1921 Mr. Kuhn was convicted and sentenced to four months im-
> prisonment for petty theft. He had ransacked the pockets of the
> overcoats of his fellow students in the university building of Munich.
> When he was released from jail it was difficult for him, as a former
> convict, to find a position. Upon urgent request of his parents, a
> Jewish friend of the family by the name of Mr. Reinhold Spitz took
> him into his warehouse. Mr. Kuhn rewarded the old friend of his
> family and his benefactor by stealing merchandise in the value of
> 2,000 marks. It was only upon the urgent request of Mr. Kuhn's
> parents that his benefactor refrained from notifying the police, and
> Mr. Spitz discharged Mr. Kuhn; his last good deed to the family by
> Mr. Spitz was that he participated in setting up a fund in order to
> send Mr. Kuhn abroad to Mexico.[20]

Benefactor Spitz, now a resident of the United States, presented this
information in an affidavit. Segar published the facts in his newspaper and challenged Kuhn to bring suit against him for libel. Although Kuhn has frequently instituted libel suits he has never accepted
Segar's challenge. Nor did he ever publicly deny the charges of theft.
Naturally, Kuhn's subsequent conviction in 1939 for embezzling Bund
funds, lent substance to Segar's charges.

While in Mexico from 1923 until 1927, Kuhn worked as an industrial chemist. He entered the United States in 1927 and obtained a
position at the Ford hospital laboratory in Detroit. Several years
later he was transferred to Ford's Rouge River plant in Dearborn.[21]
In 1933 he became an American citizen.[22] Exactly when he became
affiliated with the Friends of New Germany is not known, but the
group's own paper has declared that he joined the organization at its
inception, which presumably means June 1933.[23] For two years he
was leader of the Detroit local; and from September, 1935, until
December of same year (when he was made national head of the
organization), he was the leader of the *Gau Mittelwest* (the Mid-West
District), one of the three areas into which the organization was
divided for purposes of national administration. The procedure by
which Kuhn originally obtained the national leadership is not entirely
clear. All that is known is his confirmation as the national leader at
the 1936 convention of the Friends. At the next convention, held on
July 4, 1937, he was unanimously reelected for a four-year term.

Kuhn's leadership ended in December 1939 when a New York court sentenced him to four years in the penitentiary for stealing Bund funds. His successor and the present head of the Bund is G. Wilhelm Kunze. Kunze first distinguished himself as leader of the Philadelphia local, which he built up into a powerful organization, although small in membership. Later he became the National Director of Public Relations and National Field Representative, posts he held until his rise to his present position. He is one of the few leading Bundists who speaks perfect English as well as perfect German. All his actions have indicated that he is a capable leader.

The relations between the leaders and the rank-and-file members of the German-American Bund are not particularly democratic. Generally, the Nazi *führer prinzip* (leadership principle) applies. The pledge of applicants for membership in the Bund includes this statement: "I acknowledge the leadership principle according to which the League is being directed." [24] Similarly, the code of an *Ordnungs Dienst* man (Storm Trooper) states: "Like the whole movement, he stands for the leadership principle." On the other hand, the management of the Bund is not wholly undemocratic to judge by its constitution of 1936. The organization's national convention is empowered to "elect a National Leader, who in turn shall have the power to nominate and with the advice and consent of the national convention, shall appoint" nine other national officers.[25] District (*gau*) Leaders are supposed to be appointed by the National Leader with the advice and consent of the national convention,[26] but local leaders, appointed by District Leaders, are subject to the approval of the National Leader.[27]

To what extent are Bund leaders subservient to orders from abroad? Are they puppets in the hands of Nazi officials in Germany or are they leaders in their own right? Evidence obtained by both the McCormack and Dies Committees plainly shows that they have frequently taken orders from Berlin.

> The testimony also shows that the Friends of the New Germany had a select committee . . . appointed by the party leaders to hear all complaints against members for violations of the rules, regulations, and orders of the movement in the United States, and that some of the recommendations of such committee were forwarded to the proper officials in Germany for final action.

When under cross-examination, Fritz Gissibl, one-time head of the Friends, admitted unequivocally that he was taking orders from abroad.

> Questioner: You were taking orders, of course, from Germany. There is no question about that?
> Gissibl: I was taking orders, yes, sir. . . .
> Questioner: In any event, you took instructions from high officials in the party in Germany.
> Gissibl: Yes, I did.[28]

Another significant instance of a leader's taking orders from abroad was indicated by the following cable from Spanknoebel to Rudolf Hess, Secretary of the National Socialist German Labor Party:

> Party member Richard Schollbach possesses letter supreme party office containing announcement his installation confidential agent party U. S. A. Reestablishment party organization or installation additional party representatives gravest political consequences unavoidable. Schollbach irresponsible trouble maker. Such incomprehensible measures destroy everything built up so far. Urgently request finding out which office responsible. Confirm by cable my sole responsibility otherwise uncalculable consequences.[29]

Clearly, Spanknoebel was not head of the Friends of the New Germany in his own right. When a question of authority arose, he had to turn to someone higher to settle it and this someone higher was an important member of Hitler's cabinet.

Foreign domination of the movement has been evidenced in many other instances. Nazi secret police have kidnapped to Germany both Spanknoebel,[30] and a Mr. Weber.[31] The latter was very active in the Brooklyn local; his immigration papers "were not in such good shape" and when his arrest by American authorities appeared imminent and would have been embarrassing to the organization, he vanished. In another instance, Bohle, head of the Foreign Department of the National Socialist German Labor Party, ordered Reinhold Walter to replace Gissibl as leader of the Friends of New Germany.[32] When Rudolph Hess issued his deceptive ukase that all German citizens living abroad refrain from mixing in the politics of their resident country, the Bund promptly complied by limiting its membership to American citizens and by requiring its alien members to become naturalized. The ukase appeared on the front page of the New York *Deutscher Weckruf und Beobachter* on December 19, 1935, accompanied by an editorial stating that the Bund was "firmly resolved to carry out the order strictly."

Many German Consuls in the United States have cooperated closely with the Bund. Typical was the evidence brought out in a letter written by Spanknoebel, head of the Bund: "Our office here leans heavily on the Consul-General. . . ."[33] Another instance was Gissibl's testimony that after he resigned the nominal leadership of the Bund, Dr. Johannes Borchers, the German Consul-General in New York cautioned him to keep out of the Bund since membership in it was incompatible with membership in the Nazi Party.[34] In a letter to Spanknoebel, Reinhold Freytag, the Consul in St. Louis, assured him of close cooperation, and furnished him with the names of St. Louis

residents who could help form a Bund local.[35]   Consul-General Baron
Manfred von Killinger of San Francisco has spoken before Bund locals
several times. On one occasion he accompanied the Los Angeles Consul to a picnic of the local Bund group. The Vice-Consul at Pittsburgh
has been well known for his active participation in Bund meetings.
Schwinn, the Bund's District Leader on the Pacific Coast, and the
Los Angeles Consul, Dr. Gyssling, have been on particularly good
terms; the Consul once gave Schwinn $145 to further Bund activities.[36]
Films of important activities in Nazi Germany, which are frequently
shown at Bund meetings, are sent to the Bund in care of the German
Embassy in Washington and the Consul-General in New York.[37]
Although the Consuls have not necessarily given orders to the Bund,
they are sometimes instructed to aid the Bund. As proof, Fritz Kuhn's
boast to an aide, who subsequently turned out to be a secret investigator, may be cited:

> You see, I have a certain special arrangement with Hitler and
> Germany that whenever any of our groups have trouble with the
> Consulates in their districts they are to report it to me at once in full
> detail. I then take it up with the Ambassador, and Germany is not
> to be troubled with it unless I get no satisfaction from the Ambassador.
> That is exactly why there is a new Ambassador to the United
> States and this is exactly why many Consuls have been and still are
> being removed. All new Consuls are National Socialists and under
> special instructions to give us the fullest cooperation in every way.[38]

Other instances of German control abound. Severin Winterscheidt,
for three years managing editor and advertising manager of the
Deutscher Weckruf und Beobachter, visited Erlangen, Germany, on
September 10, 1936, and was sworn in by Julius Streicher as a representative of Nazi propaganda. Since then Winterscheidt has spoken
at numerous rallies of the Bund. (These facts came out in connection
with Winterscheidt's sentence to the New York County Penitentiary on
charges of indecent exposure and endangering the morals of a minor.)
In the summer of 1937, Schwinn, the West Coast Bund leader, and his
assistant, Karl Hein, spent six weeks in Germany taking a course in
propaganda offered by Dr. Goebbels' Ministry of Propaganda and
Public Enlightenment. The trip was paid for through a secret agree-
ment between Kuhn and the Nazi Government.[39]   Schwinn made a
practice of visiting German ships while they were in port in order to
give the captains material he wanted sent back to Germany—usually
reports of the status of Bund activities in America.[40]   In at least one
instance visiting German naval officers have been used to check on the
work of Bund leaders. In 1936 several officers from the German cruiser
Karlsruhe were instructed to make such a report.

The Bund's frequently repeated assertion that it is subject to no foreign control is disputed by the very statements of high Nazi officials. The head of the *Auslandsdeutsches Institut* (League of Germans Abroad), Wilhelm Bohle, spoke with full authority when he said:

> Loyalty, discipline, and blind obedience are the foundation pillars of every branch of the National Socialist government. The loose contact and the distance in mileage between party comrades abroad, *even though the organizations for Germans abroad is a solid unit,* render these three virtues more necessary than ever for those of us in foreign countries. Therefore we are doing right when we keep our organizations abroad free of all racial comrades who are not ready to adhere to *the absolute discipline customary with us.*[41] (My emphasis—D. S. S.)

Moreover, the Bund's assertion hardly squares with the following decree issued by the Reich Minister of Education:

> I therefore order that all persons subject to my ministry who travel abroad for study, research, or lectures, or for congresses, or similar purposes, shall on their arrival in a foreign country forthwith get into contact with *the foreign organization of the Nazi party. . . .*[42] (My emphasis—D. S. S.)

Nor does the Bund's assertion jibe with the role of Nazi group leaders in foreign countries, as defined by the official publication of the League of Germans Abroad:

> Just as the Ambassador, the Envoy, and the Consul represent the government of the Reich abroad, so is the National Socialist group leader the standard bearer of the foreign organization, the representative of the movement for German reconstruction and German conservation. He is the representative of the German nation abroad.[43]

And by its own admission the Bund is the authorized representative of the Nazi dictatorship, for one of its yearbooks boldly proclaims:

> We stand here as the heralds of the Third Reich, as preachers of the German world viewpoint, of National Socialism, which has displayed before the eyes of the world the incomparable German miracle, the miracle of National Socialism.[44]

MEMBERSHIP

Applicants for membership in the Bund must take the following pledge:

> I herewith declare my entry into the League of the Friends of the New Germany. The purpose and aim of the League are known to me and I obligate myself to support them without reservation.
> I acknowledge the leadership principle according to which the League is being directed.
> I do not belong to any secret organization of any kind (Freemasons, etc.). I am of Aryan descent, free of Jewish or colored racial traces.

Various membership restrictions have not always been enforced. Reinhold Walter has testified that "everyone applying for membership has been accepted." [45] No reference to American citizenship appeared in the Bund membership requirements until December, 1935, when Rudolf Hess made his guileful statement concerning the political conduct of German citizens living abroad. As a strategic move of self protection against being labeled foreign, the Bund recently revised its membership qualifications and its constitution now contains the following clause:

> Membership in this Bund is primarily open to all American and prospective citizens of Aryan blood, of German extraction and of good reputation. Membership may also be extended to other national elements filling the requirements of our membership application. (Article IV, Section 1.)

The phrase "other national elements" probably excludes resident aliens of other than German extraction. The provision for admitting "prospective citizens," however, leaves the Bund's door open to an influx of aliens. To what extent this has occurred will be considered later.

The number of Bund members has been greatly exaggerated. Newspaper and magazine articles have estimated the number at 100,000 or 125,000. On July 27, 1937, Representative Samuel Dickstein told his fellow Congressmen that the Bund had 350,000 members. These figures are absurdly high; 25,000 is a generous estimate of even the peak membership. In October 1933 the national membership was only 400 or 500, but during the next nine months it expanded rapidly and by summer 1934 reached 5,000. Late in 1935 the membership rolls suffered losses when Anton Haegele and his followers seceded to form the American National Socialist Party; and in December of the same year the order from Hess forcing aliens out of the organization caused a further loss.

In September 1937 the *Chicago Daily Times*, which had three reporters making a careful study of the Bund from within, estimated the membership at 20,000.[46] In January 1938 the Department of Justice, after a cursory investigation, put the figure at 8,500.[47] In August 1938 a special investigator for the Dies' Committee estimated the number of members at 25,000. When questioned on this point a year later by the Dies' Committee, Fritz Kuhn replied, "Well, very roughly, around 20,000." Thus, the best available, recent estimates put the membership at between 20,000 and 25,000. Incidentally, the imprisonment of Kuhn and the change to a new leader has not produced any disintegration of the movement or loss of membership.

The number of Bund locals, geographically well-distributed, has been growing steadily. In 1934 there were 40 locals;[48] in 1937 there were 55;[49] in 1939 there were 71.[50] All local units are distributed among three districts or *gaue*. The following list of locals was recently presented by Kuhn to the Dies Committee:[51]

Eastern District (*Gau Ost*)

Albany (N. Y.)
Astoria (N. Y.)
Baltimore (Md.)
Bergen County (N. J.)
Boston (Mass.)
Bridgeport (Conn.)
Bronx (N. Y.)
Brooklyn (N. Y.)[1]
Buffalo (N. Y.)
Glendale (N. Y.)
Greenwich (Conn.)
Hartford (Conn.)
Hudson County (N. J.)
Jamaica (N. Y.)[2]

Lancaster (Pa.)
Lindenhurst, (N. Y.)
Nassau County (N. Y.)
New Britain (Conn.)
New Haven (Conn.)
New Rochelle (N. Y.)
New York (N. Y.)[3]
Newark (N. J.)
Ossining (N. Y.)
Passaic County (N. J.)
Philadelphia (Pa.)
Pittsburgh (Pa.)
Poughkeepsie (N. Y.)
Providence (R. I.)

Reading (Pa.)
Rochester (N. Y.)
Rockland County
  (N. Y.)
Schenectady (N. Y.)
Sellersville (Pa.)
South Brooklyn (N. Y.)[4]
Stamford (Conn.)
Staten Island (N. Y.)[5]
Syracuse (N. Y.)
Troy (N. Y.)
Utica (N. Y.)
White Plains (N. Y.)

Mid-West District (*Gau Mittelwest*)

Chicago, (Ill.)
Cincinnati (O.)
Cleveland (O.)
Dayton (O.)
Detroit (Mich.)
Fort Wayne (Ind.)
Gary (Ind.)

Indianapolis (Ind.)
Kenosha (Wis.)
Milwaukee (Wis.)
Minneapolis (Minn.)
Omaha (Nebr.)
St. Louis (Mo.)
St. Paul (Minn.)

Sheboygan (Wis.)
South Bend (Ind.)
South Chicago (Ill.)
Taylor (Tex.)
Toledo (O.)

Western District (*Gau West*)

Los Angeles (Calif.)
Oakland (Calif.)
Petaluma (Calif.)
Portland (Oreg.)

San Diego (Calif.)
San Francisco (Calif.)
San Gabriel Valley
  (Calif.)

Santa Barbara (Calif.)
Seattle (Wash.)
Spokane (Wash.)

---

[1] A borough of New York city.
[2] In the borough of Queens, New York City.
[3] The borough of Manhattan, New York City.
[4] In the borough of Brooklyn, New York City.
[5] A borough of New York City.

It is noteworthy that 17 of the 69 locals are within the metropolitan region of New York. Among these 17 are the largest locals. Kuhn has testified that about 40 percent of the Bund membership is in the Greater New York area.[52]

Citizenship Characteristics

Aliens outnumbered citizens in the Friends of the New Germany in its early years. Table 2 lists as of early 1934 the number of citizens and aliens in each of the 13 important locals. Not only did aliens make up 64 percent of the membership of the organization but the remaining 36 percent consisted of naturalized rather than native-born citizens. In other words, second generation German-Americans and persons of more remote German ancestry showed virtually no interest in the organization.

Table 2

NUMBER OF CITIZENS AND ALIENS IN THIRTEEN LOCALS OF THE BUND

Local	Membership	Citizens	Aliens
Brooklyn.	458	126	332
Buffalo.	106	38	68
Chicago.	237	88	149
Cincinnati.	69	22	47
Clifton (N. J.).	54	21	33
Detroit.	276	171	105
Hudson County (N. J.).	162	65	97
Los Angeles.	118	45	73
Newark.	100	25	75
Philadelphia.	200	62	138
Rochester (N. Y.).	17	5	12
San Francisco.	99	24	75
White Plains (N. Y.).	40	9	31
Total.	1,936	701	1,235

Table 3, compiled from another source,[53] shows that the Chicago local in 1934 had only two native-born citizens in a membership of 237!

Table 3

ALIEN, NATURALIZED, AND NATIVE-BORN MEMBERS OF BUND'S CHICAGO LOCAL

Aliens:		Naturalized Citizens:		Native-born Citizens: 2
Germans	146	German birth	84	
Austrian	2	Austrian birth	2	
Swiss	1			
	149		86	
Total: 237				

That the Chicago local is not exceptional is shown by the testimony of Mr. Kruppa, a Bund official.[54]

Questioner: The old-line American of German blood has not been involved in the movement, has he?
Mr. Kruppa: Very little.

THE GERMAN-AMERICAN BUND

Questioner: That is what the evidence before this committee discloses. Outside of a very few . . . the American of German blood, the old-line American of German blood is more or less passive.
Mr. Kruppa: Correct.

The smallness of the recently-formed locals in such cities as Cincinnati, St. Louis, and Milwaukee, which have a large population of German extraction, is a further significant indication. As a St. Louis Bund member has put it, "The old Germans of St. Louis are so American they don't want anything to do with us." [55] This does not mean that the members are all recent immigrants. The Chicago local has some men 60 or 70 years of age who came to this country in their teens.

Conditions have not changed considerably since 1934. To be sure, the order from Hess has supposedly banned German citizens from the Bund, and the Bund's spokesmen and its literature have taken great pains to make the organization "American". But all the evidence indicates that the Bund now has almost as large an alien membership as it has ever had. At its secret convention in New York on April 21, 1938, the Bund admitted that 45 percent of its members were German citizens.

The Bund has resorted to devious ruses to conceal its alien membership. In Chicago it formed a separate group for aliens, the *Deutscher Volksbund*.[56] Other locals have used similar subterfuges. Sometimes the names of alien members are kept in a different part of the membership book. For all practical purposes, however, there is no difference. Alien members participate in all Bund activities and are subordinate to Bund officers in every way. The attempt at separation has been made to avoid embarrassment in the event of further Congressional investigation.

It is possible to make reasonably accurate generalizations concerning the economic status of Bund members. One approach is to note in newspaper articles the references to the vocations of Bund members. Accordingly, the membership in New York includes, for example, a retired physician, a perfume salesman, a watch importer, an electrical contractor, a barber, a delicatessen dealer, a pastry chef; in Cleveland, a dentist, a hotel bartender, the sports editor of a local German paper, and a designer of bronze gadgets; in Pittsburgh, a mechanical engineer and a "naturopath"; in Chicago, a photographer, a bartender, and an expert hairdresser; in Milwaukee, a designing engineer; in South Bend, Indiana, a cobbler, a contractor, and a janitor; in Oakland, California, a waiter and a cook. According to Dr. Erick von Schroeder, a prominent anti-Nazi leader, Bund members are definitely "middle-class". He attributes the paucity of workmen in the Bund to the fact that workmen who have emigrated from Germany have been Social Democrats.

A more scientific approach is to study the addresses of Bund members in the light of census data on median rentals. The addresses of Chicago Bund members, for example, can be "spotted" in various census sub-communities and the median rental for these areas noted. In their volume, *Census Data of the City of Chicago*, Ernest W. Burgess and Charles Newcomb have divided the monthly rentals of 832,291 homes into five approximately equal classes designated as highest, high, middle, low, and lowest. Each class has a range of rentals. If no one economic class predominates in the Bund, 20 percent of the members should fall in each of these classes. The results of this analysis are shown in Table 4.

Table 4

ECONOMIC CLASS DISTRIBUTION OF CHICAGO BUND MEMBERS

Economic Class	Number of Homes	Median Rentals per Month	Percent of Bund Members
Highest	166,525	$43.6—$178.6	3.9%
High	167,612	36.9— 43.5	17.7
Middle	168,101	29.3— 36.8	17.7
Low	164,326	21.1— 29.2	37.
Lowest	165,727	8.9— 21.0	23.5

The outstanding fact is that 60.5 percent of the Bund members come from the low and lowest rental groups, whereas only 21.6 percent come from the high and highest groups. These statistics, together with von Schroeder's opinion and the virtual absence of manual vocations in newspaper references, clearly indicate that Bundists are "lower middle class."

The foregoing examination justifies a few valid conclusions. Almost all members of the Bund were born in Germany and about half are still German citizens; economically, they are predominantly lower middle class; geographically, they are spread all over the country, though in the Greater New York region they are numerically stronger than anywhere else.

PROPAGANDA

The main channels of propaganda used by the Bund are weekly newspapers, pamphlets, and public meetings. The four official newspapers serve various parts of the country. The New York newspaper first appeared about August 1933 as *Das Neue Deutschland*, a bi-weekly with an

English supplement. In January 1934 it became the *Deutsche Zeitung*, a weekly also with an English supplement, and ten months later it assumed the alias, the *Deutscher Beobachter*, a weekly. Since July 1, 1935, however, it has been published weekly as the *Deutscher Weckruf und Beobachter*. Three other papers—the *Chicago Deutscher Weckruf und Beobachter, Philadelphia Weckruf und Beobachter*, and the *California Deutscher Weckruf und Beobachter*—are almost facsimiles of the New York publication. All four papers contain the same news, partly in German and partly in English; each carries advertisements from its own region. The papers, of full news-sheet size, are published in Philadelphia. Only fragmentary figures on circulation are available. In 1934 the circulation of the *Deutsche Zeitung* was 20,000 or 21,000.[57] A subscription campaign to build the circulation proved a failure, and at the time of the convention in April 1938 the total for all the Bund papers was down to 10,000.

"The National Socialist German Labor Party . . . furnished tons of propaganda literature, which in most cases was smuggled into this country." So read the final report of the McCormack Committee.[58] The hearings of the Committee are full of details about vast quantities of miscellaneous printed propaganda arriving on German liners. A typical example is the testimony of a United States Customs official reporting on the seizure of some literature aboard the German vessel *Estes*.[59] "I stopped at the cook's quarters. . . . In his room I found fifty-three packages of printed matter, about three or four hundred pounds of pamphlets, booklets, postcards, and newspaper articles." A similar report read:

> He told me . . . he had been invited to go aboard the Hamburg-American boat, the S. S. Vancouver, and he engaged one of the crew in conversation. He innocently asked whether they had any material on board which contained recent word from Germany, since he had not been in touch with developments there for some time. He was taken to a storeroom and there saw large stacks of German newspapers, which he estimates would total 2500 copies. He was given about 200 papers and was told he should visit other ships as they came into port, and no doubt they all carried similar supplies when they arrived from the other side.

Most of the miscellaneous propaganda is in German, though some of it is in English. Its distribution takes place through sales at the meetings of Bund locals. Accounts of these meetings invariably describe long tables piled high with Nazi books, pamphlets, and newspapers. A number of bookstores also sell this material. The following publications are characteristic:

ORGANIZED ANTI-SEMITISM IN AMERICA

Der Sturmer
Volkischer Beobachter
Das Schwarze Korps

BOOKS AND PAMPHLETS

Positive Christianity
Blood and Race
Wer Wir sind und Was Wir Wollen
The Riddle of the Jew's Success
Who are the Rulers of Russia?
Bolshevism in Theory and Practice
The Destruction of Domestic Life through Bolshevism
Bolshevik Atrocities in Spain
The Truth About the Jews in Germany
Bolshevism Unmasked
Die Juden—by Feder
Die Geheimnisse der Weisen von Zion—by Beek
Jude und Arbeiter—by Schulz
Handbuch der Judenfrage—by Fritsch
Freimauer, Weltrevolution, Weltrepublic—by Wichtel
The International Jew—by Henry Ford
Communism with the Mask Off—by Joseph Goebbels

Not all material has come from Germany. Pamphlets such as the following have been published by the Bund here in the United States:

The New Germany Under Hitler—by Frederick F. Schrader
Lifting the Pall—by R. C. Dasker
Litvinoff—by E. N. Sanctuary
The Snake in the Grass

PUBLIC MEETINGS

The Bund makes intensive propagandist use of the public meeting. Sessions of the Chicago, New York, and Brooklyn locals, which have attracted the largest audiences, have been frequently held at the Bund camps (of which there are 22). At Camp Yaphank, Long Island, several meetings have drawn as many as 5,000 persons. The smaller locals, however, often have sparsely attended gatherings. Sometimes meetings have been held aboard German liners, with the steamship company acting as host in behalf of the fatherland.

Some locals—including Hammond (Indiana), Chicago, San Francisco, Los Angeles, and Portland (Oregon)—have made use of the radio as a medium of propaganda. But a much more important medium has been the youth summer camp. Nineteen locals have had youth groups connected with such camps, the nature of which was condemned from the very first by the McCormack Committee:

> The organization . . . conducted so-called "youth summer camps" at different localities, at which nothing of American history or of American principles of government were taught. . . .
>
> On the contrary, the children were taught to recognize Hitler as their leader, to salute him on all occasions, and to believe that the principles of government taught by him were superior to the principles of our government.

Other evidence has indicated that Bund camps as well as the youth organizations are used to inculcate in children the Nazi philosophy. A letter written by the Chicago youth leader in answer to an inquiry about the youth groups said:

> We find that today there is no institution for our young people . . . that, on the contrary, everything is done to deride our race and people, so that the U. S. A. is influenced if not dominated by personalities hostile to everything German . . .
>
> Our boys and girls are banded together in their youth organization in order . . . to serve the aims of the German element organized in the nationwide German-American Bund for better understanding of the two countries . . .

As North American "Commander" of Nazi youth groups, Theodore Dinkelacker knew whereof he spoke when he said at a meeting in Brooklyn:

> We must make every conceivable effort to obtain a tight grip on all German-American youngsters. Never mind these American schools; they have to be educated to become useful fighters for our German unity. It is the duty of every person of German blood in this country to support this phase of our work. In this way you will help our youth who are destined to carry forward our Nazi ideals, and who will ultimately bring victory to the glorious German ideals here.[60]

More spectacular than the youth groups, though not yet as important, is the *Ordnungs Dienst*, the Storm Troop auxiliary of the Bund. The uniform of this branch is so similar to that of the German Storm Troopers that it has attracted a considerable amount of attention. All the larger locals have an *Ordnungs Dienst*, a select group of members whose avowed purpose is to police the Bund gatherings. In the background is the thought that the *Ordnungs Dienst* may be useful in some period of internal strife coming in the not too distant future. The Bund viewpoint on this matter is set forth in the chapter on "Propaganda."

FUNDS

The income of the Bund is derived from the following sources: dues, sale of literature and advertising, collections at meetings, profits of social events, donations from wealthy German-Americans, and subsidies from Germany.

Dues are 75 cents a month; the initiation fee, $3. The sale of books and pamphlets as well as of subscriptions to the *Deutscher Weckruf und Beobachter* are steady sources of income. The Bund newspapers and the programs of the numerous Bund-sponsored festivals invariably contain scores of advertisements. A highly lucrative source is the collection taken at every public meeting and the pledges members frequently make for specific Bund objectives. Albert Zimmer, head of the Cincinnati local, has helpfully explained the circumstances under which wealthy German-Americans contribute to the Bund treasury:

> No one knows this, but we have a permanent list of silent contributors. Most of them are wealthy Germans who feel they cannot afford, for political or business reasons, to support us openly, but who are sympathetic with our movement.
>
> You see, more than sixty percent of Cincinnati is of German extraction. . . . Of course most of these people do not agree with Hitler, but at the same time Hitler represents Germany to them. And they will not tolerate any criticism, verbal or written, of Germany. They consider it a reflection on themselves.

In some cases, the wealthy contributors are Bund members, as in the following instance.

> The Brooklyn local boasts of having "the only millionaire member," said to be an elderly Brooklyn woman who thrillingly greets the marching O. D. men (Storm Troopers) as "Oh, my boys!" and finances many of the Bund activities. She is said to have a weakness, when thus overcome by emotion, for contributing $100 bills for various Bund ventures.[61]

Contributions by American citizens not of German extraction is rare. The only instance on record involved two Californians who made a contribution to the Pacific Coast branch of the organization.

The chief form of known subsidy that the Bund gets from the Nazi government is steamship and railroad advertising in the Bund paper. The report of the McCormack Committee revealed:

> Documentary evidence before the committee obtained from the companies (Hapag-Lloyd and the German Railways) shows that this subsidy was ordered from Germany and amounted, in the case of the steamship lines, to $600 per month and in the case of the railways to $200 per month without regard to the amount of space used.

The phrase "without regard to the amount of space used" meant that the paper might give the companies a smaller-than-usual advertisement in a particular edition without ever affecting any financial adjustment or space compensation. The $200 and $600 monthly rates were established when the Bund paper had just started and had a circulation of only four hundred.

The only other evidence of money from the German government concerns gifts from West Coast Consuls to the Los Angeles and the San Francisco locals of the Bund. While conducting one of three Bund radio programs on the coast, Henry Lage, San Francisco leader, declared that the local Consul was so interested in these programs that the Bund looked to him for financial help to keep them going. When queried on this matter, Fritz Kuhn replied: "Yes, yes, I know all about the financial angles in regard to the Bund and the Consulates." A witness before the Dies Committee asserted that Dr. Gyssling, the German Consul at Los Angeles, once gave $145 to Herman Schwinn, the Pacific Coast *gau leiter* (District Leader) in order "to tide over a deficit at the German House." [62]

None of this evidence, however, indicates that any large proportion of the Bund's total expenses is defrayed by money sent from Germany. The fees for the steamship and railroad advertisements are small in proportion to the Bund's total income. The few contributions by Consuls do not prove that there is any systematic, widespread plan of financing the Bund from Germany. Moreover, it is entirely possible that some Consuls have been imposed on for a personal contribution or have volunteered personal contributions because they felt that doing so would look well on the record. Though it is possible that Germany sends the Bund large sums of money, several considerations make it seem improbable. First, the Bund has ample sources of income in the United States. Secondly, Germany is in no position to be exporting capital; it carefully conserves capital in order to pay for the vital raw materials it imports. Finally, money has on occasion gone the other way. Bund funds have been given to the Nazi Government. When Kuhn and other Bund leaders went to the Olympic games in Berlin in 1936, they gave Hitler $3,000 for German winter relief. This money came from the Bund treasury.[63] To reiterate: the amount of money the Bund receives from Germany makes up only a very small proportion of its total income.[64]

CHAPTER IV

The Silver Shirts

THE Silver Shirts and the other organizations yet to be discussed differ somewhat from the German-American Bund. For better or for worse, they have some distinctly American characteristics. As has been noted, the Bund is made up almost entirely of German-born persons (about half of whom are German citizens) and it is both controlled and subsidized from Germany. Despite all protestations to the contrary, Bund members are Germans first and last. The organizations about to be examined, however, seem part of the American scene. Their membership is predominantly old American stock and rarely includes recent immigrants. Nevertheless, these groups have much in common with the Bund.

The Silver Shirts, the most publicized and probably the most important of these groups, came into existence in February 1933 and reached its high point of 15,000 members in the summer of 1934. While it has members throughout the country at the present time, the majority are concentrated on the Pacific Coast.

Congressional investigation started the organization on the downgrade in 1934. Most of its posts broke up and many members went into such dissident splinter groups as the Constitution Legion of America, the American White Guards, and the Anti-Communist League of the World. In January 1935 another blow fell when William Dudley Pelley, the head of the Silver Shirts, and two associates were indicted for selling worthless stock of their Galahad Press. Pelley was convicted by a North Carolina court, sentenced to five years in the penitentiary, and fined $3500, but the sentence was suspended on grounds of "good behavior". The first half of 1935 saw the organization at its lowest ebb; it was practically inactive. In August of that year Pelley reorganized the Silver Shirts under an alias—the Christian Party. The latter disseminated the same ideas and consisted, to a large extent, of the same membership. The new organization was based upon cells called Councils of Safety—usually made up of nine men. Each cell member was required to organize a Council of his own, a process to be continued indefinitely. By December, the organization was beginning to grow again and by 1936 Pelley was brash enough to run for President on the

Christian Party ticket. His campaign efforts were greatest in Washington, the one state that permitted his party to be entered on the ballot. Although he stumped tirelessly for six months, he received only 1,598 votes out of a total of 700,000 cast in the state. For a few months after the election, the organization was without funds and completely inactive. It has since resumed its publishing ventures.

LEADERSHIP

The Silver Shirts, like all other groups in this study, has a leader whose personality dominates the organization: William Dudley Pelley or "Chief Pelley" to his cohorts. Born in Lynn, Massachusetts, in 1885, Pelley has let it be known that his paternal forebears are "of purest English stock".[1] In an autobiographical sketch, he has declared:

> I was born the only son of an itinerant Methodist preacher. Soon after my birth my parents began that old-fashioned Odyssey of traveling from "call" to "call" in the northern Massachusetts back hills.
> Orthodox Protestant theology, as it was forty years ago, was far more plentiful in my father's household than bread, butter, clothes, and fuel. Camp meetings and quarterly conferences, the higher criticism, predestination, free will and election, infant damnation, hell fire and the day of judgment constituted the household converse in my young and "tender" years. God early shaped up to me as a weird combination of heavenly Moloch and sublimated Overseer of the Poor.
> Parish poverty forced my father from the ministry, but with grim New England determination he saw to it that his relinquishment of the pulpit did not lessen my surfeit of conventional theology. Three times to church on the Sabbath day and twice during the week—left me small opportunity to forget my Maker and the gratitude I owed Him. Just what this gratitude was owed Him for troubled my small soul exceedingly in those far-off years, because I found myself created a perpetually hungry, shabbily dressed, and none-too-happy youngster who had to start his life labor at fourteen years of age and stay with it thereafter, even to the present.[2]

His life's labor was apparently begun in his father's toilet paper manufacturing establishment—the Pelley Tissue Corporation—at Springfield, Massachusetts. He rose to treasurer of the company in 1909, holding this position until 1912.[3] He described his life during these years as follows:

> In the years between fourteen and twenty-two I was a smouldering young Bolshevik against every kind of authority—particularly religious authority which had apparently sanctioned these injustices against me—and by picking up the rudiments of a denied education through promiscuous reading, I went far afield from accredited Christianty. . . .
> At twenty-two in a little town in Northern New York, I was

publishing a brochure magazine of heretical leanings (the *Philosopher Magazine*). I had discovered myself possessed of a certain facility with iconoclastic language. Fresh from a wry, lonely, misunderstood childhood . . . revengeful that I had been denied social and academic advantages for which my hunger was instinctive, I proceeded . . . to make things hot for several godly people . . . later I came to see that I took out on God what I should have taken out on an inhibited environment. . . .

I shopped around in my religion. I read still queerer books. For ten years I was one of the worst agnostics that ever had books come to his postoffice box in plain wrappers from freak publishing houses.

I had brains enough to see that my life had been started all wrong and was "getting no better fast", but had not the academic or social equipment to alter existence and start myself about-face.

Those were cruel, cruel years . . . looking back on them now. A couple of my business projects went to whack. So did my marriage. With each additional snarl I got more and more vindictive . . . I wrote a couple of novels . . . I knew my life was a ghastly mess, that I was cynical and caustic . . . that we got nothing in this world unless we fought for it with the ferocity of a Siberian wolf-dog.

The "business projects" mentioned in the above statement were the publishing of small town New England newspapers, among them the *Chicopee* (Massachusetts) *Journal* in 1913 and the *Wilmington* (Vermont) *Times* in 1917-1920. For a time he was on the staff of the *Bennington* (Vermont) *Banner*. In 1917, he was one of five men chosen by the Methodist Centenary and the Rockefeller Foundation to journey out to the Far East and make a survey of Protestant Foreign Missions. America's entry into the first World War found him in Japan. During the Siberian Intervention he accompanied the Japanese forces in the capacity of Y. M. C. A. official, Consular courier, and newspaper correspondent.

After the war he returned to the United States and devoted himself to writing. He wrote a novel or two and a great number of short stories for such periodicals as *Colliers, Good Housekeeping, Redbook,* and *American Magazine.* He wrote movie scenarios, too, and eventually made his home near Hollywood. Though his literary skill did not take him to the top rank of the profession, he was good enough to make the 1924-25 *Who's Who in America* and subsequent editions. This modest degree of success, however, brought Pelley no satisfaction. He recalled these post-war years bitterly:

I . . . came back to the United States to find a newspaper business in ruins. . . .

To save my newspaper creditors from loss, I went to Hollywood to labor among the Flesh Pots. I made a score of motion pictures, most of them flops because I had the uncanny facility for roiling the very persons whom I should have made my friends. I wrote a couple of

books which my publishers refused. I fought with them in conse-
quence, still taking life by strong-arm methods. I wrote many stories
that editors rejected. I fought them too.

When an editor wouldn't buy a certain story, I sat down at my
typewriter and contrived to tell him I thought him an ass. . . . You
see, I had the unfortunate complex that the attainment of success
meant a knock-down-and-drag-out scrap. It made me a lone wolf at
life, getting me the least bit mangy as I reached my forties.

Time after time I tried to correct my psychology and get back
certain religious (not theological) cues I felt I had lost with the pass-
ing of boyhood. I plunged deeper than ever into eleven pound
volumes on all sorts of race traits and behaviorism. I was a walking
exposition of how a man may reach middle life and be the worst
internal mess that ever got into *Who's Who*.

Ever since childhood I had lived under such a tremendous nervous
tension that it had kept me underweight, put lines on my face and an
edge on my voice, shattered me psychologically so that opposition
of any kind infuriated me and made me want to crash through it
like an army tank flattening out a breastworks.

Suddenly all this had departed.

I was peaceful inside.

The great change referred to was described in considerable detail for
the benefit of the readers of the *American Magazine* in a sensational
article entitled "My Seven Minutes in Eternity". According to the
article, he died for seven minutes sometime in 1928. It seems that he
left this world of strife, talked with several deceased friends and, after
exactly seven minutes, returned to earth a "new Pelley" with calm
nerves, an agreeable personality—and a determination to give up
smoking. The transformation was easily explained:

What is this thing that happened to me, and why did it happen?

First, I believe my subconscious hungered after what the Bible
terms, "the things of the spirit" . . . that is the sincere desire to
penetrate behind the mediocrity of three-meals-a-day living and
ascertain what mystery lies behind this Golgotha of Existence. . . .

Third, these experiences immediately revealed to me that there is a
world of subliminal or spiritual existence, interpenetrating the ordinary world in which most of us exist as ordinary two-legged Americans full of aches and worries, *and that this subliminal world is the
real world* . . . that it is waiting for the race to learn of it and "tap"
its beneficent resources, without waiting for what we call physical
death; that our dead dear ones are existent in it—alive, happy, conscious, and waiting for us to join them either at death or at any
time we reach that stage of spirituality when we can make contact
with them.

Despite the absence of more detailed psychological data, three things
may be said about Pelley's personality in his early years. First, he
was a frustrated intellectual. Second, his reaction to privation was

usually expressed by raging against whoever he thought was responsible. Third, he had an acute, unresolved religious problem. His frustrations dated back to the time when his family's poverty kept him from continuing his schooling after his fourteenth year. With the failures of some of his small-town New England publishing ventures, his frustrations continued. In 1921 separation from his wife caused additional injury. In the 1920's, though he made a reasonable amount of money through his short stories, novels, and scenarios, he was unable to rise above his competitors. He made a living but was not an outstanding success as a literary figure. He did not win considerable fame or fortune. He was still just a literary hack whose writings publishers frequently rejected. His mediocrity obsessed him as he entered his forties, conscious that his raging brought him no relief. He continued to live under a "tremendous nervous tension". Finally, he found a way out. He became a spiritualist. He abandoned the world of hard-boiled editors and keen competition, and entered the spiritualist's world of unreality. Here in the "world of subliminal or spiritual existence", where one could talk with "dead dear ones", Pelley found relief from his frustration and mediocrity. The fact that he was a second-rate literary hack no longer mattered because *this subliminal world is the real world*. The world of strife and frustration was only a delusion.

Exactly why Pelley chose this method of escape is difficult to say. Perhaps he came in contact with some of Southern California's many esoteric religious sects. Certainly, his unsolved religious problem predisposed him toward this escape. Never in adult life had he found anything to take the place of the Methodist Fundamentalism that had played such a dominant role in his adolescence. He outgrew his boyhood religion but found no substitute for it.

Though Pelley took up spiritualism as an escape from reality, he soon discovered that by talking and writing about it to others he could improve his mundane pecuniary resources. Hence, in 1930 he established in Asheville, North Carolina,[4] four interlocking spiritualistic enterprises—Galahad Press, Galahad College, the Foundation for Christian Economics, and the League for Liberation. The Pelley enterprises published great quantities of tracts on spiritualism and a monthly magazine called *Liberation*. Typical tracts included: *What is the Holy Spirit and How Does It Create?, That Great Migration of Souls to This Planet, How Divine Thought Operates on Matter, Which Souls Make Up the Dark Forces, Do Those Who Are Dead Meet God?, Identifying Your Soul in Eternity,* and *How to Understand the Workings of Karma.*

According to the title page, the magazine *Liberation* offered "in-

struction and inspiration from sources above and behind mortality"
and the "contents of this magazine, unless otherwise designated, were
received 'clairaudiently' via the Psychic Radio, from Great Souls, who
have graduated out of this three-dimensional world into other areas of
Time and Space".

Galahad College gave most of its instruction through mail order
courses, but it had some resident students whom it offered classes in
ethical history, public stewardship, spiritual eugenics, social meta-
psychics, (sic!), Christian philosophy, educational therapy, music, public expression, cosmic mathematics. The results were financially quite
satisfactory. In a four-month period of 1932, for example, more than
500 persons paid $60 apiece for the mail order course in "metapsychics".[5]
According to a Congressional report, nine out of ten of Pelley's followers
were women who gave him, and from whom he borrowed, varying sums
of money, in one case receiving bonds valued at $14,000.[6] The $14,000
came from a Mrs. Marie Ogden in return for an interest in the Galahad
Press.[7] The Pelley enterprises were not all uniformly successful.
Liberation did not appear regularly because of recurrent financial difficulties. Moreover, there were other similar difficulties, to judge by the
testimony of Pelley's business manager, George S. Anderson:

> During November and December [1932] the receipts decreased
> considerably, and I had difficulty in financing the payroll and other
> obligations. . . . In the latter part of November I urged Mr. Pelley
> to undertake some fiction writing again, believing that he could pull
> the institution up by its own bootstraps, if he could get out and do
> some fiction writing again. He went to New York and secured a
> new literary agent, and during the latter part of November and the
> early part of December, 1932, wrote—some seventeen short stories.[8]

Even after his swing to anti-semitism, Pelley remained just as much
a spiritualist as ever. In an issue of *Liberation* in early 1933 he informed his readers that "Chief Pelley has by long practice and training,
schooled himself to form his Clairaudient Contacts wherever he happens
to be". More recently, he addressed a group in California entirely on
his conversations with God and Jesus.

Until 1933, Pelley's activities and writings were devoid of political
consciousness. No reference was made to either the revolutionary
menace or the Jewish menace. His publications confined themselves
primarily to the world of the spirit and ignored the realm of the carnal
and the political. The transition from spiritualism to politics occurred
in January 1933. Business Manager George S. Anderson described the
change in this manner:

> When he [Pelley] returned to Asheville the day before Christmas [1932], he began to talk to me about organization of a militant character. . . .
> During January he began to talk about what might happen on January 30, which he called a "pyramid date." [9] He seemed quite certain that some great event was going to take place on January 30, 1933, and when the papers announced the rise of Hitler to power in Germany, Mr. Pelley announced that that was the "pyramid event" unquestionably; and from that point on he seemed to lose all interest in everything that had gone before in the way of his publications, and appeared to become possessed with the idea that something was going to happen in America similar to what was happening in Germany, and at one time he wanted me to have printed and sent out to all newspapers a page-size sheet headed "Is he the American Hitler?" And his rough draft for this proposed broadside . . . contained his picture [accompanied by sketches showing men uniformed in khaki shirts and riding breeches] and the history of the Liberation movement.
> The first issue of the weekly magazine [*Liberation* was changed from a monthly at this point] was devoted primarily to the Silver Shirt propaganda rather than for the benefit of the students and old readers for whom I had designed *Liberation*.[10]

In the first weekly issue of *Liberation*, Pelley outlined the new aspects of his movement:

> I knew as far back as the early days of 1929 that the ultimate aim of the Liberation Gesture was not religious. Spiritual, perhaps. But not religious.
> I have known privately—that despite all that has transpired in the last thirty months, the true Liberation movement has not even been born. . . .
> Now I proceed to a program of Action. . . .
> I shall use this journal—to talk to you about great issues of Cosmic and Civic Elucidations, and to make their application to practical problems something more than a thesis.
> The real work of Liberation must now be commenced.

The language in the revitalized publication was at first murky, but soon it became clearly anti-semitic. Three months after the Silver Shirt organization was started, Pelley was counseling his followers in *Liberation* not to despair at the magnitude of their task.

> The Hitler Movement in Germany started from a sign painter making a speech from the top of a barrel.
> It is not too early to begin casting up our slates.

Pelley is unique for the frank, naïve manner in which he has expressed his dictatorial ambitions. In the May 28, 1938, issue of *Liberation* he wrote:

> A clairvoyant child in Tennessee, who knows nothing of the Silver Shirts, has been insistent to her parents since 1934, that "Mr. Pelley

follows Roosevelt!" and has given extraordinary apt details concerning a Red dictator who lasts a matter of days, in between the two men. . . . A psychic woman in western Pennsylvania drops into a trance, unaware that Silver Shirts are in the group, and informs her audience: "This whole period comes to an end through the leadership of a man wearing a Van Dyke beard, who appears from the mountains of North Carolina."

The psychological implications are obvious. Spiritualism did not provide adequate expression for Pelley's desires. Anti-semitism, on the other hand, salved his feelings of inadequacy by offering delusions of grandeur. He would lead a nationwide movement of Silver-Shirted men to drive the Jews and revolutionaries from power! He would be the savior of his country! Here was a channel not only for externalizing his aggressions but also for releasing the bitterness generated by years of frustration.

As second in command, Robert C. Summerville, ran the Silver Shirts from the Asheville headquarters while Pelley was away on his frequent trips. Summerville was more the head of a resident secretariat than an active field organizer. He first became associated with Pelley in 1931, when he was 24 years old. An excellent picture of him was offered in an affidavit submitted by Miss Baird, a former employee of the Pelley enterprises:

> His father died when he was thirteen, and he was reared on a farm in Indiana, went to work at fourteen selling papers in Chicago. He has been a reporter on the *Chicago Herald,* real estate salesman, editor of the Montgomery-Ward catalogue, professional dancer, and is now with the Silver Shirt movement as a writer of propaganda. He says he is not like the general run of people since he sees humanity as a whole and not as individuals. He thinks his psychical powers are marked and receives inspiration for his writings from spirits of those who have passed into the beyond. He receives most of his spirit messages in dreams, says that he had found himself in the Silver Shirt movement, that it is his whole life, and that he is willing to give his life for it. . . . He has been on the stage, batted around backstage in New York. He writes most of the articles published in the Silver Shirt magazines, pamphlets, and newspapers, or at least he says he does. He is known to the Silver Shirts as "Captain Bob".

Miss Baird graphically described her reaction to a "date" with Summerville:

> I went with him, but I thought he was crazy. For everything he said was just a lot of high-sounding words meaning nothing. I figured that anyone who could keep up a conversation for two hours and not say one coherent sentence must have a "screw loose" somewhere. . . .
> He said that Pelley had often been protected by the spirits against the Jews. . . .

Another Silver Shirt bigwig, "Major" L. I. Powell, was formerly an organizer for the Ku Klux Klan and one of its principal executives and money-makers. A letter from a Shreveport, Louisiana, police official had the following to say about him:

> Powell's reputation in Shreveport is far from good. He has lived by his wits for many years—in fact, I have never known him to do any work. He pays no bills, and he is a man utterly without standing in the community. He presents a good superficial appearance and is a good speaker, and in that way he got control of the organization known as the Khaki Shirts of America. I am reliably informed that his misuse of the funds of the organization was the primary cause of its disbandment.
> Powell attempted to organize the Silver Shirts in Shreveport but failed signally in this move. . . I am . . . certain that no organization sponsored by Powell could make any headway here because Powell has neither the respect nor the confidence of anyone who knows him.

An important Silver Shirt organizer in Seattle, Dr. Howard Merrill, has been described in these unflattering terms:

> He is a big, strapping fellow, of an extremely nervous type. . . . He has a persecution complex, feeling that the Olympia Hotel, which has locked him out of his room for non-payment of rent, was run by a bunch of crooks, etc. He had occupied an adjoining room with a woman. Her husband had divorced her and thereafter commenced an action in the King County courts to obtain the custody of their two girls, whom she was bringing up as prostitutes. The woman herself had been operating several houses of ill fame in the city of Bremerton and was a rather notorious character. She was known at the Olympia Hotel as Dr. Merrill's secretary.

Very little is known of Roy Zachery, the Silver Shirts' National Field Marshal, except that he is a former lumberjack who has believed in Pelley implicitly. When interviewed by the Rev. L. M. Birkhead, National Director of the Friends of Democracy, he baldly declared:

> Of course, Pelley has sources of information not open to others. He has a clairaudient ear. He hears voices that no one else hears.
> Pelley does nothing without divine orders. It only takes him a few minutes to get in touch with God. Pelley has been chosen by God for this special work. . . .
> Pelley has been providentially prepared for all this work. . . . If you study Pelley's career you will find that every step of his way God has been preparing Pelley for this great work. Well, it's wonderful the way Pelley can get in touch with God. It only takes him a few minutes to get into direct touch with divine powers.

Silver Shirt leaders appear to be rather unstable persons. Zachery, the least unstable, is the case of a simple-minded lumberjack stricken with admiration for the first spiritualist with whom he has ever come into contact.

PROPAGANDA

The Silver Shirts' two chief channels of propaganda have been *Liberation*, a weekly magazine, and the *Silver Legion Ranger*, a weekly newspaper. Although *Liberation* dates as far back as 1930, it did not become the organ of the Silver Shirts until the issue of February 18, 1933. Adequate figures on its circulation are not available. A former Pelley employee stated in an affidavit that in December 1933 some 50,000 copies were printed and, evidently, distributed. In 1934 the publication of *Liberation* was suspended from the middle of April until the end of August; this was part of the general collapse of the organization following Pelley's conviction for violation of North Carolina laws. At the end of August it reappeared as *Pelley's Weekly*. The gap in publication lost the organization many readers. "Before me," wrote Pelley in this connection, "lies a national list of 1,708 people who were formerly enthusiastic readers of *Liberation* but who have not yet permitted me to hear from them in the matter of our present publication". The circulation of 50,000, attained in 1933, marked the high point, and, by and large, one-third of that figure has been the usual maximum.[11]

The *Silver Ranger* began publication as a weekly newspaper in Oklahoma City in November 1933. Shortly thereafter it was transferred to Los Angeles, where it was printed from January 1934 until August of that year. Its usual press run in Los Angeles was 10,000 copies per issue. The largest issue was 13,000 and a few issues were as small as 5,000 and 6,000. The list of individual subscribers was only about 1,300. Most copies were sent out in bundles to posts and to members who bought them for free distribution.

Pamphlets and folders have been a much less important means of propaganda. Pelley has put out some half dozen leaflets, two of them in quantities of 9,000 or 10,000. In addition a special set of handbills was used in connection with the Christian Party campaign in 1936. The Silver Shirts distributed a large number of copies of such pamphlets and books as Hitler's *Mein Kampf*, John E. Waters' *Red Justice*, Pelley's *No More Hunger*, Irvin L. Potter's *The Cause of Anti-Jewism*, F. Roderich-Stoltheim's *The Riddle of the Jew's Success*, G. F. Stevenson's *The Cuttle-Fish* ("a history of Manipulations of gold by Jewry in the advancement of their world conspiracy"), Carveth Wells' *Kapoot* ("Laugh and shudder with this author and lecturer"), and *The Protocols of the Elders of Zion*.

In the early part of 1934, Pelley attempted to use the confidential news-letter, the propaganda medium employed by the James True

Associates so successfully.[12]   A special appeal was made to business-men. The sales argument was stated succinctly in the letterhead of Pelley's letter of solicitation: "You should know what the Silver Shirts know to help in the conduct of your business". The letter continued:

> Once each week, out of the exhaustive information I possess and which has largely contributed to putting my organization of the Silver Shirts in the nation's headlines, I am going to write a four-page closely-typed letter to them, which will treat with many of the impor-tant men, and the government and commercial situations now baffling the rank and file of our people, giving the dossiers as I happen to know them on many individuals in the news, telling who they are, where their hookups and real ramifications lie, and what information the Silver Shirts possess about them in the former's private archives.
>
> I am compiling a very special list for this letter, and I want to place it in the hands of those bankers, industrialists, and other commercial interests who will properly value what I have to offer them.
>
> The cost of this personal service will be $25 per year, payable in advance, in order that bookkeeping and overhead costs in its produc-tion can be kept at a minimum.

Here was confidential "inside stuff" that could be learned through Pelley alone—and all for a mere $25 a year! The letter lasted only six issues.

Public platform propaganda has, of course, been used by the Silver Shirts. Pelley, an indefatigable speaker, was especially active during his campaign for the Presidency. He was assisted on the platform by W. W. Kemp, his running mate and leader of the West Coast Silver Shirts. In the early months of 1938, Zachery, the National Field Marshal, made a transcontinental speaking tour.

Although the chief function of the Silver Shirts has always been the dissemination of propaganda, the San Diego unit of the organization was for a time ready for violent action. The unit purchased arms and ammunition from members of the United States armed forces. W. W. Kemp, its leader, offered a Marine $10 for each rifle he could steal, $50 for each machine gun, and $20 for each case of ammunition. According to sworn testimony, at least 2,000 rounds of ammunition were assembled. Silver Shirts themselves have boasted of possessing 12,000 rounds. A Marine, who later turned out to be a spy for the Naval Intelligence Office, instructed Silver Shirt members on tactics in riots and street fighting and in the methods of approach to cities. The purpose of the training was preparedness in the event that Communists attempted to stage a revolution in San Diego on May Day, 1934; the Silver Shirts planned to counter-attack and seize the City Hall.

MEMBERSHIP

"Either men or women over the age of eighteen years may be members but only persons of the Christian faith are acceptable or will be recognized". These are the membership qualifications as stated in Silver Shirt literature. The membership in July 1933 was 700 or 800, scattered through 40 states; consequently, many states had just a state organizer and one or two associates. In early 1934 the membership reached its peak in numbers—15,000. During this period, the Los Angeles post, probably the largest in the country, attracted as many as 500 or 600 persons to its meetings. In January, 1938, however, Pelley could place the national Silver Shirt membership at only 5,000.

The Silver Shirt organization has always been strongest on the Pacific Coast, particularly in California. Another stronghold has been the Oklahoma City region. Only a few Silver Shirt posts have appeared east of the Appalachians. But from these mountains westward to the Pacific Coast their numbers increase. This analysis of membership distribution checks with the results of the Dies Committee's inquiry into the destinations of Pelley's literature. The Committee found that in 1937 Pelley made 12 express shipments to points South of the Mason and Dixon line and 57 to points North of it but 1,022 to the West Coast; and that in the first seven months of 1938 he made 14 such shipments to the East Coast but 1,154 to the West Coast.[13] A list of cities in which Silver Shirt posts have existed follows:

ATLANTIC COAST

Lewiston (Me.)
Philadelphia (Pa.)
Miami (Fla.)
New York (N. Y.)
Springfield (Mass.)

FROM THE APPALACHIANS TO THE MISSISSIPPI

Chicago (Ill.)
Cleveland (O.)
Indianapolis (Ind.)
Lansing (Mich.)
Minneapolis (Minn.)

Norwood (O.)
Pittsburgh (Pa.)
Rockford (Ill.)
St. Paul (Minn.)
Toledo (O.)

WEST OF THE MISSISSIPPI TO THE ROCKIES

Dallas (Tex.)
Denver (Colo.)
Ft. Smith (Ark.)
Kansas City (Mo.)

Lincoln (Neb.)
Oklahoma City (Okla.)
Omaha (Neb.)
Pueblo (Colo.)

St. Louis (Mo.)
Tulsa (Okla.)

PACIFIC NORTHWEST

Bremarton (Wash.)
Everett (Wash.)
Mt. Vernon (Wash.)
Portland (Oreg.)
Redmont (Wash.)
Seattle (Wash.)
Spokane (Wash.)
Tacoma (Wash.)
Verona (Ore.)
Walla Walla (Wash.)

Alexandria
Altadena
Bakersfield
Baldwin Park
Fontana
Hollywood
Huntington Park
Imperial Valley
Inglewood

CALIFORNIA

Long Beach
Los Angeles
Oakland
San Bernardino
San Diego
Santa Barbara
Santa Paula
Ventura

What is the social and economic composition of the Silver Shirt membership? Admission to the organization is not restricted to men.

"Major" L. I. Powell once told the press that 28 per cent of the members were women. A report of a Cleveland meeting mentioned the presence of 25 women. In Indianapolis about 165 women once attended the gathering of a special women's auxiliary of the Silver Shirts.

The members are predominantly Protestant. No formal ban on Catholics exists, and the organization carries on no open anti-Catholic propaganda. In the early days of the Silver Shirts, apparently some question on whether or not to bar Catholics occurred among the leaders. One leader in a letter to headquarters seriously suggested that this difficulty be solved by admitting Catholics only after they had sworn an oath renouncing their allegiance to the Pope.[14] Pelley himself apparently toyed with the idea of excluding Catholics because in an early issue of *Liberation* he spoke of the need of building up "a Native-Son, Protestant-Christian political machine". Local leaders expressed similar sentiments. When making public addresses a Chicago leader frequently used the expression "Protestant and Aryan". Moreover, the ranks and officers of the Silver Shirts include a large number of former Klansmen. "Major" Powell was formerly a Klan official. The Silver Shirt organizer in Baldwin Park, California, was at one time the Exalted Cyclops of the local Klan. The Philadelphia post of the Silver Shirts contained two ex-Klansmen; one of them had been an official of the Eastern Pennsylvania district of the Klan. The woman who conducted the meeting of the women's auxiliary in Indianapolis was formerly associated with the Klan. The *Punxsutawney Spirit*, an Oklahoma newspaper, asserted that in its locality "many former members of the Klan are now Silver Shirts."[15] Concerning parts of his state where the Silver Shirts were particularly active, a resident of Washington wrote: "I am quite familiar with the situation around Bellingham and Mount Vernon. This section contains a large number of people who are old Klansmen. The Klan never did disband in Skagit and Whitcomb counties." Some evidence, however, indicates that the door to Silver Shirt membership is not shut to Catholics. A former Klansman resigned from the St. Paul unit of the Silver Shirts because he did not consider it sufficiently anti-Catholic. More recently, Pelley vigorously denied charges of anti-Catholic prejudices: "The villification that I have sought to revive the anti-Catholic Klan is exposed by the presence of thousands of fine Catholic boys in our ranks."[16] In another instance, Pelley attempted to woo Catholics by telling them how the Communists planned to destroy the Catholic Church.[17] Nevertheless, common sense suggests that an organization containing so many former Klansmen will attract very few Catholics. The "thousands of fine

Catholic boys in our ranks" to which Pelley referred probably existed only in his imagination.

An occupational cross section of the Silver Shirt membership reveals significant data. Among the prominent members in various parts of the country have been Protestant clergymen. The Rev. E. F. Webber was an organizer in Oklahoma. In Minneapolis and New York clergyman members have addressed meetings. In Seattle a self-styled "former Methodist minister" proselyted for Pelley. A clergyman was very active in the organizational work of the Toledo Silver Shirts and a gentleman bearing the title "Reverend" was likewise engaged in Maine. Lawyers, too, have been well represented. A Kansas City member and a business manager for the Pacific Coast Silver Shirts were attorneys. A Los Angeles cell met in a lawyer's office. In Toledo a school physician was a member and in Cleveland a physician held a cell meeting in his office. Among those who have been typical members of the organization are an electrician, salesmen, an accountant, the owner of a large distillery, a restaurant proprietor, a teacher of drama, an ex-legislator, an ex-sheriff, an unemployed metallurgist, an unemployed architect, an unemployed mechanical engineer, a motion picture operator, and some United States Navy men and Marines. The predominance of highly trained professional people and the apparently complete absence of manual workers, as indicated by the preceding occupational listings, establishes the Silver Shirt membership as middle-class. The validity of this characterization is buttressed by the number of references to members who are also thirty-second degree Masons or Scottish Rite Shriners.

That descendants of old American families chiefly constitute the Silver Shirts has been frequently asserted. In listing the names of twenty "cronies" of the late Governor Olson of Minnesota—most of the names suggested Jewish or Slavic origin—*Pelley's Weekly* truculently defied its readers to "pick out the fine old American names". Evidence to substantiate the implication that many of the Silver Shirts are possessors of "fine old American names" is found in the list of Christian Party nominees, culled from the Washington state ballot of 1936. The names of the nominees were: Dr. Dwight D. Clark, Floyd Hatfield, Rubie Sharpe Johnson, Ole J. Lien, Malcom M. Moore, Walter L. Morgan, T. L. W. Osburne, E. E. Peterson, Harry G. Picot, Orville W. Roundtree, Jack Shields, Frank H. Tousley, Fred G. Widner, and John A. Wilson. Silver Shirt correspondence has mentioned names such as Stephen Balog, P. Bruce Brockway, I. R. Crow, Earl W. Loudon, S. M. Pinkerton, and Clarence M. Wright.

Though boasting that the numerically predominant group of Silver

Shirts are descendants of early American stock, *Pelley's Weekly* has admitted that "everywhere the German-American people . . . are coming to the front rank of the Christian Party as its most enthusiastic workers.[18] At a Silver Shirt meeting in New York City three-fourths of the audience were Germans. The Silver Shirts have made vigorous and evidently, fruitful efforts to recruit German-Americans. A recruiting officer assigned to German-American societies, reported to Pelley: "We are expecting Mr. Kessemeier back early in October; joining hands with him it will be easier for me to feel my way through these scattered German-American organizations."[19] An Indiana German-American has stated that a Silver Shirt member tried to get him to organize a German post: "Mr. M——— suggested that I organize a German post and that I invite nine faithful Germans to my house Sunday." On the Pacific Coast the Silver Shirts were instructed to attend the meetings of the German-American Bund and to endeavor to recruit members there. Apparently they were successful, for the extent of cooperation between the Bund and the Silver Shirts suggests overlapping membership.

Another source of information on the character of the Silver Shirt members is the statement of an Asheville lawyer who sampled Pelley's filed correspondence of several hundred thousand letters while they were under subpoena in 1934. He reported that he arrived at the following opinions with respect to the writers of these letters:

> They were uneducated (judging from the grammatical errors); poor (many had suffered recent economic reverses); few professional people; a high proportion of neurotics (to judge from the language they employed); practically all elderly; a high proportion were female; they were seldom prominent in their community, or if prominent, they wrote either because of their metaphysical interests or because they were interested in opposing the liberal trends of the administration. They came from small communities in general, mostly from the Middle West and the West Coast. Very little interest was manifested in the South.

The sampling appears to be open to one objection: much of the correspondence from persons interested in Pelley's spiritualism was received prior to the existence of the Silver Shirts. But undoubtedly many of these people entered the Silver Shirt movement, for *Liberation* has dealt with spiritualism.

The attorney's opinion that few professional people belong to the Silver Shirts does not deny the implications of the occupational analysis previously presented—that many of the active members were professionals. Evidence, however, supports his belief that few members— professionals or non-professionals—have been prominent persons in their community. An observer, describing a Silver Shirt meeting in a small Washington town in early 1938, stated: "I have taken the auto license numbers of many who attend, but I have not found one prominent person among them in the community."

The naïve mysticism of many Silver Shirt members is indicated by a story that appeared in the September 15, 1936 issue of the *Minneapolis Journal*. This story related that one member had stored up food for a two weeks' seige because the Great Pyramid of Gizeh predicted a Jewish revolt on the day of the new Jewish year. Another member explained that the N. R. A. blue eagle was the "mark of the beast" mentioned in the book of *Revelation;* calling attention to the fact that the latter states that the beast is to be known only by a number *(viz.,* six hundred, three score, and six—666), the member said:

> Now look at the N.R.A. emblem. Count the teeth in the cogwheel. It's fifteen. Five and one. Get it? Five and one is six. Count the tail feathers on the bird. Six. That's six and six. Now how many bolts of lightning are there? (In the Eagle's claw.) Six! And that makes 666—the mark of the beast.

The Silver Shirts, like several other groups to be examined, have attracted a number of White Guard Russians. A gentleman who went around under the title of "Prince" attended a "Council of Safety" meeting in Cleveland and there entertained his audience with the story of how the Bolsheviks confiscated his vast estates. Mr. Paul von Lilienfeld-Toal, another White Guard Russian, was for a period a Silver Shirt official.

FUNDS

The Silver Shirts have the following sources of funds: dues, collections at meetings, the sale of literature, and small donations. Dues were initially ten dollars but later dropped to one dollar. Collections, frequently taken at meetings, were apparently a lucrative source, for one observer reported noticing "many bills in the basket." Although *Liberation* and the *Silver Ranger* sold subscriptions, neither was self-supporting; both were kept going by small donations sent in by mail. That these donations were *small* was emphasized by the lawyer who examined Pelley's correspondence: "The great majority of his contributions came in small dribbles, usually one or two dollars, and a surprisingly large proportion of the letters were accompanied by a small donation." Only recently did the Silver Shirts obtain wealthy backers.

Silver Shirt officials have from time to time solicited the American-German Bund and the Nazi government for financial support. An officer of the Los Angeles local of the Bund stated in conversation in early 1936 that his organization had contributed to the Silver Shirts. When Pelley first launched his organization, he was quite optimistic about getting money from the German government. He tried hard to get in touch with the right people but his efforts were fruitless, to judge by the testimony of Business Manager George S. Anderson.

> *Questioner:* At one time he (Pelley) told you he had certain information . . . that he would come to Washington, and that he could meet an agent of the German government, did he not?
> *Anderson:* That is true.
> *Questioner:* And he had some hopes of being able to get money?
> *Anderson:* That is true.
> *Questioner:* From the agent of the German government?
> *Anderson:* That is my understanding. . . .
> *Anderson:* I asked him immediately on his return (from Washington) if he had met the party he expected to contact and he said he had not.[20]

During the first five years of its existence, the Silver Shirts organization was not financially successful. Harder-headed anti-semitic leaders such as Gerald Winrod and Harry Jung [21] have always been able to induce wealthy persons to contribute large sums to their organizations. Pelley, however, was until recently too much of a dreamer to realize that an hour spent recounting the horrors of Communism to a business man who is alive and wealthy is more worthwhile than a month spent in "the world of subliminal existence" communing with even the greatest of departed souls. (To be sure, Mrs. Marie Ogden [22] had once "invested" $14,000 in Pelley's Galahad Press, but this "investment" was made before the founding of the Silver Shirts.) As a result, Pelley was constantly in debt. In September, 1933, his creditors were pressing him on every side, and he was making desperate efforts to secure financial aid. Later the same year he was even in arrears to his employees; he owed $800 to one of the faculty members of Galahad College, In January of 1934 a letter from Silver Shirt headquarters to Harry Jung spoke of "the distressful financial difficulties which we are all experiencing." Pelley had to shift the publication of the *Silver Ranger* from Oklahoma City to Los Angeles because he was unable to meet the printer's bill in the former city. Early in 1938 Pelley began to realize that an organization such as his could expect only a precarious and harried existence unless it acquired some reasonably wealthy backers. At any rate, during the years 1938 and 1939 he received $4,600 from George B. Fisher, a publishing company executive; $3,800 from Sarah C. Scott of Belmont, Massachusetts, and $630 from Dr. John R. Brinkley.[23]

CHAPTER V

The National Union for Social Justice and the Christian Front

FATHER CHARLES E. COUGHLIN is comparatively a latecomer to the field of anti-semitism. As early as 1933, the leaders of most of the anti-semitic organizations treated in this study began to present their anti-semitic ideology as explanation of the country's ills, but Coughlin did not begin spreading his variation of the ideology until 1938. He differs, too, in that he had an established reputation before he turned to anti-semitism; other leaders were unknown until they drew attention to themselves by their attacks on Jews. And he is especially important because he has brought a large Catholic contingent into an anti-semitic movement that has been chiefly Protestant.

LEADERSHIP

Coughlin was born in Hamilton, Ontario, Canada, in 1891. His family background and early life is described concisely by Raymond Gram Swing:[1]

> . . . he was of pure Irish stock. His father, grandfather, and great-grandfather were Irish-American workingmen. His great-grandfather helped dig the Erie Canal. His father, born in Indiana, was stoker on the Great Lakes, drifted to Hamilton, Ontario, became sexton of the cathedral, met a devout seamstress, also of Irish stock, and married her.
> He was educated in St. Mary's parochial school of Hamilton, then in St. Michael's College (under the Basilian Fathers), and took his first college degree at the age of twenty at the University of Toronto . . . He was able to go for a three months trip to Europe after finishing at Toronto, and came back troubled in mind as to his career. His inclinations were in three directions—the church, politics, and sociology . . . At the dock, on his return from Europe, he met his favorite college teacher, who took him away for a long talk. It ended in his being persuaded to enter the church; and he plunged into the arduous preparatory work under the Basilian order in Toronto. He was ordained four years later and spent his first year as a priest teaching English in Assumption College, Sandwich, Ontario. Then began the trips to Detroit, and the transfer to that diocese followed. For three years he was in Kalamazoo and for a short period in North Branch before Bishop Gallagher chose him for the trying task of building up the parish of Royal Oak.

In 1926, the same year he was assigned to the Royal Oak parish in Michigan, he began his radio talks. Station WJR Detroit granted him broadcasting time to build up his parish—nothing more.

> His sermons, and later his afternoon addresses to children, were broadcast for four years without bringing Father Coughlin fame. Gradually he changed the nature of his children's talks, peppering his religion with a seasoning of politics and economics. It was not until 1930, when . . . echoing letters aroused in him the first glimpse of his own potentialities, that he organized the Radio League of the Little Flower and boldly branched out. He engaged time on stations in Chicago and Cincinnati at $1,650 a week . . . Letters now came in regularly in hundreds and thousands, many with contributions for the league or the new shrine . . . The response in letters and money justified further expansion, and Father Coughlin rented time on a sixteen station hookup of the Columbia system.
>
> He became a national figure almost at once. Currency was his most popular theme . . . He assailed the bankers . . . His discourse on the subject of "Hoover Prosperity Means a New War" brought him his largest response, 1,200,000 letters . . .
>
> After many discourses on banking, money, and capitalistic greed, he devoted a series to Communism.

When in 1932 the Columbia Broadcasting Company refused to renew Coughlin's contract and the National Broadcasting Company declined to take him on, the manager of WJR came to his aid.

> He worked out the details by which Father Coughlin could hire his own stations and pay for the connecting telephone lines himself. Thus he created his own network. It embraced at first eleven stations and grew to twenty-six from Maine to Colorado, costing him $14,000 a week.[2]

During the early months of the New Deal, Coughlin reached the highest point of his popularity. He backed the administration with such assertions as "the New Deal is God's deal" and such slogans as "Roosevelt or Ruin." He commuted between Detroit and Washington, conferring frequently with Raymond Moley and other members of the "Brain Trust." Though his popularity began to decline shortly thereafter, he was still able to rally millions from time to time. When in 1935 he attacked proposals to join the World Court, his followers deluged Congress with such a flood of telegrams that the Washington offices of the telegraph companies were temporarily disrupted.

After a long period of private grumbling against Roosevelt and the New Deal, he finally broke publicly. In the 1936 Presidential campaign he was the chief backer of the third party ticket headed by Congressman William Lemke. In one of his campaign speeches Coughlin boldly announced, "If I cannot swing at least 9,000,000 votes to Mr.

Lemke, I will quit broadcasting educational talks on economics and politics." Lemke's total vote was about one-tenth that number—891,858. Three days after the election Coughlin announced, "I am withdrawing from all radio activity in the best interests of all the people."

In November, 1936, the New Deal was at the peak of its popularity. The radio priest's efforts to oppose it had ended in a miserable fiasco. In 1937 and early 1938, however, there occurred several events which affected the New Deal's popularity. Moreover, the wave of strikes and the business recession made many persons ready to listen to any leader who would tell them the cause of their troubles. Coughlin sensed this fact and returned to the fray with a simple explanation of the country's woes—the Communistic Jews were the cause of it all.

Up to this time Coughlin had never disseminated an anti-semitic ideology. He had attacked the bankers. He had supported the New Deal and then turned upon it with unqualified bitterness. And although he had attacked the Communists he had never identified them with the Jews. Not until July, 1938, did his newspaper *Social Justice* begin printing the *Protocols of the Elders of Zion* and not until November 20, 1938, did he begin his radio attacks on the Jews. The explanation might be that Coughlin became suddenly convinced of the validity of anti-semitic doctrines, or it might be simply the case of a discredited leader anxious to return to the spotlight, who seized upon this ideology as an expedient in the belief that it would build up a following.

PROPAGANDA

The most important channel through which Coughlin's current ideology is circulated is the radio. His hookup now consists of 47 stations. Second to the radio, Coughlin's weekly newspaper, *Social Justice,* is hawked on the street corners of the nation's largest cities. Its circulation of about one million copies[3] makes it the most widely read anti-semitic periodical in America. Although the offices of the paper are in Coughlin's church, it is not an approved Catholic publication. It is a private business and, therefore, is not subject to ecclesiastical censorship. It is owned by the Social Justice Publishing Company, which is in turn controlled by the Social Justice Poor Society, a holding company controlled by Coughlin. Its officers and directors are clerks and stenographers in his offices.[4] Less important channels of Coughlin propaganda are the sale of anti-semitic books and pamphlets. These publications are distributed chiefly from Coughlin's church, their sales promoted persistently in the columns of *Social Justice.*

Certain characteristics can be noted in propaganda that is disseminated through these channels. Coughlin endeavors to establish the truth of his assertions by quoting obscure authorities or material not easily available. In certain instances, however, individuals have undertaken to check on Coughlin's "authorities" and have discovered cases of outright misquotation and of manufactured "authorities." In connection with the 1940 anniversary of Lincoln's birthday, for example, *Social Justice* asserted that the American Civil War was fought not over slavery but for freedom from the Jewish international bankers. To prove this contention, there appeared what purported to be a quotation from a book by John Reeves entitled *The Rothschilds*. The book, published in 1887 and out-of-print, quoted a speech made by Disraeli at a family gathering of the Rothschilds. The version appearing in *Social Justice* was:

> Under this roof are the heads of the family of Rothschild—a name famous in every capital of Europe and every division of the globe. *If you like, we shall divide the United States into two parts, one for you, James, and one for you, Lionel. Napoleon will do exactly and all that I shall advise him.*

Howard Vincent O'Brien, veteran columnist of the *Chicago Daily News*, took the trouble to secure a copy of the volume in question and found that the quotation actually read as follows:

> Under this roof are the heads of the family of Rothschild—a name famous in every capital of Europe and every division of the globe— *a family not more regarded for its riches than esteemed for its honour, virtues, and public spirit.*

It is difficult to understand how so great a variance from the original text could have been accidental.[5]

Another instance of misinformation was the assertion of *Social Justice* that two Polish rabbis, Rabbi Rudolph Fleischman of Schochin and Rabbi Grunfeld of Swarzedz, had admitted the authenticity of the *Protocols of the Elders of Zion*. According to the chief rabbi of Wilna, Poland, no such rabbis have ever existed.[6]

Coughlin often pretends to possess highly confidential information. Quoting a non-existent authority, he declared in his broadcast of November 27, 1938:

> The chief document, treating of the financing of the Russian revolution, is one drawn up by the American Secret Service and transmitted by the French High Commissioner to his government. It was published by the *Documentation Catholique* of Paris on March 6, 1920, and was preceded by the following remarks, namely, "The authenticity of this document is guaranteed to us. With regard to its exactness, the exactness of the information which it contains, the American Secret Service takes responsibility."

NATIONAL UNION FOR SOCIAL JUSTICE-CHRISTIAN FRONT

On the following day Frank J. Wilson, chief of the United States Secret Service, issued a press release stating that "no such report was ever made by the United States Secret Service."

One other distinctive characteristic of Coughlin's propaganda is the directness of his quotation from Nazi propaganda material. All American anti-semitic leaders are influenced by Nazi ideas, and most of them read propaganda printed in Germany for distribution to English-speaking countries; but no other leader has been so unguarded in his verbatim copying of Nazi propaganda. On September 13, 1935, Dr. Goebbels spoke before the Seventh National Socialist Congress and made a bitter attack on the Jews. The speech was published in the official report of the Nazi Party Congress at Nuremberg (*Der Parteitag der Freiheit*). Later it was reprinted in English for distribution in English-speaking countries. On December 5, 1938, Father Coughlin published an article in *Social Justice* over his own signature entitled "Background for Persecution." In it, whole portions of the Goebbels speech were copied without the change of more than a few words. The speech and the article are here reproduced in parallel columns.

GOEBBELS' SPEECH	COUGHLIN'S ARTICLE
On April 30, 1919, in the courtyard of the Luitpold Gymnasium in Munich, the hostages, among them one woman, were shot through the backs, their bodies rendered unrecognizable and taken away. This act was done at the order of the Communist terrorist, Egelhofer, and under the responsibility of the Jewish Soviet Commissars, Levien, Levine-Nissen and Axelrod.	On April 30, 1919, in the courtyard of the Luitpold Gymnasium in Munich, ten hostages, among them one woman, were murdered. This act was perpetrated by the direct order of the Communist terrorist Egelhofer, and under the responsibility of the Jewish Soviet Commissars, Levien, Levine-Nissen and Axelrod.
The Jewish Tschekist, Bela Kun, made an experiment which rivaled the Paris Commune in bloodshed, when he ordered the execution of 60,000 to 70,000 people in the Crimea. For the most part, these executions were carried out with machine guns. At the municipal hospital in Alupka 272 sick and wounded were brought out on stretchers in front of the gate of the institution and there shot.	At a later date, the same Bela Kun ordered the execution of approximately 60,000 people in the Crimea. For the most part, these executions were carried out with machine guns. At the municipal hospital in Alupka, 272 sick and wounded were brought out on stretchers in front of the gate of the institution and there shot.
In November, 1934, the Chinese Marshal Chiang Kai-shek, made public the information that in the Province of Kiangsi 1,000,000 people were	In November, 1934, the Chinese Marshal Chiang Kai-shek, made public the information that in the Province of Kiangsi 1,000,000 people were

murdered by the Communists and 6,000,000 robbed of their possessions.

The Soviet statistician, Oganowsky, estimates the number of persons who died of hunger in the years 1921-1922 at 5,200,000.

The Austrian Cardinal Archbishop, Monsignor Innitzer, said in his appeal of July, 1934, that millions of people were dying of hunger throughout the Soviet Union.

The most boorish example of the interference of "Soviet Diplomats" for the purpose of creating domestic political trouble in another country is afforded by the Jewish Soviet Ambassador, Joffe, who had to leave Berlin on the sixth of November, 1918, because he had utilized the diplomatic courier to transport sabotage material which was to be used to undermine the German army and make the revolution possible.

On the 26th of December, 1918, one of the Socialist members of the Reichstag, the Jew, Dr. Oskar Cohn, declared that on the 5th of the previous month, he had received 4,000,000 rubles from Joffe for the purpose of the German revolution.

At the second Congress of Atheists, Bucharin declared that religion must be "destroyed with the bayonet."

The Social Democrat "League of German Free Thinkers" alone had a membership of 600,000. The Communist "League of Proletarian Free Thinkers" had close to 160,000 members. Almost without exception, the intellectual leaders of Marxist atheism in Germany were Jews, among them being Erich Weinert, Felix Abraham, Dr. Levy-Lenz and others. At regular meetings held in the presence

murdered by the Communists and 6,000,000 robbed of their possessions.

The Soviet statistician, Oganowsky, estimates the number of persons who died of hunger in the years 1921-1922 at more than 5,000,000.

The Austrian Cardinal Archbishop, Mgr. Innitzer, said in his appeal of July, 1934, that millions of people were dying of hunger throughout the Soviet Union.

Before the advent of Hitler to power Germany was undermined steadily by espionage of the most treasonable kind. The Jewish Soviet Ambassador, Joffe, was forced to leave Germany on November 6, 1918, because he was found guilty of utilizing the diplomatic courier to transport sabotage material which was used to undermine the German army and make revolution possible.

On December 26, 1918, one of the Socialist members of the Reichstag, the eminent Jew, Dr. Oskar Cohn, declared that on the 5th of the previous month he had received 4,000,000 rubles from Joffe for the purpose of instigating a revolution in Germany.

Remember that, when the second Congress of Atheists convened Bucharin declared that religion must be "destroyed with the bayonet."

In Germany the Social Democratic League of German Free-Thinkers had a membership of 600,000. The Communist "League of Proletarian Free-Thinkers" numbered close to 160,000 members. Almost without exception, the intellectual leaders—if not the foot and hand leaders—of Marxist atheism in Germany were Jews. . . . Not good Jews but bad Jews; not Jews who opposed Comof a notary public, members were requested to register their declaration of withdrawal from their church for a fee of two marks. And thus the fight for atheism was carried on. Between 1918 and 1933 the withdrawals from the German Evangelical churches alone amounted to 2,500,000 persons in Germany.

munism but Jews who supported it. Among them were Erich Weinert, Felix Abraham and Dr. Levy-Lenz. At regular meetings held in the presence of a notary public, members were requested to register their declaration of withdrawal from their church for a fee of two marks. With such bribes, the fight for atheism was carried on. And between 1918 and 1933 the withdrawals from the German Evangelical churches were estimated at close to 2,500,000 persons in Germany.

In 1919, during the Bolshevik regime of Bela Kun, a Jew, whose real name was Aaron Cohn, in Budapest twenty hostages were murdered.

In 1919 Hungary, a neighbor to Germany, was overrun with Communists. The notorious atheist, Bela Kun, a Jew whose real name was Aaron Cohn, murdered 20,000.

The Jew, Gubermann, who, under the name of Jaroslawski, is the leader of the Association of Militant Atheists in the Soviet Union, has made the following declaration: "It is our duty to destroy every religious world-concept. . . . If the destruction of 10,000,000 human beings, as happened in the last war, should be necessary for the triumph of one definite class, then that must be done, and it will be done."

The atheist Jew, Gubermann, under the name of Jaroslawski and then the leader of the militant atheists in Soviet Union, also declared: "It is our duty to destroy every religious world-concept. If the destruction of 10,000,000 human beings, as happened in the last war, should be necessary for the triumph of one definite class, then that must be done, and it will be done."

MEMBERSHIP

Coughlin's following must be thought of in terms of those who are exposed to his propaganda. The best estimate of the size of his radio audience was made by the American Institute of Public Opinion in its January 9, 1939, release. It estimated that 3,500,000 persons regularly listened to Coughlin every Sunday and that two-thirds of these listeners approved of him. Probably most of the one million readers of *Social Justice* are among his radio listeners. That Coughlin's followers are primarily Catholics is a safe assumption; this point will be treated in greater detail later in the chapter. Anti-Catholic feeling among Protestants, though not intense, is real enough to make it appear unlikely that a Catholic priest could build up a strong following of Protestants. (According to the findings of Dr. Gallup's Institute, most of Coughlin's followers are in the lower income group.)

ORGANIZED ANTI-SEMITISM IN AMERICA

Attention must be focused on those followers who are organized into what Coughlin refers to as the *Christian Front*. In the May 23, 1938, issue of *Social Justice* Coughlin first urged his readers to form "platoons", providing the basis for the Front.

> Let your organization be composed of no more than twenty-five members. After a few contacts with these twenty-five persons you will observe that two of them may be capable of organizing twenty-five more. Invite these capable people to do that very thing.

A few weeks later *Social Justice* (June 13, 1938) carried an article entitled "Message to Platoons" in which Coughlin stated, "You and your people are affiliated directly to me." The same issue carried an editorial declaring: "When the proper moment arrives and not before that time, Father Coughlin will assemble all those organizations whose leaders care to follow him." One of the first platoons was organized by Father Burke of the Paulist Fathers in New York. This group adopted the name "Christian Front." Two discontented New York musicians, Harry and Joe Thorne, actually coined this name back in 1935 but nothing ever came of their idea until Father Coughlin turned to anti-semitism.

As late as the autumn of 1939 all Christian Front membership cards and other literature bore the address "P. O. Box 69, Station G, New York City." This box was rented in the name of the Paulist Fathers. Meetings were held secretly in the Paulist Fathers' Rectory at 413 West 59th Street, New York City, and converts were trained and taught the need for drastic methods to save Christianity from the Jewish-Communist menace. To prevent exposure, the heads of the Paulist Fathers transferred Father Burke to a parish in the Middle West and the Christian Front's headquarters were moved to Donovan's Beer Hall at 308 West 59th Street.

In order to create the impression that the response to Coughlin's appeal was the spontaneous, independent reaction of miscellaneous groups, organizers formed "platoon" organizations in different sections of New York and gave them different names. In Manhattan appeared such groups as the American Patriots, the American Women Against Communism; in Brooklyn, the Flying Squads of America and the American Citizens Committee Against Communism; and in the Bronx, groups whose names consisted of other combinations of patriotic symbols. The term *Christian Front* now came to be used as a general term to apply to the various groups formed under the directorship of the original Christian Front officials.

Organizing efforts were pushed vigorously. By the following summer, the July 31, 1939, issue of *Social Justice* was able to proclaim that "along the Eastern seaboard during the last six months there is emerging a highly organized and rapidly growing militant Christian Front." Although "along the Eastern seaboard" is a rather misleading description of the growth of the organization, efforts were made to spread it to cities other than New York. The July 24, 1939, issue of *Social Justice* reported the meeting of "more than 8,500 crusaders" who "jammed two Philadelphia halls to hear the voice of Father Coughlin" transmitted to them by telephone from Detroit. The article continued, "Father Coughlin praised the heroism and zeal of the Christian Front in those areas where its work has already borne fruit, and urged Philadelphians to emulate their Christianity and Americanism." The psychic satisfaction of being both good Christians and good Americans can hardly be underestimated.

New York has been the real center of Christian Front activity. Each of the groups belonging to the Front has sponsored rallies at which the officers of other groups have appeared as guest speakers. During the spring and summer of 1939, an average of fifty to seventy meetings were held every week, haranguing their audiences with vituperation against Communistic Jews despoiling the country.

That the Christian Front is thoroughly controlled by Coughlin is altogether evident. The following facts indicate the extent of this control. The Christian Front of New York scheduled an anti-Communist parade for August 19, 1939. Coughlin decided to call it off. In his broadcast on August 13th, he stated that he disapproved of the parade. The following Saturday no one marched. The January 1, 1940 issue of *Social Justice* also leaves no doubt that Coughlin is the leader of the Christian Front. It said:

> These great broadcasts are YOURS. Father Coughlin is only the spokesman for a rapidly forming and tremendously powerful element of our country—the Christian Front.

New York Front activities have been led by John F. Cassidy. *Social Justice* said on July 31, 1939:

> From a modest start of only thirty-six men banded together in Brooklyn last year, the organization has penetrated all boroughs of the metropolis. Under the leadership of Mr. John F. Cassidy of Brooklyn, there are now five central units operating in the metropolitan district.

The preceding issue of *Social Justice* had also made reference to Cassidy; he had addressed a Philadelphia meeting, sketching the formation and growth of the Christian Front. Cassidy gained considerable notoriety when in 1940 the Federal Bureau of Investigation arrested him as the leader of a plot to overthrow the United States government. The ideological kindling for this plot had been supplied by Father Coughlin's advocacy of force.

On July 30, 1939, the announcer for Father Coughlin's broadcast said, "Today's discourse sounds a call to action. Following 1936, Father Coughlin retired from all active organization; today, he is encouraging the growth of the Christian Front." The Bolsheviks of America were then asked to ponder upon this fact:

> That the Christian Front is no longer a dream; it is a reality in America, a reality that grows stronger, more courageous and more determined under the threat of your ideological invasion.

Coughlin delivered an address that included this statement:

> Nevertheless the Christian way is the peaceful way until—until— all arguments having failed, there is left no other way but the way of defending ourselves against the invaders of our spiritual and national rights, the Franco way. And when your rights have been challenged, when all civil liberty has succumbed before the invaders, then and only then may Christians meet force with force.

Legal questions sometimes arise as to exactly what constitutes an incitement to violence; however, it would seem difficult to interpret Coughlin's approving reference to "the Franco way" as anything other than just that. The same type of endorsement of violence was repeated in the November 20, 1939, issue of *Social Justice*. In a contest conducted by the paper, the following question was asked: "What is Father Coughlin's most emphatic advice to the Christian Front?" The winning answer appeared in capitals: "MEET FORCE WITH FORCE AS A LAST RESORT." [7] If Coughlin has sometimes been indirect in his advocacy of force, his followers have not been. Key organizer Cassidy has been particularly forthright, as a report of a Christian Front meeting indicates.

> Cassidy then announced that a "sports club" is being organized by the Christian Front which will teach men how to take orders and accept discipline. Members of the "sports club," he said, must be ready to go into the streets and protect their rights by force. All younger members of the Christian Front should and must be members of the "sports club," Cassidy said. This unit will train the younger members in the use of "walking sticks" to protect themselves. . . . [8]

At the same gathering Cassidy said:

> We are prepared to say to the Communists that they lay down their arms or we will meet their arms with our arms—firearms. War is declared in New York on Christianity. We must be prepared to defend Christianity. [9]

In other parts of the city, groups prepared for violence. In Manhattan small groups of Christian Fronters met at Donovan Hall twice a week for drill.

On January 13, 1940, the Federal Bureau of Investigation arrested 17 members of a sports club of the Christian Front. According to J. Edgar Hoover, the group planned to "eliminate" Jews and Communists, "to knock off about a dozen Congressmen," and to seize post offices, the Customs House, and armories in New York. In the homes of the group were found 18 cans of cordite, 18 rifles, and 5,000 rounds of ammunition. The men were held on $50,000 bail apiece. The leader of the group, who was addressed as *fuehrer* by his followers, was none other than Cassidy. The day following the arrest Coughlin disavowed any connection with the plotters. In the next two weeks, however, he changed his stand, and in the January 29th issue of *Social Justice* he stated:

> We do not hold a brief for anybody charged with sedition against the government; but neither are we running out on the fine body of New York Christians who make up the membership of the Christian Front. . . .
> Recognizing also that in one sense the opposition to Communism is on trial, I freely choose to be identified as a friend of the accused. It matters not whether they be guilty or innocent; be they ardent followers of the principles of Christ or the betrayers of them, my place is by their side until they are released or convicted.
> There I take my stand.

Although the plot involved shows how effective Coughlin's incitements to violence can be, it provides little ground for characterizing the entire membership of the Christian Front as advocates of violence.

The membership of the Christian Front is predominantly Irish Catholic of the low and moderate income groups. It is concentrated in cities of large Catholic populations: New York City contains the largest portion; such New England centers as Boston and Hartford have sizeable groups. That Catholics should be overwhelmingly predominant in a movement headed by a Catholic priest is only what might be assumed. The validity of this assumption is attested by an article in *Christian Social Action*, the Catholic layman's magazine.[10] Viewing the Front with alarm, it stated: "The people in this movement are for the most part honest Catholics. . . It daily converts fresh members of our Catholic people. . . The first meeting is reported to have been attended by a New York priest. . . Now it enjoys the apparent support of Catholic agencies that should be more wary of its implications." An article in the *Christian Century*, a Protestant publication, appearing about the same time, took the same point of view about the Front's membership.[11]   Another indication of the Catholic character of the membership is the active cooperation given the movement by a number of priests, among the most active being Rev. Edward Lodge Curran, President of the International Catholic Truth Society, and Rev. Peter Baptiste Duffee, pastor of the St. Francis of Assisi Church in New York City.

The author of the *Christian Century's* article noted also the predominance of Irish Catholics in the Christian Front, declaring that "its membership is at present almost entirely Irish and Catholic, with a sprinkling of Germans and Italians."   Other evidence supports this contention.   At a meeting of the Christian Mobilizers, one of the units of the Front, a speaker said, "Thomas Jefferson, and I think he was Irish, by the way . . . ," a typical flattering reference before Irish audiences.   Moreover, among the 17 plotters appeared several Irish names—Michael J. Beirne, Michael Vill, Keegan, Walsh, Kelly, Malone, and Cassidy.

That the members come from low and moderate income groups is suggested by their occupational characteristics.   In describing a Brooklyn Christian Front Meeting, *Christian Social Action* said:

> About seventy-five people were in the hall, most of them appearing be laboring men, sincere men, people who have worked for a livelihood. There were New York City policemen present, an ex-college professor, truckmen, school teachers, and a few steamship workers. . . .

An investigation made through Mayor La Guardia showed that 407 members of the New York police department had joined the Front.[12]   Thirteen of the 17 plotters who were employed consisted of three clerks, three salesmen, a telephone lineman, a tailor, a telegraph manager, a swimming instructor, an elevator mechanic, a bus driver, and a printer.

A close examination of one of the seventeen plotters might throw some light on the type of person attracted to the Front. [13]   Michael Joseph Bierne was thirty-two years old and married. For the past sixteen years he had been a contented worker at the New York Telephone Company. At the time of his arrest he was making $60 a week as a lineman. Bierne had come from Ireland at the age of fifteen. His schooling had ended at the age of thirteen. He was a devout Catholic and attended church every Sunday. Until Coughlin began his antisemitic broadcasts, he showed absolutely no interest in such matters. He was "no heavy-duty thinker," as a relative of his said. Since he had been brought up to respect the authority of the church, Coughlin's vivid account of the dangers of Communism and the need of "the

Franco way" profoundly impressed him. A relative explained, "The fact that Father Coughlin was a priest of the church led Michael to think that the Catholic Church had given its blessing to the Christian Front movement." When the agents of the FBI roused Bierne and his wife in the middle of the night, charging him with plotting to overthrow the government of the United States, he babbled, "I was only trying to be a good American."

Bierne is typical of the thousands of Catholics of Irish extraction who make up the radio priest's following. Persons of limited educational opportunities, they do not know that the Pope has twice condemned anti-semitism and that Coughlin's superior, the late Cardinal Mundelein, had stated that he "is not authorized to speak for the Catholic Church, nor does he represent the doctrine or sentiments of the church." [14] Somehow Coughlin's followers think of him as a golden-voiced man of God speaking with the full authority of the Catholic Church.

Another unusual characteristic of Christian Front membership is the fact that it has attracted a large number of unstable personalities. (Unstable personalities prominent in the Silver Shirts were mentioned in Chapter IV, and similar types will be noted in succeeding chapters.) The Christian Front has a greater number of active members with criminal records than any of the other organizations. This circumstance is perhaps not surprising for the Front is frankest in its advocacy of violence. Joseph Hartery, alias Joseph Herman, is a Christian Front leader with an unsavory past. On January 7, 1932, he was sentenced to 30 days in the workhouse for operating a house of prostitution. On December 14, 1938, he was arrested for assault and battery with knife and sentenced to three days in the workhouse. On August 1, 1939, he was arrested for disorderly conduct and fined. John Zitter, active in the Christian Front, was arrested on October 16, 1934, for petty larceny and convicted. He was subsequently arrested several times for disorderly conduct. Edwin Westphal, a member of both the Front and the Bund, was arrested on September 27, 1929, for burglary and committed to a hospital for the insane. On July 14, 1930, he was sent to a reformatory as a wayward minor. On July 1, 1937, he was arrested for violation of the copyright law and given 60 days in the workhouse. On August 25, 1939, he was arrested for disorderly conduct when he tried to incite a crowd to rise against the police. Edmund Burke, formerly of the Front and the Bund, is a convicted burglar. Dilling, alias Dougherty, has been arrested and convicted for assault on three occasions, one of these times for assaulting a policeman. Lucienti, a *Social Justice* salesman, with several aliases, has been arrested seven times for disorderly conduct and assault.

FUNDS

About all that is positively known about Coughlin's finances is that he takes in and spends more money than the leader of any other anti-semitic group. In the December 18, 1939, issue of *Social Justice*, he pleaded for $200,000 in contributions to enable him to carry on his radio work. "Radio expense is now close to $10,000 per week," he explained. With 47 stations in his hookup this means that Coughlin has spent close to $500,000 a year on radio broadcasts alone. Statements of the assets and liabilities of various Coughlin corporations, as found in annual reports to governmental agencies of Michigan, give certain general clues. Note the rise of his assets between 1934 and 1938. [15]

1934	$ 6,298
1935	79,358
1936	205,787
1937	196,297
1938	472,539

Few exact details are known regarding Coughlin's sources of funds. Back in 1931 and 1932 he learned that an appeal for funds, coupled with a suggestion that he might have to discontinue his work, could bring a shower of letters filled with donations. Gifts, large and small, are his chief source of income. Subscriptions to *Social Justice* also produce revenue. He always pushes the circulation of the paper. It is constantly promoted in Coughlin's broadcasts and in form letters which open with subscription pleas and close with such expressions as "God bless you" or a "Remember me in your prayers." A minor source of income, and another interesting combination of commercialism and religion, is the shop—actually inside Coughlin's church—where there are sold crucifixes, the Bible, picture postcards of Coughlin, and literature on the alleged schemes of Jewish Reds.

Suggested elsewhere in this study is the fact that no anti-semitic group can live a vigorous existence without some support from the wealthy. Coughlin with his broadcasts and his newspapers operates a tremendously expensive propaganda machine. That he supports the machine entirely by small donations from his radio public is difficult to believe. Circumstantial evidence points to a greater source of income. In 1935 and 1936, when Coughlin furiously attacked the New Deal, most wealthy people were doing the same. In 1938, he fought the unionization of the Detroit auto plants. He has constantly inveighed against the menace of Communism. In short, he has invariably been on the same side of the fence as have the upper-income groups.[16]

CHAPTER VI

Defenders of the Christian Faith

The supreme need is a great sweeping revival, a spiritual awakening. Without it our doom is sealed! . . . I now affirm that America must choose between Revival and Revolution.

If we are to be spared the agonies of a bloody revolution, it will be because the Nation turns to God. . . . BACK TO GOD, BACK TO THE BIBLE, BACK TO RUGGED EVANGELISM THAT PUTS THE FEAR OF GOD IN THE HEARTS OF THE PEOPLE.

HERE is the basic creed of the Defenders of the Christian Faith. Although its membership is a mailing list, although its government is one man, this organization has taken it upon itself to deluge the nation with literature compounded of fiery Protestant Fundamentalism and bitter anti-semitism. Ever since 1925, when the organization was born, the Rev. Gerald B. Winrod, its founder, has been a foe of modernism in religion; but not until January (or February) 1933, did he discover that behind modernism—and every other evil in the materialistic world—was "Jewish Bolshevism."

LEADERSHIP

Winrod entered the ministry by following in the footsteps of his father. The elder Winrod spent his early life as a bartender in a Wichita saloon that was among the first to feel the wrath of Carrie Nation and her hatchet. During Carrie's raid, Winrod the elder looked on philosophically, making no effort to protect the property. He came to see the error of his calling, abandoned it, and, eventually, became an evangelist. As he put it, [1] "We [Mrs. Winrod and himself] felt directed to begin a distinctly evangelistic testimony in Wichita." Offspring Gerald, born in 1898, spent all his youth in Wichita. Early in his life he was taken in charge by a traveling evangelist, who tutored him for several years and made a "boy preacher" out of him. This is important to note, for Gerald Winrod has never had any formal theological training. His degree of D.D. is an honorary one conferred upon him in 1935 by the Los Angeles Baptist Theological Seminary. The president of that institution stated:

Our academic records show that on June 2nd, 1935, the degree of Doctor of Divinity was conferred upon Gerald B. Winrod of Wichita,

Editor of the *Defender,* and a distinguished minister of the Gospel, in recognition of his valuable leadership both in the field of Christian Journalism and Theology.

Young Winrod worked with his father and eventually took over the burden of the evangelism and religious tract writing. He soon organized the Defenders of the Christian Faith and built the large Defenders' Gospel Tabernacle. At no time has he ever held a pastorate[2] nor has he been connected with any denomination. His work is non-denominational. As his secretary has stated, "Dr. Winrod has no church of his own. The entire United States and Canada are his congregation."

Winrod is a man of no small ambitions. In 1938 he entered a four-cornered race in Kansas for the Republican nomination to the United States Senate. He staged an elaborate campaign, using, among other media, sound trucks and the radio. For a time his candidacy looked promising. Finally, John Hamilton, Chairman of the Republican National Committee, expressed the party's disapproval of Winrod on the ground of his "intolerance." As a result, Winrod placed third in the election.

Winrod attributes all his important acts to divine guidance. For instance, in one letter he said: "It was back in the year 1929 that God directed me to form this inner circle." In another, he wrote: "While I was in Wittenburg, God gave me inspiration for a new book which I have just written entitled *Martin Luther and the Reformation.* Beyond doubt this is one of the most important books the Holy Spirit has ever prompted me to write."

PROPAGANDA

The Defenders have utilized nearly all channels of propaganda. The monthly magazine, the *Defender,* and the monthly newspaper, the *Revealer,* have been the most important media. In addition, the followers of the Defenders distribute a vast quantity of books, tracts, and pamphlets. They hold Bible conferences and revival meetings all over the country and make considerable use of the radio. For a few months they experimented with a Washington news bureau. The first issue of the *Defender* appeared in April 1926. By 1937 this magazine—an annual subscription to which costs only 50 cents a year—had a circulation of 100,000 copies per issue. In addition, Winrod has published a Spanish edition of his magazine, *El Defensor Hispano,* which circulates in Puerto Rico, Cuba, and Mexico. The *Revealer* appeared in April 1934 and, by February 1935, had a circulation of 50,000. Winrod attempted to extend its influence beyond its immediate subscribers. One of his "Inner Circle" letters urged: "Don't let a copy of the *Revealer* die. As soon as you have finished reading it, hand it to a Friend." In January 1937, however, he discontinued its publication.

Pamphlets constitute a highly important part of the Defenders' propaganda. In addition to carrying a large part of the writing burden of his two periodicals, Winrod has written a great number of pamphlets, the majority of which are of an anti-semitic nature. A list of such pamphlets with their publication date and the number printed includes: *Three Modern Evils—Modernism, Atheism, and Bolshevism* (1932—6,000 copies), *The NRA in Prophecy and a Discussion of Beast Worship* (1933—8,000 copies), *The U. S. and Russia in Prophecy and the Red Horse of the Apocalypse* (1933—5,000 copies), *Mussolini's Place in Prophecy* (1933—4,000 copies), *Communism and the Roosevelt Brain Trust* (1933—30,000 copies), *The Hidden Hand; The Protocols and the Coming Super Man* (1933—22,000 copies), and *The Truth About the Protocols* (1935—4,000 copies). Concerning the following pamphlets no data on the number printed is available. *World Trends Toward Anti-Christ* (1934), *The Anti-Christ and the Tribe of Dan* (1936), *The Harlot Woman and the Scarlet Beast* (1936), *The Curse of Modern Deism* (1936), *The Jewish Assault on Christianity* (1935), *Subversive Movements* (1937), *Americans, Drop Your Chains* (1938), and *America Facing the Present Crisis* (1938). These pamphlets apparently went through only one printing of 2,000 each—the rate at which most Winrod pamphlets have been published—for any additional printings have been usually indicated in the pamphlet concerned. The two listings suggest that about 95,000 anti-semitic pamphlets were printed in the years 1932-1936. Since 1937 Winrod has also sold pamphlets by other authors. Among these have been Blomgren's *The Red and Yellow Peril*, Sullivan's *Wolves in Sheep's Clothing* and *Hundreds of Questions and Answers on Socialism and Communism*, and Elizabeth Dilling's *Dare We Oppose Red Treason?*

Other forms of printed matter distributed by Winrod's Defenders are tracts—leaflets of twelve pages or less. Although most of these tracts are purely religious a few deal with political matters, as the following titles suggest: *Is America Seeing Red?*, *The Mark of the Beast, Blind Leaders of the Blind, The Coming Financial Octopus*, and *Revival or Revolution*. During the month of August 1935, no less than 75,000 tracts were distributed. Members of the "Defenders Tract Club" receive, in return for 25 cents monthly dues, a quantity of tracts, which they contribute to jails, hospitals, and CCC camps.

The Defenders sell a large variety of books. In addition to works of a strictly religious nature there are such volumes as Elizabeth Dilling's *The Red Network*, Dr. Arno C. Gaebelein's *The Conflict of the Ages*,

ORGANIZED ANTI-SEMITISM IN AMERICA

E. M. Hadley's *TNT*, E. H. Peterson's *The Underlying Causes of Our
National Depression*, E. N. Sanctuary's *Are These Things So?*, and *The
Protocols of the Elders of Zion.*

Winrod never tires of organizing meetings and of traveling about the
country to address them. Although apparently exaggerative, the following statements excerpted from one of Winrod's letters are substantially
accurate:

> We have reached audiences reaching into hundreds of thousands at
> Defenders Conferences in all sections of the United States and parts
> of Canada. We have been instrumental in getting hundreds of
> Revival meetings and Bible Conferences started in communities
> over the country.

In another letter written in May 1935, Winrod asserted that in the preceding ten months he had traveled 36,472 miles "in the service of our
Lord and Master." Among the communities in which he has spoken
are Beaumont, Texas; Memphis and Chattanooga, Tennessee; Abilene,
Manhattan, and Peabody, Kansas; and Peoria, Illinois.

When Winrod broadcasts, he tempers his hatred for the Jews; consequently, the radio as a medium for his anti-semitic propaganda is of
less importance than the others. During his campaign for the Republican Senatorial nomination, he spoke weekly for several months over
a Kansas station, flaying Communism and the New Deal.

Early in 1937, Winrod tried unsuccessfully to establish in Washington, D. C., what might have turned out to be a very powerful propaganda instrument. This was the Capitol News and Feature Service,
a bureau designed to furnish its version of current events to editors of
2,000 country papers. No charge was to be made for this service and
the editors were to be permitted to use the material in whatever way they
saw fit. The ambitious enterprise, directed by two former associates
of William Dudley Pelley, began in January and, because of lack of
funds, collapsed in April.

The Defenders of the Christian Faith has no formal membership
organization. It collects no dues, issues no membership cards. Its membership roll is merely a mailing list of those who read its literature.
Some 6,000 people who are Winrod's most faithful readers and who
contribute the funds in response to his frequent appeals comprise what
Winrod calls his "Inner Circle". The subscribed circulation of the
Defender, the most important publication, offers the best numerical
estimate of Winrod's following. In 1930 the circulation was about
25,000; by 1934, 50,000; by October 1935, 80,000; and in January 1936,

100,000. According to Winrod, the states that have the greatest number of subscribers are Pennsylvania, California, and Illinois. Other states strong in subscribers include Michigan, New York, Ohio, Kansas, and North Carolina.

Winrod's crusades carry the colors of Fundamentalism, attracting recruits from H. L. Mencken's "Bible belt". Indicative of this religious appeal is the following advertisement about the *Defender:*

> If you would like to know how Current History can be interpreted in the light of Fulfilled Bible Prophecy;
> If you want to see Modernism exposed and refuted;
> If you want to know how the rising tide of Atheism is being stemmed;
> If you are interested in warning people against the dangers of Communism;
> If you want Scriptural and Scientific arguments against Evolution;
> If you would know prophecy and understand "the signs of the times";
> If you want to see the Historic and Evangelical Faith defended;
> THEN YOU ARE LOOKING FOR THE DEFENDER MAGAZINE.

Another indication is the titles of books reviewed in the *Defender.* These include *Modernism Cross-Examined, Evolution Cross-Examined, Crucifying Christ in Our Colleges, When the Trumpet Sounds, Modernism Unveiled, The Carnival of Death, or the Modern Dance, Studies in Prophecy, Amazing Fulfillments of Prophecy,* and *The Scriptures' Reply to the Arguments Against the Second Coming of Christ.*

Reports of Winrod's Bible conferences show that his followers have much in common with the crowds that attended Billy Sunday's revivals. His audiences are described as being "aroused to a frenzy." Anti-Catholic attacks both in the columns of the *Defender* and the speeches of Winrod—though infrequent—leave no room for doubt that his adherents are Protestants. [3] The limited educational opportunities of these adherents is suggested by their strong Fundamentalist belief in prophecy, *i.e.,* the interpretation of current world happenings in terms that the Bible has foretold. Winrod has succinctly expressed this belief:

> We are seeing that an ever-increasing constituency of Christian believers are becoming interested in the matter of Bible Prophecy. Indeed, there is no way to understand the strange events taking place in the world today except as they are understood in the light of prophecy. Communists may have taken the Bible out of Russia, but they did not take Russia out of the Bible.

This explains the appearance in the *Defender* of such articles as "Mussolini in the Searchlight of Prophecy", "Ethiopia in the Bible", and "A Biblical Analysis of the Nation's Plight." Winrod's faith in prophecy leads the *Defender* to make such observations as the following: "Students of Bible prophecy have been watching Mussolini for several years, because exactly such a man is described in the book of Daniel, to arise during the end-time of this age and revive the old Roman Empire." Winrod's belief in prophecy is not confined to Biblical versions but includes the Great Pyramid variety. [4]

> Furthermore the Great Pyramid's secret is hid to all but the scientists of our own day who are Christians. Skeptics see in it a pile of stones. Believers, who search, find that it contains deep spiritual teaching. Its message is unintelligible except to those who come to it still holding the validity of the *units of Biblical measure* in terms of the Pyramid inch and cubit.

That the Defenders are primarily small-town and rural folk is shown by the rarity of Winrod's speeches in large cities. Occasionally he has talked in Kansas City, but apparently in no other large city. Indicative reports describe him as speaking at Manhattan, Kansas, before a group of "earnest souls from the Nazarene and Free Methodist Churches" or at Peoria, Illinois, under the auspices of the Peoria Tabernacle, an evangelistic organization, or at Peabody, Kansas, under the auspices of the local American Legion post.

A letter written as an aftermath of his speech at Peabody suggests the type of audience to whom Winrod appeals. The speech had been entitled "The Real Significance of Communism and the C. I. O.", but its anti-semitism had made Legion officials elsewhere in Kansas wonder if Winrod would be an appropriate speaker for their posts. Anxious to learn whether Winrod had been objectionably anti-semitic, a Legion official wrote to the Peabody post and received the following reply:

> Winrod . . . did not in his address here say anything against Jews as a race—nothing which could be construed by *good* Jews of our land as antagonistic toward them. . . .
> Your post can sponsor this lecture by Dr. Winrod without fear his remarks will be other than a real patriotic Biblical exposure of Communism and a defense of fundamental Americanism.

The letter was signed by a group of the town's most prominent citizens —the president of the Peabody Ministers' Association, the clergymen of the First Presbyterian and First Baptist Churches, the second vice-president of the Peabody State Bank, and the Commander, Past Commander, and Adjutant of the American Legion Post. The key phrase of the letter is "a real patriotic Biblical exposure of Communism and a defense of fundamental Americanism." Communism is thought of in Fundamentalist terms as something that can be foretold and exposed through a proper understanding of Biblical prophecy. The term, "fundamental Americanism," is of particular significance. The people of Peabody are Protestants. They are descendants of old American stock.

They hold to an individualistic economic philosophy. They are firmly convinced that their moral standards should be accepted by the entire American people. Cities—with their labor organizations for collective bargaining, with their polyglot and "alien" populations of Jews and recent Catholic immigrants from Southern Europe, with their multiplicity of moral philosophies—represent to Peabody townsmen the centers where their "fundamental Americanism" is threatened by "Communism"—as they conceive of Communism.

Several factors indicate the economic status of Winrod's followers. The fact that their educational opportunities appear to have been limited suggests that they come from the lower-income groups. The nature of the advertisements in the *Defender* suggest the same thing. The magazine carries no advertisements for such standard products as cars, life insurance, and cigarettes—the advertisements that are found in most magazines. Instead, the *Defender* advertises mail-order courses in public speaking, cures for asthma, and preparations for keeping false teeth from slipping. If national advertisers thought the *Defender* appealed to a public with any buying power, they would have advertised in it, for a magazine with a circulation of 100,000 is not to be ignored. A final factor is the low price of a subscription to the *Defender*—fifty cents a year. Apparently, the price is kept down in order to reach a low income group. The economic status of the Defenders may, then, be best described as "lower middle class."

FUNDS

Winrod asserts that his weekly expenses are $1,200. In view of his many activities, this does not seem improbable. He meets the expenses by drawing on at least four different sources: income from his publications, collections at public meetings, contributions from the "Inner Circle," gifts from the wealthy. Income from publications includes not only the sale of the literature but also the advertising in the *Defender*. Collections are taken at all public meetings of the Defenders. The "Inner Circle," people of moderate means, is the source to which Winrod turns to most frequently. A special mimeographed letter goes out to the Circle about every month or six weeks. Almost invariably it ends with an appeal for funds. Some special emergency has always to be met: an accumulation of unpaid bills, the purchase of a new car for Winrod, the launching of a new tract, or the expenses of radio broadcasting. In letters to the Circle, flattery and quotations from the Bible are used to encourage contributions. A letter written in connection with the launching of the *Revealer* was truly revealing:

You people have been the very heart-throb of the movement. Without your support during the last five years, the movement would have perished. . . . Your part in the work is as important as mine. If we were to cease our combined efforts, all would be lost. . . .

Who can invest $50 in order to give the *Revealer* a running start? Can someone send $100? DO HELP QUICK. Think how wonderful it would be if twenty friends could send $20 each. Or if one hundred could send $10 apiece. Let many, many contribute $5.00. . . . But if you can only send a dollar to two . . . send what you can.

On another occasion, Winrod declared:

Upon arriving in Washington I found an accumulation of over $2,000 in unpaid bills staring me in the face. My heart fairly sinks as I bring this load before you. . . . Yet, I think of the Scriptures which tell us to cast our burdens upon the Lord. And another verse, Gal. 6:2, "Bear ye one another's burdens, and so fulfil the law of Christ."

Winrod has not found his way into the pocketbooks of any great number of affluent businessmen and industrialists. Nevertheless, he has had certain successes. On at least one occasion, he is said to have obtained contributions from two wealthy Oklahoma oil men. The appeal to such men is, "We are fighting Communism". Perhaps the menace of Communism seemed real and near at hand to the oil companies when the C. I. O. conducted a drive to unionize oil field workers.

CHAPTER VII

The Edmondson Economic Service

TO REFER to the Edmondson Economic Service as an "organization" is definitely to stretch the meaning of the term. Robert Edward Edmondson, the head of this center of anti-semitic propaganda, has no organizational inclinations. He is primarily important as an energetic free-lance writer and distributor of anti-semitic literature.

LEADERSHIP

Something of Edmondson's highly interesting background can be gleaned from the autobiographical sketch he published in the January 28, 1936, issue of his weekly publication:

> Robert Edward Edmondson was born in Dayton, Ohio, in 1872, son of Edward Edmondson, artist. My business career includes nearly forty years in journalism as reporter, editor, publisher, financial writer and investment economist from coast to coast. Politically, I am non-partisan, pro-Constitution, pro-National, anti-International and anti-Communist; not a member of any secret society. Financially, modestly independent, with no entangling alliances. Religion, not a churchman but a believer in Christian principles. Ancestry, native American, chiefly Scotch descent, pre-Revolution, from Maryland.

> I began in Cincinnati, Ohio, as reporter and then sub-editor for the *Cincinnati Post*, later representative for the Scripps-McRae Press Association. Was news correspondent in New York City for the *Louisville Times, Milwaukee Journal, Minneapolis Journal,* and twenty other western newspapers. Sub-editor on James Gordon Bennett's *New York Herald*, following reportorial service on *New York Mail and Express* under Editor Stoddard. Economic writer for the Fairchild Publications. Financial editor for the *New York Journal.* For a few months I was on the staff of financial news reporters employed by the manager of the Daily Financial News Bureau of the now defunct *Town Topics Weekly*, once run by Jewish scandalmongers. J. A. Joseph was chosen to operate the bureau.

> I regard my short connection with this agency in the New York financial district as the most valuable of my entire financial experience because it provided knowledge which enabled me to identify positively the sinister Jewish Leadership forces which were then subverting American finance through economic power, and who later similarly prostituted politics. The knowledge gained during this association was what determined me when I established on a capital of $300 thirty-three years ago my own independent and unsubsidized financial news analytical Edmondson Service. . . .

[79]

The Edmondson Service established later the *American Stock-holders' Weekly,* the *New York Daily Financial News Bulletin,* and *Coming Events.* Finding it necessary in 1923 to take a prolonged vacation owing to overwork—undermining of health, I disposed of *Coming Events,* then yielding $50,000 a year net, and traveled for a few years on the Pacific Coast. With recovering health, I returned to New York City in the latter part of 1932 and reestablished the Edmondson Service, going on the staff of the *New York Daily News Record* as Economic writer. I soon found a mysterious wall against recovery. . . .

Edmondson continues with his version of the origin of his hatred for Jews and revolutionaries:

On March 27, 1934, I issued a bulletin headed: "Bankrupt Leadership," declaring that Republican leadership had shown bankruptcy by refusing to reform anything, and . . . A prominent investment interest asked me why I had published this. I replied that it was a patriotic duty to expose bad political leadership. "Is that all?" I was asked. "Yes," I answered. The questioner then held me spellbound for an hour. He and his associates had studied the Jewish Problem for years. He unfolded a story of politico-economic subversion of France, Britain, Germany and Russia, producing historical suppressed records of fact and authority, largely Jewish, furnishing documentary evidence that Jewish Leadership had caused the depression and was moving to take over the United States through the Jewish-Radical Roosevelt administration.

When he finished I asked: "What are we going to do about it?" He said: "I don't know." "I do," I declared. "There is but one course. Pitiless publicity is the only cure for public evils, and I am going to broadcast Jewish anti-Americanism and expose the plot. The Real Issue is: Shall a minority rule?"

In April, 1934, the Edmondson Economic Service entered the field of anti-semitism. At that time it was located at 84 Washington Street, New York City. In April, 1937, it moved to 400 West 160th Street and in 1939 it forsook New York for Stoddartsville, Pennsylvania.

PROPAGANDA

Although it is difficult to arrive at an accurate estimate of the circulation of Edmondson's material, it is safe to say that the total volume has been exceeded only by that of Father Coughlin, the German-American Bund, and the Rev. Gerald B. Winrod. Much of his material is distributed through other anti-semitic organizations—groups too small to publish their own literature, such as the Order of '76 and the Military Order of the Loyal Legion of the United States. His publications have turned up in such widely separated points as Montgomery (Ala.), Aberdeen (Wash.), San Antonio, Boston, Philadelphia, Galveston, Chicago, Toledo, Cleveland, and Sioux City.

THE EDMONDSON ECONOMIC SERVICE

Edmondson asserts that in his first year of operation he distributed over a million pieces of literature, pamphlets and weekly letters.[1] After two years of operation, he boasted that he had circulated over five million pieces of literature. Assuming that his figures are accurate, Edmondson's average weekly circulation over the first two years was approximately 50,000.

Prior to the 1936 presidential election Edmondson periodically published the *Edmondson News X-Ray* and *Freedom*. Neither publication ever achieved extensive circulation. In 1937, Edmondson began to distribute pamphlets frequently. They were of ten to fifty pages, selling for five or ten cents each. Among these were Elizabeth Dilling's —*Dare We Oppose Red Treason?*; Edmondson's—*The Jewish System Indicted, Anti-Semitic Causes of Today,* and *Women of America, Rescue the Republic.*

Though primarily a writer, Edmondson now and then makes use of the public platform as a channel of propaganda. On several occasions he has addressed German-American Bund groups. The American National Labor Party, a group that split off from the Bund, and the American Nationalist Party, one of the smaller anti-semitic groups, have both had him as a guest speaker. In February, 1937, he accepted the invitation of the Cardinal Newman Club of New York to address a group of 500 Catholic youths. His address, entitled "Anti-Semitic Causes of Today," is one of the rare instances of an anti-semitic address to a Catholic audience prior to the opening of Father Coughlin's anti-semitic campaign in July, 1938.

MEMBERSHIP

Edmondson has no membership organization. His followers are the readers of his weekly bulletins, equivalent in number and in geographical distribution to the circulation—about 50,000—scattered all over the country. Many reader-members are members of other anti-semitic groups. Since Edmondson's material sells quite cheaply, his followers are undoubtedly from a lower income level than those who purchase James True's $12 per year *Industrial Control Reports.*[2]

FUNDS

The Edmondson Economic Service receives its financial backing from four sources—Edmondson's private income, sale of literature, small solicited contributions, and the gifts of at least four financial "angels". Edmondson tells of starting his campaign by "using several thousand dollars of my own resources to get it on a self-supporting basis." Probably a much more important source than the sale of literature is the small solicited contribution. Typical of Edmondson's appeals for such contributions is the concluding sentence of one of his bulletins: "Carry on your patriotic crusade against aliens seeking to destroy American Liberties. I enclose contribution therefor. Please acknowledge receipt." Similar solicitations were made in connection with the Edmondson Defense Fund. Mayor Fiorello La Guardia of New York and other persons brought suit against Edmondson for libel against the Jewish people. Edmondson was shrewd enough to sense the opportunity to become a martyr and to achieve considerable publicity. Numerous Edmondson rallies were held in New York to raise funds for his defense. At least one such meeting was held in the New York *Turnhalle*—in a room adjoining that in which the Bund was holding a meeting. In Chicago, Harry Jung, head of the anti-semitic American Viligant Intelligence Federation, solicited contributions for the defense fund. Apparently the plaintiffs realized that the novel idea of libel against a race was a weak basis for a case and that they were playing into Edmondson's hands by making a martyr of him. The case was dropped. Prominent among Edmondson's financial "angels" is Howland Spencer, the wealthy owner of the *Highland Post*, an Ulster County (New York), journal. Spencer is violently anti-semitic and anti-New Deal in his paper and in the pamphlets that he writes under the pseudonym, the Squire of Krum Elbow. At least three other persons have been at one time or another Edmondson's financial "angels": a very prominent Newport, Rhode Island, lawyer; a banker now deceased, and a New York stockbroker. In 1937 the stockbroker, evidently alarmed about "the destructive influences of alien bankers in this country", gave $5,000 jointly to Edmondson and Colonel E. M. Sanctuary, leader of the anti-semitic American Christian Defenders, to further their work.

CHAPTER VIII

The American Vigilant Intelligence Federation

THE American Vigilant Intelligence Federation was incorporated under the laws of Illinois as a non-profit corporation in December, 1927. From that date until April, 1933, it was not a membership organization. It consisted only of a general manager, his secretary, a few solicitors and undercover men, and some very extensive files on persons and organizations considered subversive by the Federation. The files were the organization's chief basis of income, for from them came the information for which businessmen and others paid substantial fees. In April, 1933, the Federation became a membership organization. The high point of activity was reached in the spring and summer of 1934. At that time, meetings of the Federation's Inner Circle in Chicago were held regularly and ambitious national plans were laid. Some organizational work was carried on in certain parts of Michigan. After the McCormack Committee investigated the Federation in August, 1934, it became less conspicuous. During the 1936 Presidential campaign, however, the organization threw off some of its old secrecy, conducted public meetings, and de-emphasized spying on the "Reds." Since 1936, it has avoided public attention although it has remained quite active.

The Federation's present objects and purposes, as set forth in the literature sent to prospective members, are:

> To combat and counteract the insidious work of anti-American propagandists, including those who have invaded American shores in order to belittle the patriotic efforts of American heroes and to tarnish their fair name.
> To combat and counteract the efforts of anti-American organizations which are expending huge sums to destroy American institutions and to create a Socialistic or Communistic World Government.
> To combat and counteract the rule of insidious minorities, bureaucracies, and lawless elements.
> To refrain from being a party to any religious, political or racial controversy unless such controversy contains a political element that is inimical to American Liberty and American Civilization.
> To consummate its educational program by the means of patriotic

donations made by those who are in sympathy with the perpetuation of American Liberty and American Civilization.

To establish an endowment fund to perpetuate its work in future generations, so that our posterity may enjoy the same heritage handed down to us by our ancestors.

The Federation does not carry out its purposes in broad daylight. It uses the "secret" society technique that so many Americans find irresistible. An excellent description of this technique is to be found in the set of confidential instructions given each Federation recruit upon admission to membership.

Confidential Instructions
FROM: GENERAL HEADQUARTERS

These instructions are for your eyes only. They must be preserved and read carefully. They are our property. On occasion they will be recalled and new ones issued. If any subjects are not covered or are not clear, do not hesitate to ask about them.

In brief the following instructions cover (A) your conduct, (B) your duties, and (C) your responsibilities, all voluntarily undertaken as a working patriot, tritely but truly stated as—For God (against anti-God)—For Home (against Nationalization of Man, Woman, and Child)—For Country (Americanism not Internationalism).

A. YOUR CONDUCT

You are cautioned to:—

1. Sign communications by your number only, your signature is not necessary.

2. Address all communications to Post Office Box 144, Chicago, Illinois.

3. Since your sponsor, and members you sponsor, know of your association and work, it is not necessary to tell of it, unless you want to, and it might act as a handicap to good intelligence work, should your stand be "broadcast." Use your own best judgment, however.

4. Confidential matters of the organization should only be discussed in private and in confidence. Therefore use discretion on street cars, taxi cabs, buses, the streets, restaurants, and anywhere in public where you might be overheard or others might listen in. This should be especially watched when you are talking to friends whom you want to enlist or enroll.

5. Your identification tag (please remove from under seal on last page) is to be carried with you always. It should be displayed only to identify yourself to other members or as a test to find out if another is a member. It is purposely made inconspicuous and meaningless almost like an ordinary telephone slug, so that if lost, it can mean nothing to the finder and is readily replaceable. Meritorious service is rewarded by the issuance of tags of increasingly finer metals. In this way the various members are given rank or rating.

6. The pass-word, recognition word, and distress-shout will be told you by your Sponsor.

7. The Enlistment and Acceptance blanks are all numbered and placed in your care, confident that you will be able to use them. If you can not use them, they must be returned, because a record is kept of each one and they must be accounted for in either new Enlistments and Enrollments or returns. Also as a double check, when received, they are acknowledged. This verifies as to genuineness of applications.

8. Enlisting or Enrolling new members. *Be sure of the man or woman you enlist or enroll.* For your own sake as well as others, sponsor only persons whose background, training, likes and dislikes, you are familiar with, know about, and can vouch for as being sound. "Well-chosen" must be our watchword.

B. YOUR DUTIES

1. Report faithfully any and all information that comes to your notice. This means matter that you overhear or that falls into your hands more or less by accident.

2. Do whatever duties are assigned to you if possible.

3. Keep yourself informed by sending in your subscription promptly and in advance. If for any reason you must delay, please write in saying so. Neglect plus Silence can have only one interpretation.

C. YOUR RESPONSIBILITIES

1. You will find that anti-God, anti-Home, and anti-American material usually run along the following lines. This listing is given you so you may readily label, put your finger on, and recognize for what it is, and not for what it tells you what it is.

(a) Communist or communistic.
(b) Socialist or socialistic.
(c) Anarchist or anarchistic.
(d) Atheist or agnostic.
(e) Pacifist or internationalistic; anti-nationalism.
(f) Occult; psychic; mystic; metaphysic.
(g) Racial—creedal or cult.
(h) Derogatory of Army, Navy, Marine, National Guard, Reserve Officers Training Corps (ROTC), Citizens Military Training Camps (CMTC).
(i) Off-color educational, religious, "liberal" academic propaganda and activities.
(j) Sexy or pornographic.
(k) Subversive of the *Golden Rule.* (Business is Business attitude typifies this.)
(l) Neurotic Philosophical.
(m) Anti-law and order.
(n) Class legislation (local—state—national).
(o) Subversive of constitutional government.

2. *Speeches, pamphlets, conversation, programs, articles, reports, etc.,* which come under any of the above subheads should be reported or copies cut or sent in in toto to headquarters.

3. When you are given a job to do such as the Special Assignment Sheet attached hereto, do it if possible to the best of your ability.

4. *When you are directed to cover a meeting, forum, address, lecture, or sermon,* remember:—

(a) Type or write in ink on plain paper with date of report in upper left hand corner, signing it at end with your number only.

(b) Begin report with (1) address of hall or meeting place, (2) time of meeting, (3) and a careful estimate of the number of people present.

(c) Do your best to get the name of each speaker. If you fail to, then describe characteristics, and any peculiarities, marks or emblems.

(d) Get hold of any literature distributed, programs, etc. Send this along by all means.

(e) The markedly disloyal or destructive statements should be reported as nearly as verbatim as possible.

(f) Report any persons present who are in the public eye (important) or who appear to be persons of importance.

(g) Signed statements of eye-witnesses or attendants are highly valuable regarding poisonous revolutionary declarations on the part of speakers.

(h) Please report everything heard and seen in as great detail as possible, because even apparently irrelevant items, while seemingly meaningless to you, may, when checked with other reports, assume great importance, or even inadvertently give an inkling of something of real moment that is secret. Slips of the tongue often do just this. Therefore, be voluminous.

5. *Report even casual conversations* overheard or taken part in, when the speaker seems unsound, or persists after being objected to or after being given an American viewpoint by yourself or others. Do not hesitate to proclaim the Truth and to be American, if you can do so in good taste, or it might be well to do so regardless.

6. *Literature and periodicals* are especial items of scrutiny. Anything coming under the before-mentioned headings should be clipped and sent in, fully identified as to publication name, date and page. If you can tear out the entire page or pages, do so. Many members will be assigned this duty with reference to certain periodicals. All are asked to do it, if they can, regardless of specific assignment.

7. MEMBERSHIP:

(a) Men, women or children are eligible, *if you know them well and can vouch for them.*

(b) There are three kinds of Memberships, dependent upon financial capacities, but without demarcation or limitation because of it, since any class can Sponsor members for either of the other two. They are:

1. *Acceptance*—by enrollment as a Member of the Board of Underwriters. This classification voluntarily undertakes a monthly financial responsibility to the organization for a reasonable sum, payable monthly.

2. *Enlistment*—by undertaking to serve as a Confidential Intelligence agent and to keep informed by sending in $1.25 every 3 months for educational material disseminated by the organization.

3. *Remitted Enlistment*—identical with Enlistment except that the $1.25 subscription is remitted because of unemployment or financial distress. As soon as the distress time is over regular enlistment status must be resumed or taken up.

(c) Your Sponsor will give you additional instructions regarding membership.

(d) You are reminded that your membership was solicited by nothing more or less than another "working patriot." *There are no paid membership solicitors.* This means therefore that the growth or lack of growth, strength or weakness, effectiveness or ineffectiveness of the organization you are aligned with, depends solely upon yourself and how well you work at this patriotic job.

(e) While members are and must be "Well Chosen," there is truly strength in numbers, and you are earnestly encouraged to be alert in the Enlisting And Enrolling of your friends and associates whom you know will be equally ready to serve as "working patriots."

(f) Attention is directed to the fact that Membership is open to Men, Women, and Children. Women especially can do excellent work since they are being made the subject of concentrated propaganda.

(g) The Membership Committee, of course, passes upon all enlistments and enrollments, and can assure you of sound and necessary reasons for rejections when made.

8. IN CASE OF AN EMERGENCY

(a) On the index card herewith are recorded several telephone numbers, for your use in emergency cases and after business hours. You should be able to reach one of the members at one of these numbers. These numbers should not be used unless imperatively necessary. In talking over the phone identify yourself as Number so-and-so.

(b) Unless you are otherwise instructed, when mailing reports, etc., use always just "Post Office Box 144, Chicago, Illinois."

(c) Telegrams can be dispatched to the same Post Office Box address, without the use of any name. In signing telegrams, spell out your token number—for example: thirty-one, or whatever it happens to be.

9. *When you want proof or information* on any subject—do not hesitate to write in for it. Within limits it will be promptly supplied to you.

10. Prepared addresses will be sent to you from time to time which you are encouraged to deliver in a talk to formal or informal groups.

11. *The Bulletins of Information* which are sent you are for your use and knowledge. Broadcast it to the uninformed and the misinformed. Tell it to the World without hesitation because it is absolutely authenticated and documented, every bit of it fully proven and established.

12. *Your Immediate Assignment* is attached, please report regularly and not less than once each month.

The text of the "immediate assignment" clipped to the above confidential instructions follows:

SPECIAL ASSIGNMENT

Your special assignment until further notice will be the reading and clipping of the magazine *Literary Digest*, according to Confidential Instructions, Page 3, Item 6. Anytime you are in the near vicinity, you are privileged to visit headquarters office.

Aside from the appeal to secrecy evident throughout the above documents, the most striking feature is the fantastic classification of subversive writings and utterances. With such an approach the Federation obviously can classify as subversive anyone it does not happen to like. Moreover, not only must a Federation "Agent" do a good deal of research work, but he must pay $5 a year for the privilege.

The man who leads and has always been the dominant figure in the American Vigilant Intelligence Federation is Harry A. Jung.

During the World War, Jung served on the western side of the Atlantic doing espionage work for the Military Plant and Protection Department of the War Labor Board.[1] In the period of industrial unrest following the war, he found that his skill in espionage had definite commercial value. He set himself up in Chicago as "Labor Commissioner" of the National Clay Products Industries Association. The Association was, essentially, Harry Jung. Strictly speaking it was not a trade association of manufacturers. It was a business for Jung, the business of labor-spying and strike-breaking for any clay products manufacturer who would pay for his services.[2] Since this business thrived on labor unrest and languished during labor tranquillity, Jung did not limit himself to handling labor troubles that arose naturally. It is asserted that he fomented strikes in order that he would be called upon to settle them. Herewith is the text of a document indicating several characteristics of his operations. It appeared on the stationery of the National Clay Products Industries Association, dated September 25, 1926:[3]

General Manager,
North River Brick Co.,
R.F.D. 4,
Saugerties, N. Y.

DEAR SIR:

Find herewith excerpt from confidential report received from one of our staff representatives in connection with the Connecticut strike situation:

"Lowrie did not speak tonight of using any violence, but begged the men to stick for the sake of their wives and children, saying next spring when this battle opened up again, the Hudson River district would be organized so that no influx of negro labor could occur, as is now the case, and with this road blocked, the CBMA would have to come to time."

It is essential that this fall, winter and next spring, the Hudson River operators get together and formulate a definite labor policy and it would be advisable to have the writer address you on the subject matter of "What is the U. B. and C. W. of A.?" [4] "What do they do?"—"What have they done?" and "What Should We Do to Offset Their Activities?"

Very truly yours,

H. A. JUNG,
Commissioner.

The term "staff representative" used in the first paragraph is, of course, a euphemism for "labor spy," "Lowrie" was apparently the union organizer. Note that one of the functions of the "Commissioner" was that of traveling lecturer on the evils of labor unions and that of advance information expert on the best ways to defeat unionism.

Among the persons who attest to Jung's strike-fomenting activities as well as his espionage and strike-breaking work is the late Speaker of the House of Representatives, Henry T. Rainey. When he found that Jung was distributing printed matter attacking him among his constituents in Illinois, Rainey wrote Jung the following letter:

For a long time I was the ranking member of my party on the Labor Committee in Congress, leading the fight for labor bills and during that period of time and since that time on account of my interest in the subject I have kept a record of the activities of paid emissaries of the organizations whose object it is to foment strikes in industry and to fight the efforts of labor organizations to better their conditions. . . .

My files show that you are a sort of a detective, worming your way into the homes of the most trusted members of labor organizations and obtaining information with which to combat the efforts of labor organizations to better their conditions, and that you obtain this information for the purpose of assisting "strike breakers."

The data I have show that you foment strikes in the districts where there is no union and then settle the strike for a price.

The information I have with reference to you is that you are the man who does the slimy, stool pigeon work necessary for the purpose of destroying organized labor wherever it has contractual relations with employers.

Another document showing evidence of the same type of activity on the part of Jung is an affidavit by William Tracy, Secretary-

Treasurer of the United Brick and Clay Workers of America. The following are excerpts from Tracy's affidavit:

> This man, Jung, first showed up in our organization quite a number of years ago in the state of Iowa, where we had a number of strikes on hand, and where he circulated petitions throughout non-union plants in which he attempted to show that our organization was not financially able to take care of the number of strikes at hand, etc.
>
> In other words he was the tool of the employers. He appeared in a number of other places shortly thereafter, but we really got the low-down on this gentleman at a strike at Nelsonville, Ohio, which was conducted by the Vice President Thos. Hutson of our organization. We had a member by the name of F. A. Bonn, who was not only secretary at the Nelsonville, Ohio, Local, but Secretary of the Ohio District Council, a newly formed district, and we were informed by a friendly plant superintendent that he was a reporter for the Jung Organization, and that he was not only giving the minutes of the Nelsonville Local Union, but the minutes of the district council meetings to the Jung Organization in Chicago in return for a salary of $300 per month.
>
> We secured some of these reports which were classed as "Field Reports," from Mr. Bonn, and we likewise secured instructions from Jung's organization in Chicago to Mr. Bonn in which he was ordered to create dissension among our members and if necessary to get them out on strike.
>
> He appeared on the scene of our organization a few years ago during the terra cotta strike at Chicago Heights and it is a matter of record that he came into the County Police Department late on a Saturday afternoon when no one had a chance to appear in Court, or even to find an official and influenced them to the end that they sent a large number of County Police out on the job at Chicago Heights, which was done and had its effect, but to prove that there was no need for such action the police were removed as soon as we were able to get in touch with Sheriff Graydon on Monday morning.
>
> He appeared in Brazil, Indiana, during one of our strikes, and is ever on the job not only to break strikes but to create them.

[Signed] WILLIAM TRACY, Secretary-Treasurer,
UNITED BRICK AND CLAY WORKERS OF AMERICA.

Signed and sworn to before me this 25th day of May 1935.
[Signed] JAMES M. RILEY,
Notary Public.

The late Edward N. Nockels, secretary of the Chicago Federation of Labor, expressed similar ideas in a letter he wrote Jung in October, 1934:

> Be advised that you and your . . . so-called AVIF we consider as nothing more or less than a racketeering, strike-breaking, detective

agency outfit, using the alibi that you are fighting communistic propaganda and appealing to "open shoppers" and labor-baiting employers for financial assistance, when, as a matter of fact, these communists are your own hired hirelings, used in the dissemination of propaganda to destroy organized labor, in order to bring business to you for the carrying on of your nefarious racket in strike breaking.

Jung's strike-fomenting is worthy of special attention. However unethical labor-spying and strike-breaking may appear to a labor sympathizer, this business implies at least an honest relationship between the manufacturer and the detective agency he hires. Not so with Jung. The National Clay Products Industries Association seems to have double-crossed its own clients. Though paid to keep labor peace, the Association continually stirred up trouble. Jung's technique of strike-fomenting proceeded somewhat in this fashion:[5] In a non-union plant Jung's representative would discuss the idea of union organization and a strike. He would even suggest that the Brick and Clay Workers' union be requested to send down an organizer or, if a new local had already been formed, he would agitate for an immediate strike.[6] Bonn, Jung's hireling mentioned in Tracy's affidavit, was, for example, instructed to get the Nelsonville local out on strike. Such strikes lacked the approval of the central headquarters of the union; the national officials believed that the local could go further by holding the threat of a strike over the heads of the owners than by actually striking and that it was wiser not to call a strike until the local was stronger and its chances of winning better. Consequently, both employers and responsible trade union officials suffered as a result of Jung-fomented strikes. Jung alone profited by these strikes.

Strike-fomenting tapped two sources of income for Jung: payment for settling strikes and the sale of confidential information on union activities. The more strikes Jung secretly fomented, the more the industrialists felt dependent upon the labor espionage service that the National Clay Products Industries Association could furnish. It was as if a fire insurance company anxious to induce more farmers to take out policies were to hire a "firebug" to set fire to barns.

The nature of the reports sent out by Jung was such as to keep industrialists in a continual state of insecurity. The menace of violence was emphasized frequently. In Jung's letter to the North River Brick Company, for example, the spy's report said, "Lowrie did not speak tonight of using violence," a sentence creating the impression that Lowrie had done so at other meetings or that it was usual for labor organizers to advocate violence. Trade unionist Tracy tells of a report that falsely quoted him as suggesting dynamiting a plant if certain employers did not come to terms promptly.

For a time Jung apparently had the confidence and fees of many employers in the clay products industry. After his union achieved recognition, Tracy became friendly with manufacturers in the industry and asked them about their relationships with Jung. Time and again they registered embarrassment in confessing that they paid him considerable fees.

The foregoing offers an idea of Jung's chief activities. However, these were by no means his only activities. Early in the 1920's he began to collect files on persons and organizations he considered "Red", the files that were to form the basis for the American Vigilant Intelligence Federation. Jung's literature asserts that the Federation was established in 1919. His files were quite possibly started that early, though the Federation as a corporate body was not organized until considerably later. At any rate when Norman Hapgood's *Professional Patriots* appeared in 1927, Jung received but brief notice. Hapgood said:

> The association (the National Clay Products Industries Association), according to Commissioner Jung, is a sort of clearing house of patriotic information on radical movements. Besides receiving all the literature of various professional patriotic societies, the association also has its own source of information "for which," says Mr. Jung, "we pay good money." [7]

And further on:

> This gentleman (Jung) issued a statement in 1926 to the effect that Lenin was once in America and that while he was here he associated with such "anarchists, murderers, disloyalists, and dynamiters as Emma Goldman, Robert Minor, Eugene V. Debs, etc." [8]

A sample of Jung's early anti-revolutionary work is the following letter, written May 5, 1926, on the stationery of the National Clay Products Industries Association:

Mr. John V. Farwell
229 Lake Shore Dr.
Chicago, Ill.

Dear Mr. Farwell:

> If you haven't time to read the attached report, turn it over to your women folks, and if they are members of any clubs, let them get started spreading the gospel to their friends about the activities of Miss Jane Addams and others of her ilk, who are doing their level best, some wittingly, and others as mere pawns, to break down the morale of our citizens and eventually emasculate our national defense. . . .

Very truly yours,

H. A. JUNG

The letter was apparently directed against Miss Addams' activities in the Women's International League for Peace and Freedom and her other efforts. In December, 1927, this aspect of Jung's work had advanced far enough to justify incorporating the American Vigilant Intelligence Federation under the laws of Illinois. By 1930, Jung had achieved something of a reputation as an authority on "subversive" persons and organizations. In May of that year the *National Republic*, a magazine of distinctly red-baiting tendencies, spoke of him as "Harry A. Jung, of Chicago, one of the most active combatants against revolutionary radicalism in this country."[9] A few months later, Jung appeared before the Fish Congressional committee investigating Communism and boasted that he was "considered an authority on the subject". In the autumn of 1930 he obtained widespread publicity from the publication of his blacklist of dangerous "radicals."

Sometime after November, 1931, Jung abandoned the National Clay Products Industries Association and began to devote his efforts completely to the Federation.

At present, Jung carries on his work under the aura of secrecy that might be expected of an ex-labor spy. His organization is not listed on the directory in the lobby of the building where his headquarters are located and the sign on his door is simply the mysterious A.V.I.F. His collection of data on "subversive" characters has become so voluminous that one whole side of his office is covered with neat steel files full of it. On the opposite wall are shelves and shelves of related as well as unrelated books.

PROPAGANDA

The channels of propaganda used by the Federation are a weekly leaflet, a monthly leaflet, special memoranda, confidential reports, pamphlets and books, public meetings, and the activity of a field representative.

The four-page monthly leaflet, the *Vigilante*, first appeared in May, 1932. Its purpose seems to be to present "radical" trends in such a menacing light that its readers will be kept in a constant state of *delirium tremens*. The weekly leaflet is entitled, *Items of Interest on the Patriotic Front*. When it first appeared in late 1930 or early 1931, it consisted of only a few mimeographed sheets and contained much the same material to be found in the *Vigilante*. A typical issue of this period "exposed" a questionnaire on war and peace, American engineers working in Russia, tours sponsored by college professors, pacifist pastors, etc. Later it began to appear in printed form and its scope became more specialized. It confined itself to two matters—"Notes on the Radicals", a section offering news about the latest activities of such organizations as the League for Industrial Democracy and the Young Communist League, and "Personals", a section of brief thumbnail biographies of liberal pastors, professors, labor leaders, and, now and then, a real revolutionary. If a subscriber were to keep a scrapbook of all these "personals", as suggested by Jung, he would gradually build up the equivalent of Mrs. Elizabeth Dilling's *Red Network*. A typical item charges Harold D. Lasswell, University of Chicago professor, with being an "internationalist who calls himself a Socialist, but acts and speaks like a Communist," alleges that he has been guilty of "a scurrilous attack upon Nationalism and the American Flag," and announces that he is associated with the American Civil Liberties Union, the executive committee of the Chicago Chapter of the League for Industrial Democracy, the Chicago Workers Theatre, and the Chicago Workers School.

The combined circulation of the monthly and weekly leaflets has never been very great; the paid circulation of both publications probably never exceeded five or six thousand. The subscribers have resided primarily in Illinois, Indiana, Michigan, and Wisconsin. Issuance of both sheets was discontinued in November, 1936.

Occasionally the Federation has sent out special mimeographed bulletins on organizations or individuals considered particularly dangerous. On January 15, 1932, there appeared a special bulletin "exposing" a pacifist group calling themselves Peace Patriots. Somewhat earlier appeared a memorandum on Dr. Karl Borders, which concluded: "Dr. Borders is an adept and faithful propagandist for Soviet Russia and the BOLSHEVIKI murder regime in power in that unhappy land and apparently serves his masters well."

The circulation of the Federation's confidential reports has been restricted exclusively to those businessmen who can afford to pay $100 a year to obtain them.[10] The earliest definite record of the appearance of one of these confidential reports is June 4, 1930. The reports have appeared at frequent intervals, sometimes daily. Between June 4, 1930 and December 20, 1931, some 159 appeared. The material usually contains the reports of Jung's spies in Pennsylvania, Illinois, and Wisconsin. A typical report describes the activities of Communist groups in Milwaukee and surrounding environs. Another report is on the Chicago meeting of the Communist Party; the report covers six single-spaced typewritten pages. Another report contains a list of the factories to be represented by "revolutionary" employees at a Metal Workers' Industrial League Conference held in Youngstown, Ohio.

Another medium through which the Federation spreads its ideas is that of books and pamphlets. A partial list follows:

The Immigration Crew on the New Deal Railroad
Pastors, Politicians, and Pacifists
The Red Network
Bartering our Birthright
Fish Committee Communist Investigation Report
Left Wing Peace Organizations
Christianity, a Practical Business Philosophy
Are We Aliens in Our Own Country?
Have Americans Become a Nation of Spineless People?
The Alien Menace to America

The Federation keeps up to date in the literature it distributes. For instance, in early 1937 its literature reflected its fight against the Committee for Industrial Organization and President Roosevelt's plan for reorganizing the United States Supreme Court. Such pamphlets include:

Carter Glass' *Constitutional Immorality,* a reprint of his radio attack against the President's plan
Josiah W. Bailey's *The Living Soul of Democracy,* a reprint of a radio address of the same nature as that of Carter Glass
Join the C. I. O. and Help Build a Soviet America, an effort to connect the C. I. O. with Moscow
Americans, Avoid the Chains of Vicious Dictatorships, a reprint from the *National Republic*

Other literature distributed by the Federation are:

The Man Behind the Men Behind the President
The Protocols of the Elders of Zion
Halt! Gentile, and Salute the Jew
Questions and Answers

The publications in the third group are anti-semitic. *Halt! Gentile, and Salute the Jew* originally appeared in England. Jung brought out the first American edition of this pamphlet. *Questions and Answers,* an eight-page mimeographed sheet of nineteen questions and answers dealing with the Jews, is a brain-child of Jung; he distributed between 1,500 and 2,000 copies in 1934. Data on the number of pamphlets the Federation has distributed is too fragmentary to be of much value. Although 50,000 copies of *The Man Behind the Men Behind the President* were known to be distributed jointly by Jung and Colonel E. N. Sanctuary, the authors, this number is too large to be a typical figure for Jung's pamphlet distribution.

The printed word is by no means the only channel of propaganda used by the Federation. The group spreads its ideas through public meetings as well. This channel was used a good deal during the 1936 Presidential election campaign, when the Federation worked hard to demonstrate a link between Moscow and the New Deal. Most of the meetings of this period were held at the Real Estate Building in Chicago. Admission for non-members was upon the recommendation of a member-sponsor and the payment of twenty-five cents. Attendance was reported as having been at times as high as two and three hundred. The speakers at these gatherings included Dr. Hugh S. Magill, president of the American Federation of Investors; Dr. James Oliver Buswell, president of Wheaton College; Major John L. Griffith, "Big Ten" Athletic Commissioner; and Jung.

Jung has long been active in speaking before groups of all kinds. He is particularly well received before small town Chambers of Commerce and business clubs in Illinois and in Michigan. On February 18, 1934, he addressed Chicago's Highland Park post of the American Legion in a meeting held in a public school. Apparently this was not the only time Jung spread his ideas through the medium of the American Legion, for Edward N. Nockels wrote in 1935, referring to Jung, "We find he has sold his ideas to the American Legion who take him to be a super-patriot." In at least one instance Jung addressed an anti-New Deal organization during the 1936 election. On October 14, 1935, he spoke before the Constitutional Protective League in Lansing, Michigan.

FUNDS

The Federation's sources of income may be classed as follows: miscellaneous minor sources, the sale of confidential information, fees for labor espionage, and gifts from the wealthy. The minor sources consist of the sale of books and pamphlets, subscriptions to the *Vigilante* and to *Items of Interest*, admission fees to meetings, and the five dollars annual dues of the regular members. Dues paid by the members of the "Board of Underwriters", i.e., wealthy Federation members who supposedly undertake to support the organization by regular contributions every three months, would not ordinarily fall into the category of minor sources; however, these dues have apparently been paid sporadically rather than regularly. The second source, the sale of confidential reports on revolutionary activities, was highly important until 1933, when the Federation became a membership organization. These reports have been distributed to an exclusive list of subscribers for a fee of $100 per year. Gifts constitute the most important source of income. The sums Jung received from this source during the years 1931-1934, inclusive, follow:[11]

AMERICAN VIGILANT INTELLIGENCE FEDERATION

Table 5

Date		Donor	Amount
1931			
July	18	Rockford Bank & Trust Co.	$500
	18	Central Trust Co.	100
August	6	Rockford National Bank.	500
	13	First National Bank, Joliet.	500
	13	Baldwin National Bank.	100
	13	Commercial Merchants National Bank of Peoria.	100
	19	American National Bank of Peoria.	100
	28	First National Bank of Joliet.	500
	29	Rockford National Bank.	500
September	2	Peoria National Bank.	136
October	24	Continental National Bank.	200
	24	Rockford National Bank.	100
1932			
January	4	Rockford National Bank.	175
	16	" " "	175
February	3	" " "	175
	19	Mrs. Finley J. Sheppard.	1,000
	19	H. B. Joy.	1,000
May	5	Mrs. Finley J. Sheppard.	1,000
June	20	" " "	1,000
July	8	Sears, Roebuck Co.	250
	22	William Wrigley.	500
September	29	First National Bank.	500
	19	Donnelly & Sons.	100
October	11	International Harvester.	1,000
December	2	William Wrigley, Jr.	50
	10	First National Bank.	250
	20	John H. Harding.	200
	28	Mrs. Finley J. Sheppard.	250
1933			
February	10	Mrs. Finley J. Sheppard.	800
	24	Harris Trust & Savings Co.	50
March	22	William Wrigley.	250
June	6	First National Bank.	100
	9	Sears, Roebuck Co.	100
	10	A. B. Dick.	100
July	5	Corn Products Refining Co.	100
	12	Sterling Morton.	50
	31	Stewart Warner.	100
August	22	International Harvester Co.	250
	23	General American Tank Car Co.	100
	25	Northern Trust Co.	100
	29	Bendix.	105
September	20	Mrs. Finley J. Sheppard.	200

Date	Donor	Amount
1934		
February 14	Mrs. Finley J. Sheppard............................	$1,000
June 5	Edison General Electric Appliance Cp................	50
8	Corn Products Refining Co..........................	100
12	Mrs. Finley J. Sheppard............................	25
13	Stewart Warner Co.................................	100
16	A. B. Dick..	100
July 11	Florsheim Shoe Co.................................	50
26	Victor Manufacturing & Gasket Co..................	25
August 10	Phoell Manufacturing Co...........................	50
15	Northern Trust Co.................................	100
Total...		$15,511

What motives induced these firms and individuals to contribute so liberally to Jung's organization? The opinions of Lieutenant Mike Mills, head of the "Red Squad" of the Chicago Police Department, expressed in the course of a Congressional hearing about radicalism in Chicago, are somewhat illuminating in this connection.

> Congressman Weideman: There are certain men who promote organizations that are constantly fighting the "reds." Is this not so?
> Lieutenant Mills: Yes, sir.
> Weideman: And the more newspaper publicity we have on all this communistic proposition, do you think, or will you give your idea as to whether or not it makes it easier for them to do a lot of "faking" and collect some money in fighting an imaginary foe?
> Mills: The societies and associations that are always howling about communism or any other "ism" are doing it for their own benefit.
> Weideman: For their personal gain, would you say?
> Mills: To make a little money.
> Weideman: In other words, there are some men who are executive directors of some organizations that keep themselves in a job by keeping the public mind aroused on the subject?
> Mills: They can go up to some of the wealthy members of the society and say "We are trying to fight communism and we would like to have a little donation"—and they are getting them.

An examination of Table 5 will indicate the nature of the large contributors. Of the $15,511 collected, Mrs. Finley J. Sheppard (the former Helen Gould), banks, and businessmen each donated approximately one-third—about $5,000. Lieutenant Mills' testimony probably explains Mrs. Sheppard's interest. The businessmen's contributions were undoubtedly motivated by an additional factor—the service of small-scale labor espionage. In the midst of the depression when manifestations of popular discontent made the wealthy feel insecure, Jung's suave solicitor would visit an industrialist and increase his insecurity by exaggerated accounts of insidious Communist power—perhaps with particular reference to the situation in his own plant. The Federation offers to be of service by sending several "representatives" to his factory to ferret out any Communists. The industrialist becomes panicky. He reaches for his checkbook. Along with his check he gives Jung's solicitor a list of his employees. A week later the list comes back with four or five names checked and perhaps the notation, "These men are Communists and should be fired."

Seven Jewish enterprises have contributed to the Federation's coffers. Obviously, Jung's solicitor did not mention that their contributions would be used to spread anti-semitic propaganda. The McCormack Committee's report was quite accurate when it concluded, "the contributors had no knowledge of the purposes for which the money was used."

Why the banks paid a total of $5,000 is more difficult to explain. Perhaps a clue is to be found in the following type of article appearing in the *Chicago Tribune*, July 28, 1932. It was headed:

RAID BARES RED PLOTTING OF RUNS TO RUIN BANKS

The sources of propaganda causing runs on many Chicago banks was believed to have been exposed yesterday with the seizure of literature in a hotel room at Pontiac, Michigan, detailing the operations of a communist plot to wreck the financial structure of the American nation. . . .

When apprised of the seizure of the letters, Melvin A. Traylor, president of the First National Bank, said that there was no doubt that runs on Chicago banks were caused by false rumors spread by telephone and anonymous letters. . . .

According to the American Vigilant Intelligence Federation, which has records of communists and their activities, "Comrade H. G." is Harry Gannes . . . Gannes, officials of the Federation said, was in Chicago in the spring of 1931 when bank runs first became serious. (*Chicago Tribune*, July 28, 1932.)

In July of the same year Melvin Traylor believed the revolutionists were causing runs on banks; in September and December his bank paid the Federation $750, and the following June it contributed $100 more. What specific service the Federation performed can only be conjectured. Probably, it furnished confidential bulletins on the operations of the "Reds", giving the bank's officers the pleasant feeling of possessing "inside" information. As for the contributions by the Rockford and Joliet banks, Jung's secretary [12] explains that they were payment for "Americanization campaigns". Possibly the need for such campaigns was felt in Rockford because it is close enough to the Wisconsin border to have been influenced by the Wisconsin progressive movement; and in Joliet because that city is an industrial town with a large foreign population which may have been restive during the depression. These circumstances may have made local bankers uneasy.

The success of the Federation in eliciting funds from businessmen and bankers is attributable to C. Ralph Burton—an extremely able gentleman. Jung seems to have valued Burton's services greatly; the latter has received forty percent of everything he has collected.[18]

Two other small items confirm the fact that Jung has obtained most of his income from wealthy persons. One is a report of the Chicago Better Business Bureau; in discussing the Federation, the report stated: "The Bureau is advised that this organization has the support of some very prominent men in Chicago. . . ." The other is a letter written by Jung in which he boasted, "Its (the Federation's) influence to large taxpayers and prominent citizens is not sneered at." Since August, 1934, no definite records of large contributions to the Federation have been known. The revelations of the McCormack Committee may have resulted in the drying up of some of these sources of funds or may have compelled Jung to shroud in secrecy his further solicitations.

CASE STUDY

A clear conception of the Federation as a functioning whole may be best obtained by an examination, or "case study," of the correspondence between Jung and Peter Armstrong, his field representative. The letters quoted herein indicate Armstrong's illiteracy, his propaganda technique, Jung's preoccupation with money matters, and the type of persons interested in the Federation. Most of the letters were written between January and April, 1934; at that time, the Federation's field headquarters were at Grand Rapids, Michigan. In his letters Armstrong identified himself as "No. 31" and Jung as either "No. 1," or "A. G." He penned his first letter from Grand Rapids on January 14, 1934. It read:

Dear No. 1,

Yours of Twelfth instant received and Mr. Shera delivered your package to me last Saturday.

Mr. Thompson and Mr. Tolliefiero were out of town so I'll try to get in touch with both on Monday. Saturday a.m. I had one hour and 20 mi. talk with editor of G. R. *Herald* Mr. Frank Sparks. He read my credentials and after conversing a while we agreed upon that something should be done and done in a hurry. I left with that chap our three documents—memo on Foster, AVIF programme, blue C.P.U.S.A. chart. Facing the Facts, and Vigilant. I think it will be a good idea if you send him a few lines mentioning how glad you are e.t.c.

Same evening I received invitation to attend dinner at Dr. Ferris N. Smith (639 Plymouth blvd. Grand Rapids, Mich.) He is a very prominent, rich and internationally known Plastick Surgery specialist. In my honor we had two bottles of champaign and other things beside. . . . So last night she (Mrs. Smith) pledged herself to AVIF and will sign card on my return back to Grand Rapids.

About a month later No. 31 had made a truly promising contact and wrote:

Dear A. G.

Send Set of "Vigilante" to Mrs. Eastman J. Sheehan, 211 E. 62d St., New York City, N. Y. She is a Catolic and so is She Lousy with money, may become members.

On February 15, No. 1 wrote:

Dear No. 31

Enclosed find herewith . . . a letter of introduction from Art Young to Senator F. C. Walcott. . . .[14]

Did you collect any money from Fred C. Oldham, No. 631, or from Margaret A. Norris, No. 1103, or Clark Drury, No. 1115?

On February 23, No. 1 again wrote:

We now have fifteen members at Grand Rapids. All of them have received their instructions and some literature.

You have done some splendid work in making contacts, but we have got to be getting some financial aid from some of these contacts, or we will be getting nowhere.

And again on March 6th:

Understand from your telephone conversation with Miss Rose that you are to meet the ex-governor.[15]

Then came a long report from No. 31:

3/19/34 Grand Rapids

Tomorrow noon I am to talk before the Army & Navy Club about 75 invitat send out. At 4:30 Rev. Brown will come and take me for another meeting where I have to talk also.

Peninsular Club Sunday Forum has put me on program on second Sunday in April month. Khiwany's and Rotary are approaching Mr. W. about me talking there. Mr. Buist (The Bookman) yesterday was selling here Protocols at 50¢ a piece (same as our edition). It was sold out in no time. Is he a member? A. G. that new book by Col. Sanctuary made a present to Dr. Ferris Smith. Oh, boy, Is he hot on protocols? He bought from Buist two copies one for himself personally and other he expect to put into circulation amougst his friends. He is 100%....

*   *   *

Next Thursday I have to talk befor group of Mrs. Rowe. Saw Mr. Stickney he want me to meet some of his friends. Mrs. Stickney asking me to come in May to Traverse City and start our chapter over there. . . .

Sometime between March 19 and 27, No. 31 reported:

. . . Tonite I have to go to Hudsonvill and speak before group of dutch farmers in that vicinity. Capt. Crowhaw made arrangements about my appearance on 2 more meetings in April.

Cherio. Yours as usual

P.S. Sending G. R. Herald commentary on my speech at Army & Navy Club.

On March 27, No. 1 replied:

Dear No. 31,

I'll endeavor to write to our Grand Rapids friends as rapidly as I can get around to it.

It was good to have the account of your talk in the Grand Rapids Herald. I congratulate you on the good work you are doing. . . .

On April 9, 1934, No. 31 listed his speaking engagements for the week:

Dear No. 1,

. . . sometime next week to Toledo, Ohio to talk before High school audience in school auditorium. Will stop Ann Arbor to talk on campus, on 15th will go to Middleville to talk before congregation of 300 at morning service. Tomorrow have to talk befor group where Jew-lawyer Shoulsky will be present.

The following day No. 1 wrote:

Dear No. 31,

. . . Of course we will accept Dr. Brown's membership as a remittance. . . .

Sometime between April 9 and 13, No. 31 queried:

. . . P.S. How's about late relises?

Dr. S. has one. Am I entitled to my copy or not. Send me also Mrs. Dilling Book. Please. Send you money shortly.

No. 31

A Federation member evidently should never, never lower himself to arguing with a Jew.

Dear No. 31,

I sent two copies of "The Red Network" via parcel post, addressed to No. 28. It should reach you Monday. . . .

I cannot understand why you should have permitted yourself to get into an argument with Harry Shouldsky, and I am certainly disgusted to think that No. 483 would lend herself and her home to a debate between yourself and a J. . . .

If I had been down there I would certainly have vetoed the idea unless there are some circumstances that I know nothing about which might have altered my considered judgment in having you demean yourself to have any truck with any representative of the Tribe. They are tricky and will probably misquote you. You know how they intrigue and say things that are definitely derogatory. I am distressed that No. 483 did not have the courage to turn down the request for the use of her home for the debate between S. and yourself.

. . . be a gentleman as you always have been and hold your ground and you will win out.

On "April 14th-16th", No. 31 dutifully reported:

Dear No. 1,

This Sunday I was speaker at church meetings at Middleville . . . Church was packed to limit. My talk began at 10:30 a.m. and ended at 1:30 p.m. Good crowd and good talk. . . . Coming Wednesday starting for Toledo, O. to talk before High school students group in a luncheon and talk in Ann Arbor befor group of Students. . . .

P.S. G. R. general meeting will be held coming Tuesday at Pantling Hotel. Expecting around 50 or 60 peoples:

On April 21 Mrs. J. Eastman Sheehan, the Catholic lady that is "lousy with money" reappears in the correspondence. She is to be duly scared by the "Communist" conspiracy, though kept in the dark about the Federation's plot against part of her fortune.

Dear No. 31,

. . . In the meantime tell No. 28 that we have sent "The Red Network" to Mrs. J. Eastman Sheehan, Mr. John A. Parks and Mr. William Hatton, and will follow this with a brief note. We also sent two copies of the book to No. 28.

A day later No. 31 replied:

Dear No. 1,

On our way to Detroit we had a chance to stop and see Mrs. Smith friends at Ann Arbor. You may expect at least one order on Red Network from there. Big prospects for cracing open of all University for A.V.I.F.

Now speaking of Moamee, Ohio, I had three meetings there. . . . I talked before assembly of high school students (around 200-250). Same day at 3 pm I had Womens group of Moamee one hour and half and at 8 pm till 10 pm we had a forum for men and women in Presbeterian Church.

In only one period—April, 1933 to late 1934—was the American Vigilant Intelligence Federation a membership organization.[16] Prior to April, 1933, it was merely a business that sold confidential information on "radicalism." Since late 1934 it has resembled the groups headed by Winrod and Edmondson in that its membership has consisted solely of its mailing list. Nevertheless, this change is not as significant as it may seem. The kind of person connected with the Federation has remained about the same throughout. Businessmen who had taken the confidential information service were among the first persons Jung approached when he organized his membership group. His present mailing list, incidentally, includes the names of people associated with him in his earlier enterprises.

The McCormack Committee has revealed that the Federation has had between 600 and 700 members.[17] However, Jung has been the only really active member. As both Jung's secretary and a volunteer worker at his office testified at the committee hearing, Jung virtually *is* the Federation.[18]

At the time of the McCormack investigation, the Federation had no regularly elected officers such as a president or vice-president, as most organizations have, nor did it have any by-laws. Nevertheless, for a period an élite group of enthusiastic members did constitute what was called the "Inner Circle." Its functions probably pertained to policy formation. During the summer of 1934, the "Inner Circle" met sometimes as often as once a week. Usually less than a dozen attended the meetings, but once, in July, 1934, a dinner meeting attracted thirty-seven persons.

What may be said concerning the persons associated with the Federation? An examination of the correspondence previously presented shows that the persons mentioned as members or prospective members had what are popularly called "good English names." The names, literally transcribed, are:

Dr. Brown	Fred C. Oldham	Mr. Shera
Capt. Croshaw	John A. Parks	Dr. Ferris N. Smith
Clark Drury	Gerry D. Pettibone	Mr. Stickney
William Hatton	Mrs. Rowe	Mr. Thompson
Margaret A. Norris	Mrs. J. Eastman Sheehan	

Not a single name ends in "ak," "witz," or "ski." While a few of the names may not be those of "true Anglo-Saxon aristocrats," the list suggests that most members may come from very old native stock or may be descendants of early American immigrants. The list of persons reported attending "Inner Circle" meetings leads to the same conclusion:

Cantwell	Nichols	Clemens
Gail Carter	Saunders	Studebaker III
Lawrence Harper	Sims	Webber

Middle-class people have been most interested in the Federation. Substantiating this generalization is the fact that field representative Peter Armstrong addressed such groups as Kiwanis, Rotary, and Army and Navy clubs—undoubtedly using these clubs as recruiting grounds —and that in his correspondence with Jung he specifically mentioned as membership prospects such persons as the wife of an "internationally known" surgeon and a woman "lousy with money." Although upper-class people—industrialists and bankers—have contributed heavily to the Federation coffers, apparently none has ever attended a Federation meeting. The explanation might be that their contributions were made solely in gratitude for a specific service, e.g., ridding a plant of "Communists."

Under the heading of membership must also be considered the "hanger-on," a person who joins an anti-semitic organization either to make what money he can from it or to learn the business with the view of establishing an organization of his own. Chief "hanger-on" of the Federation was Peter Armstrong ("No. 31"), its field representative. A White Guard Russian, Armstrong was born Peter Afansieff in Petrograd in 1893 and came to this country in 1922 under that name. On the Pacific coast he assumed the alias of Prince Kushubue, but after a while changed it to Armstrong. Shortly thereafter, he got himself into trouble. On November 12, 1929, he was arrested in Chicago on two charges, viz., tampering with an automobile and forging a United States Treasury check. On December 19, 1929, he pleaded guilty to the latter charge and, four days later, Federal Judge F. J. Kerrigan sentenced him to eighteen months in the penitentiary, where he served his term under the name of Afansieff. He was next heard of late in 1933, working in Jung's office together with three other White Guard Russians on a new translation of the *Protocols of the Elders of Zion*. He soon became affiliated with the German-American Bund and the Nazi party in both New York and Chicago. Later he established himself as head of the Right Cause Publishing Co., printers of the anti-semitic *American Gentile*. In February, 1935, when Jung accused him of withholding funds, they parted company.

ORGANIZED ANTI-SEMITISM IN AMERICA

Another White Guard Russian who frequented Jung's office, though never so closely connected with it as Armstrong, was Captain Victor DeKayville (born Livok), a former officer in the Czarist army. He had entered the United States illegally by deserting the ship on which he was a seaman. He was associated with Jung's colleague, Armstrong, in the publication of the *American Gentile*.

Most interesting of all the "hangers-on" is Alfredo Caputo, an Italian with a cosmopolitan background, who was associated with Jung for some months in 1931 and who gave him much "valuable" information concerning the trend of subversive movements throughout the world. After Caputo returned to Europe, the Berlin police asked the Chicago police for information on him and received the following reply:

Der Polizei-Prasident
Landeskriminalpolizeiamt,
Berlin, Germany

Dear Sir:

Alfredo Caputo got very friendly with Mr. Jung and furnished him with all sorts of "fake" or incorrect information.

Jung paid Caputo's expenses while he was in Chicago and when Caputo was ordered deported he made him European representative of the American Vigilant Intelligence Federation.

I am attaching hereto a memorandum on Caputo, which gives a short outline of his activities while here.

The memorandum read:

Alfredo Caputo (alias Aldo Corpe-Aldo Stolle-Aldo Stolli- Stelle Schwertz). Born in Constantinople on Aug. 14th, 1885, of Italian parentage, therefore he is an Italian citizen.

He came to the United States on or about September 20, 1930, and on his arrival in Chicago made the acquaintance of one Harry Jung, head of the American Vigilant Intelligence Federation. . . .

Caputo told Mr. Jung that he was a member of the Italian Secret Service.

Caputo was wanted by the Geneva police for a theft of jewelry. During the Italian-Turkish war in 1911 he was in Turkey and was suspected of being a Turkish spy. During the Balkan war he resided at Dedeogatch, where he was disposing of stolen goods. In Bulgaria he was a spy for Greece, for which the Bulgarian authorities sentenced him to death. . . . In August of 1916 he was arrested by the English police and kept at Malta until the end of the war. He was expelled from Portugal in 1926.

I am informed by a report from Louisville, Ky., that Caputo made the acquaintance of one L—— R—— of Lydon, Ky. . . . he further offered to said gentleman a contract for the building of European buildings at said Fair [Chicago World's Fair] taking from him $275.65 as registration fee, which was paid to him . . .

furthermore Caputo requested R—— to loan him $4500 stating that he had to go to China to sign a contract for arms and ammunition and airplanes with Chang Kai Shek, the Chinese Dictator, who he claimed was his personal friend, and claiming the possibility of making a profit of $300,000. He offered part of the profits to Mr. R——. . . .

Caputo was arrested by the U. S. Immigration authorities and ordered deported to Italy. However, upon his arrival in New York, his fare was paid to Germany by Harry Jung on the steamer "Berlin." He left on Sept. 24th, 1931 in accordance with United States Department of Labor Order No. 55761-659.

An interesting commentary on Jung's gullibility is the manner in which he described Caputo in a Federation memorandum marked "Strictly Confidential". It read:

Back in the days prior to 1914, a beautiful and spacious hotel in Moscow was owned and operated by a wealthy Italian family. It was famed throughout the world for its cuisine and hospitality. Then came the dark days of the World War, followed by the two revolutions in Russia. This magnificent hotel property and estates of its owners were confiscated and nationalized. The family was divided and disappeared in the way incident to all victims of the Bolshevik terror.

One member of this family survived. . . . The rest of the family was never heard from. They were either killed or exiled to the convict camps or prisons of Siberia. . . .

. . . this sole survivor of the once prosperous family dedicated his life to combatting the menace of Bolshevism.

Jung went on to report how Caputo, the "sole survivor", came to the United States, tried to make certain officials of the United States government realize the hideous menace of Communism to this country but was ignored and even insulted. Finally:

Learning of the existence of the American Vigilant Intelligence Federation in Chicago, Mr. Aldo [Caputo] decided to come here to seek the aid and support of the officials of the A.V.I.F. . . . he immediately went into secret session with A.V.I.F. executives which continued for a period of nine days. During these extended sessions, Mr. Aldo unfolded an amazing series of Bolshevik activities in the United States under the direction of trusted Moscow agents in this country. . . .

There followed four pages detailing these activities and finally this conclusion:

Thus we find the Bolshevik program for the destruction of the United States to be all embracing and lacking in no single detail. In the face of all this, our Departments of Government . . . sit idly by wooing this menace instead of taking action against it. . . . This fatuous and willful disregard of the world's greatest menace will cost the United States dearly in the not far distant future unless the American people become aroused and demand that the Executives of Government take steps to kill the rapidly growing cancer of communism.

The fact that Jung paid both Caputo's expenses in Chicago and fare to Germany perhaps indicates that Jung really believes what he writes. This consideration may be incompatible with characterizing Jung as a smooth gentleman who, tongue-in-cheek, sent out wild tales to gullible businessmen. Jung believed a crafty international crook and was just as much deceived as the simple-minded gentleman from Lydon, Kentucky.

The "hangers-on" of the Federation have not all been real or alleged Russian emigres. Gale S. Carter ("No. 37"), a former head of the Illinois Ku Klux Klan, shared Jung's office for some time. Second to Jung, he appears to have been the most active man in the Federation. In 1934, Carl Strover and George Schaeffer, Chicago members of the Federation, tried to launch an organization with the ostensible objective of keeping Jews out of the legal profession. Few lawyers, however, were willing to pay dues and the plans dissolved.

Lieutenant Nelson E. Hewitt, a Naval Reserve officer and one of the original incorporators of the Federation, worked with Jung until April, 1934, when he and Jung quarreled and parted. Thereupon, Hewitt formed an organization of his own, the Advisory Associates. It published a leaflet called the *Advisor*, which was patterned closely after Jung's *Vigilante* and *Items of Interest on the Patriotic Front*. Never large, the organization is now inactive.

CHAPTER IX

The Industrial Defense Association

THE Industrial Defense Association was organized in 1924 and incorporated in 1926. Its stated aim is "to inculcate the principles of Americanism to industrial, religious, fraternal, and educational circles." The organization is small in importance when compared with such groups as the Defenders of the Christian Faith, the German-American Bund, or the Silver Shirts. Like the majority of anti-semitic organizations, it is a one-man affair; the entire work of the association is performed by its secretary. In many aspects it resembles Harry Jung's American Vigilant Intelligence Federation. Both organizations existed long before the depression, both wield influence in narrowly restricted geographical areas, and both have leaders with similar backgrounds.

LEADERSHIP

Edward L. Hunter, the head of the Industrial Defense Association, was born in 1875. The fact that two of his marriages were performed in New Hampshire and that his first employment was obtained there indicates that much of his early life was spent in that state. When he was married in 1908, he gave his occupation as "traveling man." About five or ten years afterward, he entered the line of endeavor that he was to follow for the rest of his life—that of unmasking and denouncing people as criminals or as revolutionaries.

He began his detective career in a humble way. At first, he worked in a Boston department store catching shoplifters and later on for the Amoskeag Manufacturing Company in New Hampshire, securing evidence for court use in cases of allegedly false accidents.[1] By 1919 he had progressed to the point where he felt competent enough to offer his detective services in murder cases. But his career in this field was not successful because of two pronounced fiascos. One concerned the murder of Herbert Clifford of Manchester, New Hampshire, in 1919. Hunter was employed by the county government to handle the case. He successively accused three persons, each of whom was found innocent. The sheriff finally dismissed Hunter and, when questioned years later, referred to him as a "fraud and a liar." The other fiasco in Hunter's life occurred when a Manchester newspaper hired him as a private detective to investigate a local murder. As a result of his investigation, the paper charged a certain individual guilty of the murder. This was afterwards found to be unfounded and the paper had to stand a heavy libel suit.

Hunter's two blunders in criminal detection probably were important in causing him to enter the field of labor espionage. The transition is indicated by an article in the *Manchester Mirror* of November 10, 1919. It stated that he visited the town "in the course of a trip here to get extradition papers for rioters wanted at Raymond." A question regarding his occupation prior to organizing the Industrial Defense Association in 1924 elicited the following answer:

> For about ten years I was employed in counteracting Communistic influences . . . largely in New Hampshire. Just prior to the formation of the Industrial Defense Association I conducted a campaign against the anarchists and outlaw unions in Lynn.[2]

Another interesting aspect of Hunter's life is his three or four marriages. The office of the Registrar of New Hampshire records three marriages—one in 1908, another in 1919, and still another in 1924. The 1908 and the 1919 marriages are both recorded as second marriages. Quite possibly Hunter, desiring not to have too many instances of matrimony on his record, omitted mention of one when applying for a license in 1919. Incidentally, one of the marriages ended in a divorce obtained on grounds of extreme cruelty.

Hunter has been an outspoken anti-semite for a number of years. In this respect he differs from the other leaders, nearly all of whom acquired their anti-semitism about the time Hitler came into power in Germany. In 1930 Hunter referred to "Jew-controlled Soviet Russia" in one of his letters. In 1933 a person who had been observing his activities for some years expressed surprise concerning "the first circular I have seen for years emanating from that office [Hunter's] in which there is no reference to the Jews as such."

The Industrial Defense Association disseminates its propaganda through its speakers' bureau as well as through pamphlets, leaflets, and books. "We conduct a Patriotic Speakers' Bureau," proclaims the organization's letterhead; and although the "Bureau" consists solely of Mr. Hunter, the number of speeches made is large. Hunter maintains that he has given "approximately seven hundred lectures on the subject of the 'Menace of Communism' before Legion groups, Rotary, Kiwanis, churches."[3] He does not say how many years these lectures covered.

THE INDUSTRIAL DEFENSE ASSOCIATION

To the above list of groups addressed should be added the Federation of Women's Clubs of Boston and several chapters of the Daughters of the American Revolution. Hunter's outspoken attacks on the Jews have resulted in loss of not only further invitations to speak before American Legion and Kiwanis groups, but also some of his influential members and financial support. His persistence may indicate the sincerity of his convictions. Were he interested only in making money, he would probably confine his attacks to persons identified with revolutionary ideologies; thus, he would keep within the mores and would be acceptable everywhere.

The most important propaganda channel for the Industrial Defense Association is the distribution of pamphlets and books. The publication that it distributes in greatest volume is the "special report," a four-page leaflet appearing at irregular intervals—whenever Hunter is moved to write one. He averages about four reports a year. A list of typical reports follows:

Special Report on World Bolshevism
Special Report on World Anti-Judaism
Special Report on Soviet Trade in the U. S. A.
Special Report—Radicalism Penetrates the Emergency Peace Campaign
Christianity vs. Judaism
The Prophets of Despair
The Fear Complex.

Hunter's literary output is not confined to such brief tracts. His long pamphlets include:

Legislation for Hatred
Does the CIO Seek to Promote Red Revolution?
Will This Arch Conspirator Rule American Labor? (Below the title is a picture of Stalin)
The Grave Diggers of Russia
The Swan Song of Hate
Jewish Jazz; Tin Pan Alley.

In addition to his own pamphlets, Hunter distributes the following publications: *Zionism* (a tract of the Militant Christian Patriots of England), Irwin L. Potter's *The Cause of Anti-Jewism in the United States,* Elizabeth Dilling's *The Lady Patriot Replies,* and *The Protocols of the Elders of Zion.* Hunter has advised his correspondents to write to Nazi Germany for detailed anti-semitic propaganda. In a letter dated September 29th, 1938, he wrote:

> I would advise you to send a couple of dollars to World-Service, 4 Daberstedterstrasse, Erfurt, Germany . . . asking them to place your name on their mailing list.[4]

World-Service prints anti-semitic propaganda in six languages and distributes it on a worldwide scale.

The volume of propaganda put out by the Industrial Defense Association cannot be accurately estimated. Hunter asserts that two of his pamphlets had a very large distribution—40,000 to 50,000 for *Grave Diggers of Russia* and about 30,000 for *Does the CIO Seek to Promote Red Revolution?* These figures may be padded in order to inflate the importance of the Association. Even if not padded, however, the figures are probably not typical. Hunter states that his regular mailing list is part of perhaps 5,000 or 6,000 address cards in his office. Assuming his regular mailing list is half this number, only about 3,000 people would get his special reports. Moreover, since his other material and pamphlets are much more expensive, their circulation is probably considerably less than 3,000.

Another activity sponsored by the Industrial Defense Association is small-scale labor espionage. Hunter speaks of "supplying confidential reports to persons who have nuclei of reds in their factories and places of business."[5] He avers that he has advance information on strikes, offering to notify not only the factory owners but also the state police and the local Chamber of Commerce. For these activities, he asserts, he receives no pay. Their extent cannot, of course, be compared with that of large agencies specializing in labor espionage.

MEMBERSHIP

Several of Hunter's letters soliciting funds state that "a contribution of two dollars will put your name on our mailing list." Actually, the mailing list and the membership list seem to be one and the same. Consequently, for two dollars or more contributors receive all or most of the literature Hunter distributes. An estimate of what part of the 5,000 or 6,000 addresses in Hunter's files definitely form the mailing list may be gleaned by noting that his total budget for 1935 was a little more than $6,500. If all contributors gave only two dollars, the membership would be 3,250. Since, as will be shown later, a small number of wealthy persons are probably the chief support of the Association—obviously donating much more than two dollars—the membership in all likelihood does not exceed 1,000.

In the past, the Association did operate on a formal membership basis and had a little more than 200 members. The change to the present basis probably occurred in 1933, when the Boston Better Business Bureau investigated Hunter. The report issued by the Bureau accused Hunter of fomenting anti-semitism and resulted in a number of withdrawals from the Association and, apparently, in the abandonment of a formal membership list. The existence of a president, a vice-president, a treasurer, and a Board of Directors is the only present vestige of membership.

As to the character of the membership, it is noteworthy that the Association has a higher proportion of persons from the upper-income group than any organization heretofore considered. This was particularly true when the Association was first founded. As one person familiar with the membership puts it, "Originally Hunter interested some very fine people in creating his corporation . . . On the Board of Directors at that time were General Edwards, prominent clergymen, and some persons of fine standing." Another observer uses nearly the same words: "When he began his activities, Hunter surrounded himself with men of standing . . . but, following his anti-semitic attack . . . all the people of standing withdrew from his Board of Directors." Although these resignations undoubtedly lost Hunter some wealthy and distinguished members, ample evidence indicates that his supporters still include many wealthy persons. The evidence reveals that active members of a predominantly upper income group, the Daughters of the American Revolution, have purchased his literature, that he has addressed many chapters of the D. A. R., and that, at the behest of one chapter, he investigated Mary Emma Woolley, famous educator and president of Mt. Holyoke College from 1900 to 1937.

On the Association's Board of Directors in 1936 were a genealogist, an attorney, a clergyman described as an "active Legionnaire", and a man who referred to himself as "active in military, naval, and insurance circles". In the following year, a consulting engineer succeeded a Baptist fundamentalist "minister and evangelist" as president of the Association.

A list that Hunter swore represented the distribution pertaining to orders for his pamphlet: *Does the CIO Seek to Promote Red Revolution?* further brings into high relief the character of his Association's membership. The list presented to a Federal officer in December, 1937, follows:

Table 6

PURCHASERS OF THE PAMPHLET "DOES THE CIO SEEK TO PROMOTE
RED REVOLUTION?"

Date (1937)	Name	Number Sent	Remarks
June 15	Brockton Shoe Mrgrs. Assn.	2–3	Never ordered
	E. C. Gray, Secretary		quantity
	M. Lawrence Turner	1000	
	Mrs. David Rumbough (DAR)	50	
	Max Rosen	50	
	c/o Western Slipper Co.		
	Blue Island Av., Chicago		

Date		Name	Number Sent	Remarks
June	16	Edith Bowdoin (DAR)	1000	
	17	Sangatuck Fairfield Co.	150	Paid $2.00
	18	American Federation of Labor by William Green	0	Inquiry on 100,000 Quoted $3.50/M
	18	E. O. Walker	50	
	21	American Tool Works Co. Cincinnati, Ohio J. B. Doan	100	Paid $2.00
		Marion B. Bishop New York State Economic Council, Inc.	15	
		Sara H. Birchell	10	
		The Home Owned Store Magazine Des Moines, Ia.	25	
		Mrs. E. T. Moulton	12	
	24	C. B. Butterfield	5	
	30	Stuart Nelson	1–2	
July	1	Women Defenders of America A. M. Saunders	2–3	Sought 500
	9	Massachusetts Spec. Commission	14	
	12	"The Defenders" [of the Christian Faith] M. L. Flowers	100	
	14	Karl Newmann	100	
	15	Mrs. Francis Copson c/o Scott's Laundry Springfield, Mass.	500	Wouldn't pay bill. Returned
	19	Mrs. M. A. Shawn	0	
		Elizabeth Knauss	25	
		" "	25	
	20	L. R. Brown	50	
		George W. Hunter American-European Fellowship	25	
	22	Rev. E. A. Dobberstein	25	
	23	F. H. Copson c/o Scott Laundry, Inc. Springfield, Mass.	500	
	23	Dr. Chas. Pichel Box 25, General Post Office, N. Y. C.	—	"Will you please send a few copies to my friend Paul M. Winter, Box 115, Shavertown, Pa. He wishes to give them to the owners of the anthracite coal mines there, who are fighting the CIO too."
	26	Karl Newmann		Further request refused
	27	H. S. Hickman	50	
	28	Doren Hadley	25	
	29	Nellie Hall	12	
	30	Paul Winter, Ph. D. Civil Intelligence Bureau, Shavertown, Pa.	25	Combatting Communism in the anthracite fields of Pennsylvania

THE INDUSTRIAL DEFENSE ASSOCIATION

Date		Name	Number Sent	Remarks
August	6	Carl Waltz	4	
	6	Keokuk Laundry	100	
	7	E. J. Walters	3	
	11	Jerry Lawson	1	
	16	H. B. Kenyon	25	
	26	Mrs. H. T. Leedon	25	
	30	Peter Holman	Quantity	
	31	American Vigilante Minute Men	5–10	
September	4	Public Building Service Employees' Union Owen Cunningham Minneapolis, Minn.	100	
	7	Lillian Remshack	4–5	
	8	Kathleen Morse (DAR)	500	
	9	Gwinn Bros. & Co. Huntington, W. Va.	1000	As per wire urging prompt shipment
	24	Mrs. J. E. Hanley	1	
	27	Mrs. H. T. Leeden	50	
	28	Lambert Castle Assn.	12	
	29	Sun Ship Employees' Assn. Chester, Pa. W. N. Appleby, Secretary	50	Parcel post collect as requested
October	5	R. H. Frye	10	
	12	R. T. Wecker (Rev.)	20	
[No date]		Virginia Constitution Crusaders	3	

Not all groups or persons named in the preceding table are necessarily on the regular mailing list of the Association. Nevertheless they are probably typical of the membership. The five types worth noting and examples of each follow.[6]

The anti-semitic organizations: the Defenders of the Christian Faith (M. L. Flowers and Elizabeth Knauss) and the Civil Intelligence Bureau.

The anti-revolutionary organizations: the Women Defenders of America, the American Vigilante Minute Men, and the Virginia Constitution Crusaders.

Industrial concern: Keokuk Laundry and Gwinn Bros. & Co.

The Manufacturers' Associations: the Brockton Shoe Manufacturers' Association and the New York State Economic Council.

The company unions: the Public Building Service Employees' Union and the Sun Ship Employees' Association.

The presence of manufacturers' associations and company unions points to the fact that the membership of the Industrial Defense Association includes the most militant foes of bona fide trade unionism.

Another point regarding the membership is the absence of anyone whose name suggests relationship to recent immigrant stock. In so far as the names of the original incorporators of the organization and of the 1936 board of directors are typical, they are almost without exception Anglo-Saxon: General Bisbee, Ross H. Currier, Miss Eva F. Dalby, General Edwards, David I. Egan, Mrs. E. M. Fales, Adeline Fitzgerald, William J. Good, Courtenay Guild, the Rev. Wallace Hayes, Harry A. Jung, Mrs. C. W. Mansus, the Rev. Charles L. Page, Eliza J. Pearson, Commander Charles H. Shaw, Jerome O. Smith, Miss Evelyn Tankend, and the Rev. Herbert R. Whitelock.

As for the geographical distribution of members, the Association may be considered a Boston or, at most, a New England, organization. Members of the Board of Directors give as addresses Boston, suburban Boston, or towns within a short distance of Boston. However, Hunter sends his literature outside of New England; his material has appeared in such distant places as San Francisco. He has spoken several times in Rhode Island, apparently with the intention of extending his activities there; but this is about as far away from Boston as the Hunter influence extends. His is definitely a localized organization as compared with the German-American Bund, the Silver Shirts, or the Defenders of the Christian Faith.

Since the membership of the Association apparently includes a proportionately greater number of wealthy people than that of the Silver Shirts or of the Defenders of the Christian Faith, its educational level most likely is also much higher. The Silver Shirts are interested in the message of the Great Pyramid; the Defenders, both in this message and Biblical prophecy. Such interest suggests limited education, a characteristic of the lower-income groups. The literature of the Association, however, contains no references to prophecy, either of the Great Pyramid or of the Biblical variety.

FUNDS

"Mr. Hunter, who gets his money by prodding D.A.R. ladies with the Red Scare," is the brief and reasonably accurate way a Bostonian, long familiar with the Association, described the source of Hunter's finance. More accurately, the Association has three sources of income: sale of literature, lecture fees, and gifts—the third being the most important. The Association developed financially until 1933 when the expose of anti-semitism caused the loss of many rich supporters. Among those lost was a lady who had given $40,000. For the year 1936 the entire budget was only a little more than $6,500. At present the finance is on a relatively wider basis. Each January the old members receive a letter urging them to make their contributions as generous as possible. Moreover, the organization is constantly soliciting non-members. As one such solicitation stated, "We are seeking new friends to enlarge our work of counteracting and suppressing destructive influences." A two-dollar contribution and the contributor's name goes on the mailing list. In some instances, Hunter's pamphlets have carried appeals for funds, and donations of as little as a dollar are held acceptable. Nothing more precise can be said of Hunter's finances, for since the McCormack Committee investigation (1934) all contributions have been recorded as "anonymous" and all records of earlier contributions destroyed. Hunter has profited by the experience of his friend Harry A. Jung, the names of whose financial backers were revealed by the McCormack Committee.

An interesting sidelight on Hunter's operations is the fact that he once tried to get money from the German Government. William Dudley Pelley, chief of the Silver Shirts, made a similar attempt in 1933.[7] On March 3, 1934, Hunter wrote to the Friends of Germany, the predecessor of the Friends of the New Germany:

> Several times I have conferred with Dr. Tippelskirch [then German Consul in Boston] and at one time suggested that if he could secure the financial backing from Germany, I could start a real campaign along lines that would be very effective.
> All that is necessary to return America to Americans is to organize the many thousands of persons who are victims of Judaism and I am ready to do that at any time.

No evidence attests that Hunter actually received any money from the German Government; he probably never did. The significant point, however, is that he wanted "to inculate Americanism" with German money.

CHAPTER X

The Paul Reveres

THE distinction between an organization that is anti-revolutionary and anti-semitic and one that is merely anti-revolutionary is not always easy to draw. The groups considered so far are openly and frankly anti-semitic; and they do not care who knows it. Among the scores of American organizations that are termed only as anti-revolutionary, however, a few are covertly anti-semitic. Often the leader is anti-semitic while the rank and file is not and, moreover, is unaware of its leader's prejudice. Such a group is The Paul Reveres. It is analyzed not because it is an important group, but because it is typical of several organizations that border on anti-semitism.

LEADERSHIP

Mrs. Albert W. Dilling, famed among red-baiters as the author of the *Red Network*, was the real founder of The Paul Reveres. The organization dates back to early 1931, when Mrs. Dilling first discussed with Colonel Edwin Marshall Hadley the formation of some sort of anti-Communism club. Nothing concrete was done, however, until October 17, 1932. On that date, Colonel Hadley and Kenneth E. Shephard called, by appointment, at Mrs. Dilling's home in Kenilworth (suburban Chicago) for the purpose of putting her idea into effect. Mrs. Dilling suggested the name—*The Paul Reveres*. Hadley formulated the purposes of the organization:

> To promote patriotism
> To advance Americanism
> To combat radicalism.

On November 21, 1932, the group obtained a certificate of incorporation. Headquarters were then set up at 120 South La Salle Street, Chicago. Shortly thereafter, Mrs. Dilling resigned because, according to her admission, Colonel Hadley, the president, had become anti-semitic. An active membership existed until 1935, but from then until early 1937 it was merely Colonel Hadley. Subsequently the name of The Paul Reveres disappeared from the door of the La Salle Street office, and the organization passed quietly into limbo. Though The Paul Reveres had several other elected officers and a national advisory council of no less than 37, Colonel Hadley was the dominant personality. As Mrs. Dilling's husband put it, "It's a one-man organization. The advisory council is only a bunch of stuffed shirts."[1]

Unlike all other anti-semitic leaders, save Father Coughlin and perhaps Colonel Sanctuary, Hadley did not earn his living by heading his organization. A wealthy retired businessman, he has ample money and time to develop his prejudices. He was born in Peoria, Illinois, in 1872. In *Who's Who in Chicago* (1931 edition) he pointed with pride to the fact that he was an eighth generation American and that his ancestors arrived from England in 1630. Again unlike all other anti-semitic leaders, save Colonel Sanctuary, he had a college education, receiving his A.B. from Northwestern University in 1895. His business experience,[2] according to *Who's Who*, was as follows: "Entered business in Chicago, 1893, occupying positions as auditor and credit man; with others organized the Dudley Coffee Co. and the Ceylon Planters Tea Co., 1898, of which he was secretary, treasurer, and director until 1906; chairman of the board of the Chicago-Cleveland Car Roofing Co., 1908-1925." During the World War, Hadley served in the Intelligence Division of the General Staff. His title "Colonel" comes by virtue of his rank of Lieutenant-Colonel in the Illinois National Guard. This title is his pride and joy; Mr. Dilling asserts that life would be meaningless for him if he were to be deprived of the title.[3] He belongs to several military organizations—the Reserve Officers Association, the American Legion, the Military Intelligence Association, and the Army and Navy Club of Washington, D. C. He is a member of the Union League Club and a thirty-second degree Mason.

Hadley's presidency of The Paul Reveres was not his first effort at combating revolutionary ideology. In 1929 he wrote a novel entitled *Sinister Shadows*, which purported to "expose" revolutionary teaching in American colleges and the corruption of youth by revolutionary and partly insane professors.

PROPAGANDA

The Paul Reveres have had no regular periodical. In late 1933 and in early 1934, a sheet called the *Paul Revere Message* appeared, lasting only a few issues. The list of literature distributed by The Paul Reveres is not long; much of it is Hadley's own creation.

> *Organize*
> The Paul Reveres
> *Sinister Shadows* (1929)—E. M. Hadley
> *T.N.T.* (1931)—E. M. Hadley
> *The Rape of the Republic* (1935)—E. M. Hadley
> *Facing the Facts* (1934)—Earnest Sincere
> *The Plan in Action* (1934)—Earnest Sincere

The last two mentioned are definitely anti-semitic; the others are fulminations against revolutionaries. The name, Earnest Sincere, looks patently like a pseudonym. As a matter of fact, Albert W. Dilling has declared that Hadley is the real author of *Facing the Facts*. In a letter to Rev. Albert D. Bell of Chicago, Dilling [3a] wrote:

> I was very much surprised to have you state that . . . the pamphlet, *Facing the Facts*, supposedly written by one "Earnest Sincere," was in reality the work of Mr. Harry Jung of the AVIF. For I happen to know that Lt. Col. Edwin Marshall Hadley is its author.
>
> You will recall that something over a year ago Mrs. Dilling and I were associated with Col. Hadley in The Paul Reveres. . . .
>
> While still associated with him, however, I read in manuscript in the Colonel's office and at home identically what later appeared in *Facing the Facts*. It was intended at the time to get it out as a "Paul Revere" publication. . . .

That Hadley also wrote *The Plan in Action* admits of little doubt; its sub-title is *A Sequel to Facing the Facts*. Moreover, the style of the two is the same and the wording of the last two pages of each pamphlet is almost identical. The Reveres never distributed any great volume of propaganda. *The Rape of the Republic*, the most widely circulated of all the organization's literature, probably reached only several thousand persons.

Though The Reveres have had no formal speakers' bureau, several prominent members have frequently spread the organization's message from the public platform. Hadley, Major John L. Griffith, "Big Ten" Athletic Commissioner, and Ray Warren, the first vice-president, are known to have addressed Rotary Clubs, chapters of the Daughters of the American Revolution, American Legion Posts, and the Executives Club of Chicago. Moreover, the central chapter of The Paul Reveres has frequently listened to speakers at weekly or bi-weekly luncheon meetings.

MEMBERSHIP

The Paul Reveres have had a membership in the strict sense of the word: those who paid dues and whose names were on the records, not merely those who read its literature. On the whole, the organization has been a failure. Though it has aspired to be a nationwide group, it has had only a few short-lived locals in and near Chicago and one in San Diego, California. As a matter of fact, the only two locals that are known to have existed beyond dispute are the so-called "central" chapter in Chicago and the branch in San Diego. Some evidence indicates that two locals may have been organized in suburban Chicago—one in Glencoe and another in Wheaton.[4] Mr. Dilling, however, thinks The Reveres have had as many as twenty chapters in the Chicago region.[5] The "central" chapter has had fifty or sixty members. Mr. Dilling speaks of his wife's addressing groups interested in forming a chapter and of sixty or seventy persons enrolling as members after such a meeting. Nevertheless, since the number of chapters are not known, no estimate of the total membership can be made.

More satisfactory information concerning the kinds of persons who have been members is available. The membership requirement specifies that applicants must be native-born citizens.[6] Jews are not eligible, according to Ray Warren, the first vice-president.[7] The existence of chapters in two rich residential suburbs of Chicago—Glencoe and Wheaton—would suggest members in the upper income groups. The fact that the "central" chapter met at noon in a downtown hotel might imply a membership of prosperous businessmen. The affiliations of certain national officers further strengthen these implications: the first vice-president has been president of the Executives Club of Chicago; the second vice-president has been described[8] as "a former Marine educated at the University of Missouri, and now an advertising consultant in Chicago"; and the national secretary bears the title "captain" and has been "for many years active in patriotic movements."[9]

Further information on the membership can be gained from examining the list of the 37 national directors, most of whom have merely lent the prestige of their names to The Reveres. The significant fact, however, is that these 37 constitute by far the most distinguished group of persons connected in any way with the organizations treated in this study. The directors include a former President-General of the Daughters of the American Revolution, three men bearing the title "Judge", a past commander of the American Legion, three college presidents, a Congressman, a former Governor of Kentucky, and the President of the American Legion Auxiliary. Of the eighteen directors residing in Chicago, eleven are listed in *Who's Who in Chicago*, eight hold an A.B. degree, and six have a degree from some professional school. In brief, The Paul Reveres has consisted of well-educated native-born Americans, primarily from the upper-income groups.

FUNDS

The organization has operated on a small budget; it has never had much money coming in or going out. The founders, Colonel Hadley[10] and Mrs. Dilling[11] started things off with money from their own pockets. The two other sources of finance have been dues fixed independently by each chapter (the "central" chapter fixed it at $5 per year) and contributions collected at meetings.

CONCLUSIONS

The degree to which The Paul Reveres have been anti-semitic merits close examination. First, Jews have not been permitted to join The Paul Reveres. When Hadley learned that some Jews were members of the San Diego chapter, he insisted that they be compelled to resign, whereupon a feud developed and, finally, the chapter dissolved.[12] Hadley has, of course, attacked the Jews in the pseudonymous writings which he has distributed secretly from headquarters of The Reveres. As Mr. Dilling has aptly stated, "He lacks the guts to write openly against the Jews, but he whispers against them constantly." Mrs. Dilling agrees with her husband.

Significant information has been volunteered by Major John L. Griffith, himself no anti-semite: "The organization has been accused of anti-semitism, but this is untrue. Some individuals may have been anti-semitic, but that does not imply that the organization has been so."[13] This suggests that Griffith was well aware of Hadley's anti-semitism and anxious to protect the name of the organization as a whole. On the other hand, several other officers of The Reveres have been known anti-semites. Ray Warren, the first vice-president, has been very much interested in the Silver Shirts. In February, 1934, he manifested his anti-semitism in an address based on the *Protocols of the Elders of Zion* and delivered before the Executives' Club in the Sherman Hotel, Chicago. Then, too, the national advisory board of The Reveres has included Colonel E. N. Sanctuary, head of the anti-semitic American Christian Defenders, and Dr. Arno C. Gaebelein, author of *The Conflict of the Ages,* an anti-semitic book. Hence, The Reveres, though not officially anti-semitic, have been so to a degree.

The difference between an organization like The Reveres and one that is openly anti-semitic lies in the general type of person associated with each. To none of the preceding organizations discussed in this study have distinguished people been willing to lend the prestige of their names. Clearly, then, anti-semitism is not quite respectable; it is "in poor taste"; the "best people" do not espouse it—not openly, at least. Anti-revolutionary activity, on the other hand, is always acceptable. People who have had the best educational opportunities and who have elicited the highest degree of deference are glad to support openly an organization "fighting Communism and promoting Americanism." Witness their presence in large numbers in the Daughters of the American Revolution and the United States Chamber of

Commerce, two groups active in the distribution of anti-revolutionary propaganda.

Since open espousal of an anti-semitic group is counter to the *mores*, whatever support such groups receive from the wealthy and socially prominent must take the quiet form of financial contributions. Moreover, when a few leaders are anti-semitic, they must express their anti-semitism furtively. They must write against the Jews under pseudonyms—and talk in whispers. Should the anti-semitism become widely known, the wealthy and socially prominent members might be faced with the possibility of being publicly embarrassed because of their connection with an organization led by anti-semites. Hence, in borderline organizations the anti-semitic work must be unobtrusive. An actual case in which numerous resignations followed a revelation of anti-semitism was one involving the Industrial Defense Association.[14]

In summary, Americans of wealth and distinction will affiliate openly with anti-revolutionary groups but, for the present time at least, not with groups both anti-revolutionary and anti-semitic. Nevertheless, should conditions favorable to the spread of anti-semitism be intensified, upper class persons might embrace anti-semitism.

CHAPTER XI

Typical Minor Groups

THE JAMES TRUE ASSOCIATES

A ONE-MAN concern, the James True Associates, resembles the Edmondson Economic Service in a number of respects. It has made no pretense at being a membership organization. It has operated chiefly through a weekly newsletter called the *Industrial Control Report*. It differs from Edmondson's organization in that its literature reaches a much smaller number of people—principally because Edmondson keeps the price of his weekly letter within the reach of the man in the street while James True charges the comparatively high price of twelve dollars a year for his reports.

The James True Associates first appeared in July 1933. Like all of the organizations in this study save the Industrial Defense Association and the American Vigilant Intelligence Federation, it was born of the depression. For a time the Associates had a subordinate organization called "America First," a channel for distributing propaganda to those persons unwilling to pay the twelve-dollars-a-year fee for the newsletter. It appears, however, that "America First" existed chiefly on paper.

LEADERSHIP

James B. True, Jr., head of the organization, was born on July 1, 1880. The earliest record of his career is his employment with the *Chicago Tribune* from 1917 through 1919. He started as an investigator in the advertising department and, when he left the *Tribune*, was an advertising salesman. From this period down to the time of the establishment of his organization, True remained in journalism. As he said in one of his bulletins:

> When the New Deal came in, the undersigned had been a newspaper correspondent, mainly in the business field, for more than twenty years. For about twelve years he had been the Washington representative of several outstanding business publications. He had been a successful free-lance feature writer,[1] and had been on the staffs of two metropolitan newspapers. His total savings amounted to about $18,000 tied up in three pieces of real estate.

With regard to the origin of his organization, True has explained:

> After the New Deal got under way, the undersigned refused to join in the propaganda ballyhoo. Because he insisted on writing facts and pointing out economic fallacies, newspapers and business magazines refused to publish his articles for the first time in his life. Then, because he was convinced that the truth was indispensable to business interests, he began publication of the reports.
>
> He was assured of adequate financial support for two years; but it did not materialize. About that time, although the writer did the work of several men, the venture was precarious, and was continued as a patriotic duty. Then the writer sold his property at a great sacrifice, and invested the return in the publication and the subsequent meagre living of his family.

True is the most profoundly neurotic of all the anti-semitic leaders. Even Pelley with his spiritualism suffers by contrast. True is sadistic. He has invented and applied for a patent on an extra-heavy policeman's club which he calls a "Kike Killer." Details on this weapon, as well as an excellent insight into True's personality, have been furnished by Dr. L. M. Birkhead, National Director of the Friends of Democracy. Shortly after an interview with True, Dr. Birkhead wrote:

> I found True to have the look and determination of a fanatic. Spread out on his desk were a half-dozen wooden pieces which looked like the lower ends of an axe handle. On examination I found that they had straps running through one end much the same as a policeman's billy. When Mr. True began to explain to me that he had a very militant organization in the South which he was equipping with arms in order to kill off the Jews,[2] I began to understand what these hip-pocket-flask billies were for. They were Mr. True's "Kike Killers."
>
> "What are you trying to do through your organizations?" I asked Mr. True.
>
> Quick as a flash he replied, "To defeat the only real enemy that America has today." That enemy, it appears, is the Jew Communism which the New Deal is trying to force on America.
>
> "We may have to do something more militant than vote," Mr. True said with the emphasis of a man who believed that bullets might have to be substituted for ballots.
>
> I asked him just what he meant by being more militant.
>
> "What I mean is that the thing has possibly gone too far for us to save the country by political methods," True replied. "I had a man in here to see me very recently. He has an organization of 1,500—a very secret organization with each man sworn to absolute secrecy. These Southern men were ready to kill the Jews and the Negroes in order to protect the white women of the South."
>
> "I don't understand the connection of the Jews with attacks on the white women of the South," I said.

"Why, I tell you what I mean," said Mr. True. "These Southern white men have discovered that rich Jews have hired 'big, buck niggers' to attack white women. These Jews give the 'niggers' plenty of money and tell them to go after the white women. Yes, these fellows down there are going to kill every Jew in their section of the South. Doesn't sound very nice, does it? Call it a pogrom if you want to, but it is the one language the Jews understand. The Jews, you see, are guilty of sex crimes just like the 'niggers.'"

"Now, wait a minute, Mr. True, what do you mean?" I asked.

"You may not know it, but mulattoes of the South are ninety percent the children of Jewish fathers and 'nigger' women," Mr. True told me. "You see, every Jew wants to sleep with a nigger wench."

"But how do you know about the mulattoes?" I inquired.

"Well, because it is an established fact that Jewish blood is yellow, and mulattoes are yellow, aren't they?" Mr. True asked with an affirmative answer expected.

Mr. True speaking: "I don't see any way out except a pogrom. We have got to kill the Jews. Ballots don't mean anything to them."

"May I ask, Mr. True, if you aren't oversimplifying the problem?" I said by way of interruption. "Suppose we could line up the fifteen million Jews up against a wall and shoot them, that wouldn't solve our problems. We'd still have them with us—the same old problems."

True speaking: "That's just where you're wrong. Our problem is very simple. Get rid of the Jews and we'd be on the way to Utopia tomorrow. The Jews are the source of all our troubles. That's plain to anyone who makes a study of this problem, and I have studied it deeply."

"Who is it that is trying to destroy our Constitution and the American form of government? The Jew.

"You take the hiring of 'big, buck niggers' by the Jews to attack white women in the South. That's right in the *Talmud*. The *Talmud* teaches the Jew that it's all right to do that. Only recently a police chief had to shoot one of these 'niggers' and he found out that he was hired by a Jew to rape a white woman.

"Communism is the major part of the Jewish conspiracy today. Why, just look at Russia where the Jews run the country.

"I want to leave with you a thought," said Mr. True as I arose to leave. "I predict a pogrom for America. I don't see how it can be avoided." [3]

PROPAGANDA

True utilizes three media of propaganda: his *Industrial Control Report*, miscellaneous pamphlets, and, occasionally, the public platform. By far the most important medium is the printed, four-page *Industrial Control Report*, the first issue of which appeared on July 10, 1933. True temporarily suspended publication after the November 14, 1936 issue—an experience shared by many of his colleagues. Not until early September, 1937, did he resume publication. Since then an *Industrial Control Report* has appeared every week.

True bragged to Dr. Birkhead that the subscribers to the reports numbered 2,500. A more accurate basis for estimating the circulation is True's statement of his organization's total income down to the 1936 election. In his report of November 14, 1936, True stated, ". . . in more than two years we have collected exactly $7,167.78 to carry on the work." The subscription rate was $12.00 a year. Assuming all income was from subscriptions and none from outright gifts (which was probably not the case) the maximum number of subscribers would be only about six hundred. A complicating element enters into this estimate if circulation is defined as the number of people who actually read a publication. In one report True asserts that

> "a checkup covering approximately twenty subscribers showed that the smallest number of readers per report was about twenty-five, and that the largest number was more than two hundred. We are confident that for at least three years the average number of readers per report has been more than thirty."

In view of his exaggeration to the Reverend Birkhead, this report must be taken with a grain of salt. If True is conceded a liberal average of five readers per report, his total circulation was 3,000. His ten months suspension of publication, however, must have cost him many readers and put his circulation below that figure.

True's circulation of pamphlets was small compared to that of other anti-semitic organizations. Among those he distributed were *Americans Everywhere* and *What Is Roosevelt?*, both apparently written by him, and *Toward Armageddon* by the Squire of Krum Elbow— (Howland Spencer,[4] a wealthy supporter of the Edmondson Economic Service). In 1938 True put out *Gold Manipulations and Depressions*, a 76-page special report selling for five dollars. His publication *Americans Everywhere*, True declared, had a circulation of 10,000.

True seldom speaks in public. The only record of a speech is that before the Rotary Club of Baltimore in October 1934. He has probably made other speeches, but, as an ex-newspaperman, he has made his forte his writing.

MEMBERSHIP

The readers of the *Industrial Control Reports* may be taken as True's membership. The number was never more than 3,000 and in 1940 was down to perhaps 1,000 or 2,000.

The character of the members is indicated by the fact that True always made his appeals to businessmen. In a letter soliciting new subscribers to the reports he wrote: "It is our desire to furnish you with authoritative information and those facts which are necessary for the intelligent management of your business." Similarly, in the last report before his ten month suspension of publication, he sketched the history of his enterprise, saying:

> We submitted to four hundred business leaders the first definite program of activities to counteract the subversion of American institutions. . . .
> We were convinced that the facts regarding the New Deal and the promotion of communism by the administration would be indispensable in the intelligent management of business. We also believed that the business interests, finding our information of value, would eventually support our work by paying the small annual fee required for our service.

Since in every case the appeal was to the business executive, the inference that many of his subscribers were business executives is reasonable. The facts that the reports cost twelve dollars a year and that True would offer a special 76-page report for five dollars further suggest a wealthy membership.[5] Unlike Edward L. Hunter's and Harry A. Jung's organizations, which drew members from a small geographical area, True's reports reached such distant places as Portland (Ore.), Hamilton, (O.), Pittsburgh, (Pa.), Mobile, (Ala.), and Rochester, (N. Y.). In summary True's membership came from the upper-income group—mostly business executives throughout the country.

FUNDS

The finance of the organization seems to have come wholly from subscriptions to the reports and from True's own pocket. True maintains that he "sold his property at a great sacrifice, and invested the return in the publication." To be sure, the subsidiary organization, America First, had a membership fee of $1.00, but this source could not have yielded much because the organization was so insignificant. True may have received a few outright grants of money, but they too could not have been large. In short, True's organization has not been a financial success. He testified to this himself when he said in his November 18, 1936, report: "We have been sadly disappointed in the financial support of industry. . . ."

THE AMERICAN CHRISTIAN DEFENDERS

The American Christian Defenders, as well as the World Alliance against Jewish Aggressiveness, consists solely of Colonel E. N. Sanctuary and his office at 156 Fifth Avenue, New York City. Of the latter organization little is known. Information on the American Christian Defenders, however, is available. It has neither a membership nor a regular publication. Its propaganda activity consists of the pamphlets that the Colonel distributes—many of which he writes himself—and of the lectures he delivers. The first mention of the organization appears in April 1934.

LEADERSHIP

Eugene Nelson Sanctuary was born on November 6, 1870, in Hinesburg, Vermont. Here he spent his boyhood and attended high school. In 1893 he received a degree in civil engineering from the University of Vermont. Sanctuary has apparently spent a good part of his life in civil engineering, and the practice of his profession has necessitated his living in many cities throughout the country. Though he was not sufficiently distinguished in his profession to appear in the *Who's Who in Engineering,* he has apparently made a comfortable living. At least, in 1936 he was in a position to make a rather heavy investment in a mining venture. During the war, Sanctuary attained the rank of major in the United States Army and held the post of "Personnel Officer, Military Railways in France, Office Chief of Engineers." His present title of "Colonel" is bona fide, coming from the National Guard. Sanctuary is a prominent layman in the Presbyterian Church. He is also treasurer of the American-European Fellowship for Christian Oneness and Evangelization, an organization devoted to evangelization, Bible distribution, and relief work in Europe.

Sanctuary gives an interesting account of the origin of his antisemitism. When questioned by the Reverend Birkhead, he explained: "Well, during the war I was in charge of the Railroad Division of the army. I saw a lot of interesting documents. I saw the documents by which Jacob Schiff transferred $1,000,000 to Lenin and Trotsky with which to foment the Russian Revolution." Sanctuary continued to the effect that these documents have been destroyed and so cannot be produced now. Moreover, he was evasive when asked to describe more precisely the nature of the documents.

PROPAGANDA

Sanctuary's one work that could be properly described as a book is entitled *Are These Things So?*, but Sanctuary has written a number of pamphlets; these include *Roosevelt Warming the Serpent* (December 1934), *The Man Behind the Men Behind the President* (Harry A. Jung, co-author), *Litvinoff, Foreign Commissar of the U. S. S. R.,* *Tainted Contacts, Blind Leaders* (December 1935), *Communism, Its Heart and Goal* (1936), and *Is the New Deal Communism?* In 1937 the Colonel seemed to be writing less, and to be distributing more material by other authors. In addition to considerable propaganda published by the Edmondson Economic Service, he disseminated such material as *The Protocols of the Learned Elders of Zion*, Fred Marvin's *Fool's Gold* and *Fruits of Paternalism*, Hadley's *The Rape of the Republic*, *International New Dealism* (by the League for Constitutional Government), and *The Key to the Mystery* (by the Montreal Women's Anti-Communist League). The only clue to the number of pamphlets distributed is Sanctuary's assertion to the Reverend Birkhead that the American Christian Defenders together with the American Vigilant Intelligence Federation had distributed 50,000 copies of their *The Man Behind the Men Behind the President*. Since the pamphlet appears to have been an exceptionally successful one and since the two organizations were distributing it, the figure 50,000 is probably far too high to be typical of the average circulation of Sanctuary's pamphlets.

Sanctuary travels and lectures extensively. In the latter part of May and early June, 1935, he lectured in New York state—in Binghamton, Rochester, and Buffalo. He has also addressed such groups as the Alexander Forum Foundation (New York City, January 1936), the Buffalo Bible Institute, the American Legion Post of Pawtucket (January, 1936), the Toronto International Christian Crusade, and the Citizens League against Communism (New York City, October 1937).

MEMBERSHIP

Though readers of Sanctuary's literature and auditors of his lectures may be considered the membership, no basis for estimating their number is available. Many of the members apparently are fundamentalists, for Sanctuary has lectured before such Fundamentalist groups as the Buffalo Bible Institute and the Toronto International Christian Crusade. Moreover, his prominence in the Presbyterian Church and in the American-European Fellowship for Christian Oneness and Evangelization suggests that his members include followers of numerous other religious organizations.

FUNDS

The American Christian Defenders obtain income from fees for lectures and from the sale of literature. Sanctuary lectures on a strictly fee basis. As James True stated, giving Sanctuary a little free advertising in one of his *Industrial Control Reports*, "He [Sanctuary] is a well known authority and lecturer on the development of Communism in the United States . . . His fee is moderate." (Sanctuary reprinted

this quotation in the back of one of his pamphlets.)   One edition
of Sanctuary's *Litvinoff, Foreign Commissar of the U. S. S. R.* was
published by the *Deutscher Weckruf und Beobachter,* the official newspaper of the German-American Bund.   In all probability, Sanctuary
received payment for the permission to reprint his work.   More important sources of finance are Sanctuary's "angels".   A New York
stock broker [6] contributed $5,000 jointly to Edmondson and Sanctuary.
Other "angels" include a wealthy woman (for a time one of Harry
Jung's chief sources of income), the head of a chain of novelty stores,
and a prominent physician of New York and Boston.

THE ORDER OF '76

The discussion of some of the foregoing organizations may give an
exaggerated impression of the strength of the anti-semitic movement.
Actually, many anti-semitic organizations are both short-lived and
insignificant.   An example of such an organization is the defunct
Order of '76.   Its existence was reported in the *American Hebrew* as
early as December 1933.   It achieved a maximum membership of 168
members in 1934, at that time having an office at 139 East 57th Street,
New York City.   After 1934 the group became inactive, and by 1936
it had formally dissolved.   For a time, Royal Scott Gulden, the founder
and head of the organization, continued disseminating propaganda
from a post office box, but his efforts grew progressively feebler.
Finally, in 1937 he announced that the menace of Communism was
over and stated that he was busy "hustling real estate" and making
himself a nice living.

LEADERSHIP

Only fragmentary information concerning Royal Scott Gulden is
known.   He is a middle-aged, New York real estate broker.   Apparently, his financial condition has not always been of the best, for
in May, 1936, he filed bankruptcy proceedings in a New York court,
listing nearly $23,000 of liabilities and no assets.

The Order of '76 never had a publication of its own.   Its literature,
which came from other anti-semitic organizations, was blessed with
the mark of its rubber stamp, and, judged by the standards of even
the smallest of the organizations considered so far, was distributed in
only small quantities.   The propaganda distributed included A. P.
Quill's *Off the Record,* John B. Trevor's *The Recognition of Soviet
Russia by the United States—an American Political Problem,* and the
October, 1935 Bulletin of the Immigration Restriction Leagues; material published by the Edmondson Economic Service, reprints of

Hearst feature articles on the Communist menace and of George E. Sokolsky's "Revolution", an article in the New York *Herald Tribune* of March 29, 1937; and reprints, with comments, of radical literature, such as *What to Do When Held for Arrest* and *What to Do When Held for Deportation*, both published by the International Labor Defense, and *Red Front*, an anti-fascist publication.

The membership of the Order, which at its height consisted of only 168 persons, was apparently almost entirely recruited from New York City. Attesting this statement is the evidence that all the charter members and the board of directors were New York residents. Since the charter members included three Army officers and one Naval officer,[7] the report in the December 8, 1933, issue of the *American Hebrew* that the Order was enrolling members from the National Guard appeared convincing. According to the magazine, "Our investigators know of instances in a famous New York regiment where the Order of '76 recently attempted and continues even now to recruit members. During the week just past activities have extended to another New York regiment." Another expose in a magazine listed in the ranks of the Order, United States Naval and Military Intelligence officers. The same article stated that the membership also embraced Union League Club members, New York City detectives, bankers, and businessmen.[8]

A former member of the Order who is in some respects typical is described as follows. He comes from an old-American family. He is wealthy and retired, possessing substantial real estate holdings. Since the Order dissolved, he has held, for the enlightenment of his friends, anti-Communist meetings in his home; once he even invited a White Guard Russian to speak.

The names of the directors and the charter members do not show the "Anglo-Saxon" domination usually found in anti-semitic organizations. The names are John Beck, Herman E. M. Bernhard, William See Buck, Allen Farrell, William H. Gubrecht, Jr., Harriette Livermore, Henry P. Nelson, Jr., Ivan Tarasoff, and Kark F. Walz. The name, Ivan Tarasoff, suggests the lone White Guard Russian mentioned in connection with several of the other anti-semitic groups.

The finance for the Order came from the sale of literature and nominal membership dues. The financial difficulties and short span of life evidenced that the Order had no wealthy benefactors.

CHAPTER XII

A United Front?

HAVE the anti-semitic organizations cooperated? Have they formed a united front? Have they shown a willingness for organic unity and for monocracy?

Only fragmentary information exists on the first abortive effort towards unity. In the summer of 1934, eleven of America's anti-semitic leaders met in Lincoln-Turner Hall, Chicago, at a conference that lasted far into the night. Those known to have attended included Peter Gissibl, leader of the Chicago local of the German-American Bund; a second Bund representative; Harry A. Jung, director of the American Vigilant Intelligence Federation; and an Englishman by the name of Strath-Gordon. Two others believed to have attended were Colonel E. N. Sanctuary, head of the American Christian Defenders, and Colonel E. M. Hadley, national president of The Paul Reveres. The purpose of the conference—to coordinate the activities of anti-semitic groups—was apparently never achieved.

The next effort was the Asheville, North Carolina, meeting of August 12-16, 1936. The American Forward Movement, a newly-formed organization headed by the Reverend Ralph E. Nollner, invited many Catholic and Protestant clergymen and laymen throughout the country to attend a conference against "Communism," for "Americanism," etc. Though the 200 clergymen and laymen who signed the invitation included 35 of the most prominent Jew- and Red-baiters in the country, nothing in the invitation implied anti-semitism. But no Jews were invited. When this omission was pointed out, two Jewish rabbis were promptly asked to speak; they accepted.

When the anti-semites arrived in Asheville and learned that Jewish rabbis were to speak, 45 of them bolted the conference, formed their own organization, and convened at another meeting place. Among the bolters were Gerald B. Winrod, Harry A. Jung, Robert E. Edmondson, James B. True, Colonel E. N. Sanctuary, George B. Deatherage, Howland Spencer, Nelson E. Hewitt (a Jung associate), and O. K. Chandler. The insurgent conference, which elected Winrod as chairman, was flagrantly anti-semitic in all its utterances; the regular conference, on the other hand, avoided anti-semitism. Although the insurgents decided to meet again in Washington, D. C., on October 15 and 16, somehow this meeting never materialized.

Several points regarding even the regular conference should be cleared up. Where did the Reverend Nollner obtain the generous financial backing? The expenses of all conferees were paid in cash, no questions asked. Equally interesting is the way Major A. Lloyd Gill, Hearst representative, seemed to be running the conference and the fact that it received considerable publicity space in the Hearst papers but was ignored elsewhere. Incidentally, Gill was closely connected with Myers Y. Cooper, former Ohio governor; the latter was an assistant to John R. Hamilton, the Chairman of the Republican National Committee.

The third effort towards a united front—the American Christian Conference held in Kansas City in August 1937—was an insignificant affair. The meeting was called by the American Nationalist Confederation, an organization which described itself pompously as "a coalition of Christian Anti-Communist Organizations" but which consisted chiefly of its director, George B. Deatherage. Although the heads of almost all anti-semitic organizations were invited, few attended. A possible explanation might be the fact that Kansas City is the home of the Reverend L. M. Birkhead's Friends of Democracy, a group that has as one of its objectives the exposure of anti-semitic activity. Anti-semitic leaders knew that they could be carefully watched. At the first session of the conference, messages were read from Robert B. Edmondson, M. L. Flowers (Winrod's office manager), and Colonel E. N. Sanctuary. Fritz Kuhn also wrote, expressing regret that he could not be present and asserting confidently, "God is with us." The conference ended without plans for a future meeting or steps toward a united front.[1]

In brief, the anti-semitic groups have shown no sign of willingness to abandon their separate operations and unite in one effective organization under a central command. This does not mean, however, that these groups do not cooperate. Their cooperation takes many forms. The most common is the distribution of each other's literature. For example, the New York local of the German-American Bund has distributed Pelley's Silver Shirt literature; the Industrial Defense Association, Winrod's pamphlet, *The Hidden Hand;* the Order of '76, Edmondson's material; and Pelley, Jung, and the Bund, The Paul Reveres' booklet, *The Plan in Action.* Frequently, the publication of one group has carried articles written by the leader of another group, *e.g.,* James True's series of articles in Winrod's *Revealer* and in the *Deutscher Weckruf und Beobachter* of the Bund.

A UNITED FRONT?

Anti-semitic organizations have frequently supplied one another with speakers and officials. For instance, a prominent member of The Paul Reveres, Major John L. Griffith, addressed a meeting sponsored by the American Vigilant Intelligence Federation. On several occasions Edmondson has addressed Bund meetings. Harry Jung has been on the directorate of Edward Hunter's Industrial Defense Association, and Colonel Sanctuary on that of The Paul Reveres.

In their survey of Bund activities on the Pacific coast, *Chicago Times* reporters obtained statements from Bund members indicating cooperation with the Silver Shirts: "We get some support from the Silver Shirts"[2] and "the Silver Shirts are with us."[3] In at least two instances, the Bund and the Silver Shirts have held joint meetings:[4] one in Chicago, one in Los Angeles.

That the anti-semitic leaders have met one another and know one another personally is implicit in the evidence of the various forms of cooperation. In fact, their leaders have openly acknowledged their friendship. Pelley has called True, Edmondson, Winrod, Jung, Sanctuary, and others his "co-workers," stating, "I know these men personally. With the exception of Winrod I have talked with them in private."[5] Hunter, in addition to boasting of fraternizing with True and Edmondson, has asserted that he has been in touch with "every patriotic group in the United States."[6] Similar instances abound. When Fritz Spanknoebel, first fuhrer of the Bund, was in legal difficulties, he asked Royal Scott Gulden, head of the Order of '76, to recommend a lawyer.[7] Colonel Sanctuary has referred to "my friend Edmondson."[8] Colonel Hadley and Harry Jung came together at the meetings of the Military Intelligence Association to discuss such joint projects as a radio program. When Edmondson was being sued for libel against the Jews, Harry Jung and Colonel Sanctuary contributed to his "defense fund";[9] the leaders of the New York Bund even permitted Edmondson to use Bund property for fund-raising rallies. Winrod, on his way home from Europe, stopped in to confer with True;[10] and once Fritz Kuhn had a long talk with Pelley in Los Angeles. Then too, the anti-semitic leaders, through their publications, have indulged in mutual popularization and admiration. Winrod's *Defender* flattered Harry Jung with the statement: "Few men are more feared by the despoilers than this great leader."[11] Edmondson in one of his reports quoted Winrod's *Defender* approvingly,[12] and Pelley in his *Liberation*, has done the same with regard to the *Deutscher Weckruf und Beobachter* of the Bund.[13] James True, the most generous of all in his recommendations, declared in his *Industrial Control Report*, "Every businessman in the country should read the special 'LaFollette Edition' of *Liberation*."[14]

The foregoing facts do not, of course, cover all instances of cooperation between anti-semitic organizations; they merely indicate a few examples of the sort of cooperation involved. Why has cooperation been so limited? Why has it not been extended to include an effective united front? Perhaps because the leaders (except Father Coughlin, Colonel Hadley, and Colonel Sanctuary) make their bread and butter through their organizations and sense in a united front not only a threat to their independent solicitation and use of funds but a possibility of losing their employment. These facts do not necessarily question the sincerity of the leaders, inasmuch as the need for making a living often leads to rivalry rather than cooperation. That rivalry does exist is indicated by a letter written by Mrs. Estelle Barnard of Grand Rapids, Michigan. She describes a meeting of the American Vigilant Intelligence Federation addressed by field representative, Peter Armstrong, alias Prince Kushubue: [15]

> After the meeting I went up to Mr. Armstrong who greeted me hopefully. I told him I was sorry I could not afford to belong to both organizations but that I am doing the same work as I am a Silver Shirt. He made a grimace. . . .
> After a little more conversation, Mr. Shera butted in, evidently afraid I was going to win the Prince over to *Liberation*. Mr. Shera says that once while in Harry Jung's office, Mr. Pelley claimed that he was the Messiah and he seems to class Mr. Pelley with all the other frauds. Over the phone . . . he maligns the leaders of the Silver Shirts. I wonder if Mr. Jung isn't afraid Mr. Pelley may "steal his thunder."

Mrs. Barnard appraised the situation accurately. Jung feared that the Silver Shirts might steal not only "his thunder" but—more importantly—his financial support in the community. Only a few months earlier, he had written Armstrong that "we have got to be getting some financial aid from some of these contacts, [in Grand Rapids], or we will be getting nowhere." Pelley also needed the financial support of Grand Rapids. Although Pelley and Jung are anxious to awaken the country to the "Jew-Communist menace," yet, since the country still slumbers, both must compete with each other in order to eat.

Both Pelley and Winrod are rivals not so much in the realm of finances as in the realm of prestige. The Defenders and the Silver Shirts are two of the largest anti-semitic organizations; hence, their leaders become logical candidates for the national directorship of any united front that may be formed. By the same token the two leaders become jealous rivals, for a united front could have only one fuhrer. An insight into this rivalry may be obtained from an article Pelley wrote for the *Liberation* of November 21, 1937:

A UNITED FRONT?

When Gerald B. Winrod made a recent address in Ohio, a group of *Liberation* readers went to him point-blank . . . as to why he did not give more recognition to the work being done by Pelley of the Silver Legion. Winrod is reported to have replied: "I consider that Pelley is doing a great work, but I can't follow him in his religious ideas," obviously referring to Pelley's esoteric researches. So because Brother Winrod can't admit there is any other religious teaching but the Fundamentalism that glorifies the Jewish patriarchs, for the good of the United States he forbears to disclose to his people that a chap named Pelley exists.

Another factor that impedes unity is the presence of a large Catholic, anti-semitic movement headed by a Catholic priest—Father Coughlin and his followers. The leadership and membership of virtually all other anti-semitic groups are Protestant. Hence, it is quite unlikely that these Protestant leaders will ever subordinate themselves and their groups to a Catholic priest and equally unlikely that Coughlin will ever call on his followers to join in a "Christian front" behind a Protestant leader.

CHAPTER XIII

The Operations of 121 Organizations

THE preceding chapters have dealt with 11 anti-semitic organizations—the most important and the most typical of the 121 that have appeared in recent years. This chapter, however, will list all 121 organizations and will comment on the regions and periods that have nurtured all of them.

Although the number of the organizations creates the impression that the country is being engulfed by anti-semitic sentiment, a great proportion of them are far less significant than the short-lived Order of '76 described in Chapter XI. In many instances, an organization flashed into view only once. Such were the cases of the Christian Protective League and the American Gentile Youth Movement; the former in June 1938 circulated a few mimeographed anti-semitic letters in Mobile, Alabama, and about the same time the latter posted an anti-semitic sticker on the window of a Chicago candy store. Nothing else has ever been heard of these two organizations—an indication of their unimportance. Quite possibly the Christian Protective League consists of three gentile tailors who feel that their poor business results from the competition of the one Jewish tailor in the neighborhood. More striking as an example of a "peanut-sized" anti-semitic organization is the National Gentile League, which has a Washington, D. C., address. The pompous name and the address suggest a powerful, nationwide organization. Actually, the League consists of an unemployed and penniless person called Donald Shea, who occasionally finds some anti-semitic sympathizer willing to buy him a decent suit of clothes and to help organize a meeting which Shea can address on behalf of the National Gentile League. The substance of many an anti-semitic group is seldom more than a pretentious name.

The list below consists of groups that are quite definitely anti-semitic. Under the name of each group are noted the location of the headquarters, the date of the first record of existence (a rough estimate of the founding date), and the status in 1940—active, defunct, or doubtful. (The word "doubtful" is applied to those groups of which nothing has been heard of recently, yet of which there is no proof of dissolution.) In some instances, complete information is not available.

The A-C Society,
St. Albans, W. Va.
1938
Active

Advisory Associates,
Chicago. Ill.
1934
Defunct (1935)

America First, Inc.,
Washington, D. C.
1934
Defunct (1936)

America in Danger
Omaha, Nebr.
1936
Active

American Aryan Folk Association,
Portland, Ore.
1937
Active

American Blue Corps,
Sharon, Pa.
1933
Defunct (1934)

American Cavalcade,
Washington, D. C.
1938
Active

American Christian Defenders,
New York City
1934
Active

American Defenders,
Coral Gables, Fla.
1934
Active

American Eagle Association, Inc.,
Chicago, Ill.
1934, 1936, 1939
Active

American Fascisti (alias Order of
  Blackshirts),
Atlanta, Ga.
1934
Doubtful

American Fascists (alias Khaki Shirts
  of America),
Philadelphia, Pa.
1932
Defunct (1933)

American Federation of Youth,
Chicago, Ill.
1939
Active

American Gentile Protective Association,
Chicago, Ill.
1937
Active

American Gentile Youth Movement,
Chicago, Ill.
1938
Doubtful

American-German Bund,
New York City
1933
Active

American Guards,
Chicago, Ill.
1938
Active

American Italian Union,
St. Louis, Mo.
1937
Active

American Labor Party,
Los Angeles, Calif.
1934
Defunct (1934)

American League Against International Jewry
1937
Doubtful

American League of Christian Women,
Pacific Coast
1937
Doubtful

American National Labor Party,
New York City
1935
Active

American National Political Action
  Club,
Chicago, Ill.
1936
Active

American National Socialist League,
New York City
1935
Defunct (1936)

American Nationalist Confederation,
St. Albans, W. Va.
Active

American Nationalist Party,
Los Angeles, Calif.
1934
Active

American Nationalists, Inc.,
New York City
1935
Defunct (1936)

American Patriots, Inc.,
Greenwich, Conn.
1938
Active

American Patriots Association,
Terra Haute, Ind.
1936
Active

American Peoples Party,
Chicago, Ill.
Doubtful

American Rangers,
Beverly Hills, Calif.
Chicago
1938
Active

American School of Christian Democracy,
Kansas City, Mo.
1937
Doubtful

American Science Foundation,
Chicago, Ill.
1938
Active

American Vigilant Intelligence Federation
Chicago, Ill.
1927
Active

American White Guardsmen,
Pasadena, Calif.
1936
Doubtful

American Workers Progressive Club,
New York City
Defunct (1936)

Anti-Communist League,
Philadelphia, Pa.
1936
Active

Anti-Communist League of America,
1931
Doubtful

Anti-Communist League of the World,
Pacific Northwest
1934
Defunct (1935)

Anti-Jewish League to Protect American Rights,
New York City
1937
Active

Arab Nationalist Party,
New York City
1936
Active

Aryan League of America,
New Orleans, La.
1938
Active

Association of American Gentiles,
Chicago, Ill.
1938
Active

Association of Leagues.
Cleveland, O.
1937
Doubtful

The Awakeners,
Highland-on-Hudson, N. Y.
1936
Defunct (1937)

Benjamin Franklin Society,
Waukegan, Ill.
1934
Doubtful

Black Legion,
Detroit, Mich.
1936
Active

Black Shirts,
Tacoma, Wash.
Baltimore, Md.
Union City, N. J.
1936
Active

Brotherhood of Builders of Business,
Chicago, Ill.
1936
Active

Casa Italiana,
New York City
1939
Active

Christian American Crusade,
Los Angeles, Calif.
1935
Active

Christian Constitutionalist Party,
San Francisco, Calif.
1937
Doubtful

Christian Democrats,
Dallas, Tex.
1935
Defunct (1937)

Christian Front,
New York City
1938
Active

Christian Mobilizers,
New York City
1939
Active

Christian Protective League,
Mobile, Ala.
1938
Doubtful

Christian Vigilantes,
Minneapolis, Minn.
1935
Defunct (1936)

Circolo Mario Morgantini,
New York City
1938
Active

Citizens Protective League,
New York City
1937
Active

Civil Intelligence Bureau,
Shavertown, Pa.
Active

Civilian Army of American Bluecoats,
Inc.,
Los Angeles, Calif.
1936
Doubtful

Committee of One Million,
New York City
1937
Active

Common Cause League,
New York City
1938
Active

Constitutional Legion of America,
Los Angeles, Calif.
1935
Defunct (1936)

Crusader White Shirts (after 1936, Crusaders for Economic Liberty),
Chattanooga, Tenn.
1933
Active

Defenders of the Christian Faith,
Wichita, Kans.
1933
Active

Deutsche-Americanischer Heimatsauschuss,
1938
Active

Deutscher Konsum Verband,
New York City
Philadelphia, Pa.
Chicago, Ill.
1935
Active

Edmondson Economic Service,
New York City
1934
Active

Father Duffy's Cadets,
New York City
1939
Active

Friends and Neighbors, Inc.,
Toledo, O.
1938
Active

Friends of Germany,
New York City
1933
Defunct (1934)

Gentile Improvement Association,
Terre Haute, Ind.
1939
Active

Gentile Workers Party of America,
Chicago, Ill.
1939
Active

Grand Lodge of the Mystic Legion,
Houston, Tex.
1935
Doubtful

The Homesteaders,
Fresno, Calif.
1933
Defunct (1934)

Industrial Defense Association,
Boston, Mass.
1924
Active

International Brotherhood, Inc.,
Chicago, Ill.
1939
Active

International Committeee to Combat
the World Menace of Communism,
New York City
1934
Active

International Legion Against
Communism,
New York City
1937
Active

James True Associates,
Washington, D. C.
1933
Active

Knights of the White Camellia,
Charleston, W. Va.
1936
Defunct (1936)

Knights Vigilante,
Washington, D. C.
1934
Doubtful

Ku Klux Klan,
Atlanta, Ga.
1915
Active

League of War Veterans' Guardsmen,
Tacoma, Wash.
1937
Doubtful

League of Young Russia,
New York City (the Bronx)
1934
Active

Loyal Aryan Christian Citizenship
Organization of the United States,
Pacific Coast
1934
Defunct (1936)

Militant Christian Association,
Charleston, S. C.
1936
Defunct (1936)

Militant Christian Patriots,
Glendale, Calif.
1936
Active

The Musketeers,
San Francisco, Calif.
1937
Active

National Blue Shirts of America,
Cumberland, Md.
1938
Active

National Christian Patriots,
Los Angeles, Calif.
1937
Active

National Citizens League of America,
Miami, Fla.
1937
Defunct (1937)

National Defenders of '76,
New York City
1937
Defunct (1938)

National Gentile League,
Washington, D. C.
1936
Active

National Liberty Party,
Tacoma, Wash.
1938
Active

National Protective Order of Gentiles,
Los Angeles, Calif.
1937
Defunct (1938)

National Socialist Workers Party
of America,
New York City
1935
Defunct (1936)

National Union for Social Justice,
Royal Oak, Mich.
1934
Active

Order of '76
New York City
1933
Defunct (1937)

Pan-Aryan Alliance,
New York City
1935
Doubtful

Patriot Guard of America, Inc.
Washington, D. C.
1937
Active

Patriotic Research Bureau,
Chicago, Ill.
1938
Active

Prayer League of America,
Chicago, Ill.
1939
Active

Pro-Christian American Society,
Minnesota (state)
1936
Doubtful

Protective League of America,
Milwaukee, Wis.
1938
Doubtful

Protestant Voters League,
Terre Haute, Ind.
1938
Active

Protestant War Veterans Association,
Kansas City, Mo.
1938
Active

Russian National Revolutionary
Party (White Guard Russians),
Putnam, Conn.
1935
Active

Secret Fifty-Three,
San Antonio, Tex.
1934
Doubtful

Silver Shirts,
Asheville, N. C.
1933
Active

Sons of the South,
Cleveland, O.; Detroit, Mich.
1938
Active

The Tomahawks,
Walla Walla, Wash.
1937
Active

Uncle Sam's Club,
Bismarck, N. Dak.
1938
Active

United American Patriots,
Terre Haute, Ind.
1937
Doubtful

United Guards of America,
Baltimore, Md.
1934
Defunct (1935)

White Band, Inc.,
Atlanta, Ga.
1927
Active

The White Front,
Coral Gables, Fla.
1939
Active

White Shirts,
Virginia, Minn.
1938
Active

World Alliance Against Jewish
 Aggressiveness,
New York City
1934
Active

World War Gratuities Bureau,
Chicago, Ill.
1935
Active

The preceding data provide the basis for certain observations on the regions in which most of anti-semitic groups have their headquarters and on the years in which these groups came into existence. The number of groups in any region is meaningful only in comparison to the population of that region. Table 7 makes this comparison in terms of percentages to the total number of groups and to the total population of the country.

Table 7

REGIONAL DISTRIBUTION OF ANTI-SEMITIC ORGANIZATIONS

Region (U. S. Census)	Number of Organizations	Percent of Total Organizations	Percent of Total U. S. Population
New England.................. (Mass., Conn., R. I., N. H., Vt., Me.)	4	3.4	6.7
Middle Atlantic............... (N. Y., N. J., Pa.)	35	29.	21.4
East North Central............ (Ohio, Ind., Ill., Mich., Wis.)	26	21.8	20.6
West North Central............ (Minn., Iowa, Mo., Neb., N. Dak., S. Dak., Kans.)	9	7.6	10.8
South Atlantic................. (Del., Md., D. C., W. Va., N. C., S. C., Ga., Fla., Va.)	19	16.	12.9
East South Central............ (Ky., Tenn., Ala., Miss.)	2	1.6	8.1
West South Central............ (Ark., La., Okla., Tex.)	4	3.4	9.9
Mountain..................... (Mont., Wyo., Utah, Idaho, Nev., Colo., Ariz., N. Mex.)	0	0	3.0
Pacific Coast.................. (Calif., Oreg., Wash.)	20	16.8	6.7

The two regions that, in proportion to population, have the greatest number of anti-semitic organizations are the Middle Atlantic States and the Pacific Coast. The former has only 21.4 percent of the total population of the country, but 29 percent of the organizations; the latter has only 6.7 percent of the population, but 16.8 percent of the organizations.

Equally interesting is the data for the South. By totaling the percentages for the South Atlantic, West South Central, and the East South Central regions, one finds that these regions represent 30.9 percent of the nation's population and 21 percent of the anti-semitic groups. The percent of the population, however, must be corrected to exclude that of the Negro in order to make any inferences from the comparison valid. In that event, the comparison reads 22.5 percent of the total population to 21 percent of the total groups and so suggests that the South, the stronghold of the Ku Klux Klan, does not have a disproportionate number of anti-semitic groups.

Table 8 gives the geographical distribution of anti-semitic groups according to the cities in which they have their headquarters. The largest cities in the country have correspondingly the largest number of such headquarters. New York has 26; Chicago has 18.

Table 8

CITIES IN WHICH 118 ANTI-SEMITIC ORGANIZATIONS HAVE THEIR HEADQUARTERS

Asheville, N. C.	1	Minneapolis, Minn.	1
Atlanta, Ga.	3	Mobile, Ala.	1
Baltimore, Md.	1	New Orleans, La.	1
Beverley Hills, Calif.	1	New York, N. Y.	26
Bismarck, N. Dak.	1	Omaha, Nebr.	1
Boston, Mass.	1	Pacific Coast [1]	3
Charleston, S. C.	1	Pasadena, Calif.	1
Charleston, W. Va.	1	Philadelphia, Pa.	2
Chattanooga, Tenn.	1	Portland, Oreg.	1
Chicago, Illinois	18	Putnam, Conn.	1
Cleveland, Ohio	1	Royal Oak, Mich.	1
Coral Gables, Fla.	2	St. Albans, W. Va.	2
Cumberland, Md.	1	St. Louis, Mo.	1
Dallas, Tex.	1	San Antonio, Tex.	1
Detroit, Mich.	1	San Francisco, Calif.	2
Fresno, Calif.	1	Sharon, Pa.	1
Glendale, Calif.	1	Shavertown, Pa.	1
Greenwich, Conn.	1	Tacoma, Wash.	2
Highland-on-Hudson, N. Y.	1	Terre Haute, Ind.	6
Houston, Tex.	1	Toledo, Ohio	1
Kansas City, Mo.	2	Virginia, Minn.	1
Los Angeles, Calif.	7	Walla Walla, Wash.	1
Miami, Fla.	1	Washington, D. C.	6
Milwaukee, Wis.	1	Waukegan, Ill.	1
		Wichita, Kans.	1
		Total	118

[1] Although these three organizations operate solely on the Pacific Coast, their exact headquarters are unknown.

Since the approximate founding years for 119 of the 121 anti-semitic organizations are known, a chronological distribution is made in order to reveal any significant groupings. The results are shown in Table 9.

Table 9

CHRONOLOGICAL DISTRIBUTION OF 119 ANTI-SEMITIC ORGANIZATIONS

Year of Founding	Number of Groups
1915	1
1924	1
1927	1
1931	1
1932	1
1933	9
1934	19
1935	13
1936	18
1937	22
1938	24
1939	9
Total	119

Apparently almost all the organizations were formed since 1933. The obvious deduction which follows is that the Nazis' rise to power in Germany in 1933 and the long, severe economic depression of the 1930's in the United States violently spurred the formation of anti-semitic groups. Save for minor American twists, the ideology of these groups is identical with that of the Nazis. Since 1933 the annual number of new groups has, by and large, increased. This significant fact should be noted in any attempt to predict the future of the anti-semitic movement in America, for it suggests that an intransient anti-semitic ideology has taken root.

Although the general trend of the anti-semitic movement in the United States has been upward, severe fluctuations have occurred frequently. Ordinarily, a graphic presentation showing trends of membership enrollments and sales of literature would provide a barometer of fluctuations; but complete statistical information unfortunately is unavailable. Consequently, the curve of the anti-semitic movement can only be drawn verbally. The curve rockets from virtually zero in early 1933 to a high point in the summer of 1934. Falling steadily until the autumn of 1935, it rises again, reaching, just before the 1936 presidential election, almost the level of its highest point. After the election the curve descends abruptly and only in late spring of 1937 does it slowly begin to ascend again. In the autumn of 1938 its ascent increases in rapidity and by 1940 it is above the high level of 1934. The rapid rise in 1933 and 1934 is to a large extent a result of the increased organizing activities of the German-American Bund and the Silver Shirts. The valley between the summer of 1934 and the autumn of 1935 represents an aftermath of the McCormack Committee hearings, which gave unfavorable publicity to the Bund and the Silver Shirts and temporarily discredited the entire anti-semitic movement. From the autumn of 1935 until the 1936 election, most of the anti-semitic groups campaigned actively with the anti-New Deal forces. They presented the New Deal as a part of the "Jewish-revolutionary" conspiracy and worked themselves into a high pitch of activity. After the New Deal's victory at the polls, their activity decreased very pronouncedly. Many groups permanently suspended operations, others did so temporarily. For three months virtually no activity was evident. Then came the proposal to enlarge the Supreme Court and the wave of strikes in 1937—events that increased the insecurity of the middle classes and made them again receptive to anti-semitic propaganda. The business recession of late 1937 and of 1938 further revitalized the Pelleys and the Winrods. In the autumn of 1938, after Father Coughlin adopted anti-semitism, he quickly proselyted a very large Catholic group to his new creed. The anti-semitic movement soon exceeded all previous proportions.

CHAPTER XIV

Propaganda Techniques

THE propaganda of the anti-semitic movement will be treated here as a whole, paying particular attention to four aspects: the channels of distribution, the philosophy, the ultimate goal, and the types of psychological appeal.

The major channels are the newspaper, magazine, pamphlet, leaflet, newsletter, book, radio, and the public meeting. The distinction between the newsletter and the leaflet requires explanation: although both sometimes resemble each other in general appearance, the former usually appears regularly while the latter is quite irregular.

The channel most frequently employed is the pamphlet. Almost all anti-semitic groups have issued one or more pamphlets. For the smaller organizations—particularly the Industrial Defense Association, the American Christian Defenders, the Order of '76, and The Paul Reveres—it is the most important channel. Next in importance are the magazine and the newsletter. Two of the magazines in the field—Winrod's *Defender* and Pelley's *Liberation* (known for a time as *Pelley's Weekly*)—have had large circulations and have been in almost continuous existence for five years or more. Edmondson's reports, James True's *Industrial Control Report*, and Harry Jung's *Items of Interest* and *Vigilante* exemplify the newsletter. Winrod's letters to his "Inner Circle" perhaps fall into this category; they have appeared on an average of about once a month. Pelley once attempted to establish a newsletter service but failed.

Four groups have used newspapers with varying success.

The German-American Bund: *Deutscher Weckruf und Beobachter* and its predecessors.
The National Union for Social Justice (the Christian Front): *Social Justice*.
The Silver Shirts: *The Silver Ranger*.
The Defenders of the Christian Faith: *The Revealer*

Six groups have turned the public meeting to useful account. For the Bund, the Christian Front, and the Silver Shirts it has been of considerable importance. The American Vigilant Intelligence Federation and The Paul Reveres have held meetings occasionally. An interesting variation of the public meeting has been Winrod's Bible conference. As used by Father Coughlin, the radio has reached a larger public than any other channel.

Table 10

CHANNELS OF PROPAGANDA USED BY ANTI-SEMITIC ORGANIZATIONS

Organization	Paper	Magazine	Pamphlet	Leaflet	News-Letter	Public Meeting	Book	Radio	Total
German-American Bund	x		x			x	x	x	5
Silver Shirts	x	x	x		x	x	x	x	6
Defenders of the Christian Faith	x	x	x	x	x	x	x	x	8
Edmondson Economic Service			x		x				2
American Vigilant Intelligence Federation			x		x	x	x		4
Industrial Defense Association			x	x					2
James True Associates			x		x				2
American Christian Defenders			x	x			x		3
Order of '76			x	x					2
The Paul Reveres			x	x		x			3
National Union for Social Justice (Christian Front)	x		x			x	x	x	5

Since anti-semitic groups lack a clear-cut, unified philosophy, it is necessary to use a "piecing together" technique in order to present the ideas embodied in their propaganda as a systematized whole. Fundamental is the idea of a Jewish conspiracy to dominate the world. "Conspiracy" is the key word. Merely to assert that the number of Jewish lawyers in Chicago or of Jewish civil servants in Washington is far in excess of the proportion of Jews to the total population does not imply "conspiracy"; but to interpret such facts as part of a Machiavellian plan to gain control of the United States is definitely an expression of the idea. The original source of this concept is that notorious forgery, *The Protocols of the Elders of Zion,* sometimes known as *The Protocols of the Wise Men of Zion,* first widely circulated by the Russian secret police during the pogroms that followed the Revolution of 1905.[1] This pamphlet, bruited about as a set of agreements drawn up by leading Jews at a secret meeting held about 60 years ago, contains a detailed plan whereby Jews will undermine and destroy Gentile civilization in order to achieve mastery of the world. Although new pamphlets revealing certain contemporaneous events as part of the Jewish conspiracy are continually published, the *Protocols* have remained the basic required reading matter for all anti-semites.

Using the *Protocols* as their starting point, the leaders of the anti-semitic organizations studied usually set forth the following intriguing series of allegations!

Communism is world Jewry in action. Communism is the Jews' weapon for obtaining world domination. The Soviet regime is a Jewish regime, for nine-tenths of the key governmental positions are held by Jews. The original plotters of the Russian Revolution were Jewish intellectuals. Russia represents the model of what the Jews hope to do to all countries and that is why they lead the Communist parties in capitalistic countries. But here in these countries the Jews' control is only slightly less absolute. England is under the heel of the Jewish money power. Republican Germany and France were run by the Jews to suit their pleasure. Had not Hitler come to the rescue and torn the burning fuse from the bomb, the explosion would have occurred and Communism would have been established. The United States under the New Deal is Jew-controlled. Roosevelt is a mere "front," a puppet controlled by such Jews as Felix Frankfurter, Bernard Baruch, and Justice Louis Brandeis. The Jewish Brain Trust really runs the country. Roosevelt himself is of Jewish extraction. He comes from Dutch Jews who originally bore the name "Rosenfeld."

All international bankers are Jews. They are so powerful that they can cause depressions at will. Moreover, they work hand in hand with the Communists. For instance, Jacob Schiff, the American Jew banker, gave Lenin and Trotsky $1,000,000 with which to finance the Russian Revolution. Once the Jewish bankers have caused depressions, the time is ripe for other Jews to circulate strange new theories to confuse and bewilder the people and turn class against class. Thus can the people be eventually persuaded to accept Communism. Frequently the persons who spread these false theories are not themselves Jews but Gentile fronts whom the Jews have duped and whom they use for their own advancement. The Jews, as in every country, have a complete control of the press. They can suppress all news unfavorable to themselves and lull the people into a false sense of security up to the very morning of the Red revolution. Patriotic Christians who see through the plot and want to expose it must establish their own periodicals to counteract the fallacies found in the Jewish dailies.

Jewish craft knows no bounds. One of the most insidious features of the Jewish plot is the corruption of the Gentiles' morals. Gentile youth in particular is to be perverted by early immorality and the use of liquor. Its moral fibre weakened by early sin, this generation will fall easy prey to the Red-Jewish conquerors. The Jews carry out this purpose through their control of the vice, liquor, and dope traffic. They fill art, drama, and the motion picture with sex. Jews absolutely run the motion picture industry and the theatre, and the filthy, sexy output of these two is just part of the plot. Lewd literature and books on birth control that explain to young people how to "get by" can also be traced to the Jews. Soviet Russia is proof of all this. In that Jewish-Communistic state the family has been abolished, women have been nationalized and made the common property of all men, and abortion is legal.

The Jews boost internationalism and pacifism in order to destroy patriotism and preparedness in all countries except Russia. The disarmed countries will then fall easy prey to the Communist revolutior iries at home and the Soviet armies from abroad. Because it is already far advanced, the plot is particularly menacing. Jewish Reds and their Gentile stooges have wormed their way into many American institutions. Red dupes have captured numerous churches and universities. The Federal Council of Churches is definitely Red; revolutionaries hold important positions in the Y.M.C.A. and the Y.W.C.A. The Reds even have their own legal aid organization, the American Civil Liberties Union, whose Jewish lawyers get Communists out of jail when patriots try to convict them. Careful watch must be kept over people who call themselves liberals, for a liberal is really a Communist in disguise. The foreign-born and the Negroes will also bear close watching—the foreign-born because they undoubtedly have brought some revolutionary and un-American ideas with them to this country and the Negroes because the Communists plan to use them as the shock troops of the revolution. The Communists have penetrated labor unions. The C.I.O. is thoroughly Communist; it is one of the outstanding successes of the Reds.

Each anti-semitic leader varies the preceding theme, adding his favorite trills and arpeggios. For instance, Winrod, a Fundamentalist above all else, sees the Jews as the inventors of Modernism and the doctrine of evolution—as the disseminators of these ideas for the sole purpose of undermining the faith of our fathers and preparing the way for Communism.

Anti-semitic propaganda is far more concerned with so-called facts than with demands for action. A meticulous examination of such propaganda uncovers only a melange of calls to militancy. Moreover, such demands as are made are, by and large, of an immediate nature. The anti-semitic movement has no explicit long-term program; it concerns itself primarily with propagandizing against the so-called menace of Jewish Communism.

There follow a number of somewhat specific demands:

No official recognition must be given the criminal nation of Soviet Russia.[2]

One of the most dangerous radicals in American public life today is the Jew, Louis Brandeis, of the United States Supreme Court. Mobilized Christian sentiment should drive him from the bench as quickly as possible.[3]

Buy Gentile! Vote Gentile![4]

Let the various states put on their statute books acts requiring every educator to take an oath of loyalty to the Republic, its Constitution, and the Flag.[5]

Urge your congressional representatives to oppose all anti-gun and registration legislation.

We propose to impose racial quotas on the political and economic structure . . . that no racial factions shall be allowed further expectancy of public or professional office in excess of the ratio of its blood members to the remaining total of all races. . . .

Why shouldn't New York's Gentile majority, defending itself against the Jewish Anti-American subversions herein recited, disfranchise Jewish voters, put them in the class of wards of the nation and segregate Jews as in the case of our Indians?

Cloudy imperatives such as these are apt to be a bit bewildering:

We must sweep out our half-baked radical theorists with whom we have been tolerant too long. We must prevent the approaching Jewish domination and insure Anglo-Saxon supremacy that is free from international control. . .
We must drive from control those organized minorities who are conspiring to overthrow the Republic and the Constitution of the United States of America.[6]
This nation, forthwith, must be purged of its scoundrels.[7]

"Intermediate" demands sometimes specify actions but obscure the recipients of the actions; "Let us deport the radical aliens for whom Madam Perkins . . . has such a fond regard"[8] and "Scoop out the Reds from our United States Senate."[9]

Few of the anti-semitic groups have a long-term program; certainly the groups as a whole do not have a clearly defined goal. They are opposed to an alleged Jewish Communist conspiracy, but precisely what they are working for is obscure. Is the objective Fascism? Three considerations are relevant to an answer for this question.

First, several anti-semitic groups are thoroughly in sympathy with European Fascist dictators. Secondly, in some instances these groups have expressed contempt for democracy, implying that democracy does not really exist in the United States. Finally, William Dudley Pelley, chief of the Silver Shirts, has admitted that his group is Fascist, and his goal, Fascism. Other anti-semitic leaders, however, have guardedly commented on the need for Fascism.

Four leaders have expressed their sympathy for German Fascism. James True has stated that "Germany has proved that its Nazi dictatorship, although repugnant to the Republic of the United States, is honest and national and vastly superior to the Jew-controlled Roosevelt new deal."[10] Robert Edmondson said in an interview with the Reverend L. M. Birkhead: "I believe in the Republican form of government. Of course, I am sensible of the great service that Hitler has rendered to Germany . . . I do not agree with all of the methods that Hitler has used. But you must remember that he had a vicious and unscrupulous foe to fight." Gerald Winrod also told the same clergyman that "I do not approve of everything that Hitler has done . . . but you'll have to admit that Hitler saved Germany from Jewish Communism." Moreover, Winrod in his newspaper dismissed the Nazis' anti-semitic policy in the following manner. "Inasmuch as a great many of the leaders and their followers were of the Jewish race, these Communistic Jews, or Jewish Communists, had to be dealt with in a fashion that was not to their liking. Jewry all over the world immediately swooped down on Germany by perverting the facts into an attack on the Jews . . ." [11] The article continued with an account of how Hitler had purged Germany of nudism, obscene literature, and homosexuality.

Pelley, in keeping with his frank acceptance of Fascism for the United States, has been the most enthusiastic admirer of Hitler. In his official publication *Liberation,* he wrote: "No one who possesses ten cents worth of second hand brains now argues the question as to whether or not Adolf Hitler is the greatest personality in Europe . . . a great leader of the Gentiles has stopped the rapacious advance of predatory Judah in Europe . . . Hitler is the Man who 'led off' on the great insurrection against Jewish ascendency in Europe." [12] In other issues of *Liberation,* recent American visitors to Germany have lauded Hitler's regime. One such panegyric is entitled "Germany, Jew-Purged, Becomes Ideal Country." Other articles in *Liberation* have given warm approval to the program of the Canadian Union of Fascists.

Father Coughlin has compared the democracies unfavorably with the Fascist dictatorships, indicating that the latter had "cured depression and stopped Communism." [13] He has even suggested that America ought to appeal for missionaries from those whom he termed "Christian dictators in other lands".

Anti-semitic groups have at times condemned the democratic process in the United States. Here again Pelley is the most outspoken: "The Jewish Reds uniformly wail thus loudly for the 'preservation of democracy' through congressional rule, because they know they can control such a congress in their own interests . . ." [14] On another occasion he wrote: "Today throughout the country we hear an unholy screech about the 'destruction of democracy' . . . Of course, it is not democracy but mob rule by Jewish representation, deceit, bamboozlement and camouflage." [15] The newspaper of the German-American Bund has questioned whether democracy actually exists in the United States:

> We hear it claimed that the Reichstag blindly approves what Hitler proposes. Since the President has a rubber-stamp Congress, democracy becomes a conception pretty much academic. One fails to be appalled by the gulch supposed to yawn between the German system of cabinet government and the White House system of dictatorship. The distinction shows an ever diminishing rate of disparity. [16]

Sometimes anti-semitic leaders have denied that the American form of government is a democracy. They assert that it is a "republic". This distinction has been made by both Edmondson and Pelley:

> The system of government in the United States is that of a RE-
> PUBLIC—not a Democracy, as the Communist Jews try to propa-
> gandize.[17]
> The Silver Shirts will attempt to restore the American Form of
> government, but it won't be a democracy—it will be Republicanism.
> That this nation is a Democracy, or has ever been a Democracy, is
> mere blatherskite smokescreen. The Silver Shirts will attempt to
> restore a Constitutional Republic. . . .[18]

Father Coughlin has been more flowery in his scorn for democracy:

> Democracy! More honored in the breach than in the observance.
> Democracy! A mockery that mouths the word and obstructs every
> effort on the part of honest people to establish a government for the
> welfare of the people.
> Democracy! A cloak under which hide the culprits who have built
> up an inorganic tumor of government which is sapping away the
> wealth of the citizens through confiscatory taxation.[19]

Fascism as the solution to the evils besetting the country—and, consequently, as the goal of the anti-semitic movement—verges on the
inevitable, according to one of Edmondson's newsletters:

> . . . prompt and broad education is the only way to action and
> results. Small, compact, militant political groups have achieved
> emancipation in Germany, Italy, and Roumania. It can also be done
> in America. "Let the people know the truth—and the country is
> safe."
> Unless Saving Leadership is welcomed, Civil War and Fascistic
> Dictatorship may be inevitable.[20]

The Silver Shirts have gone farther than Edmondson, although they
have at times shied from the label of "Fascist". Immediately after
Roosevelt's reelection in 1936, Pelley wrote:

> "Fascism," if you please, will now make its appearance openly in
> the United States as a result of what the Ash'Kanazi Tammanyites
> wrought technically throughout the nation on the past November
> 3d! . . . .
> Is it not unthinkable that the rest of the earth should arise and put
> down Jew-Communist "Democracy" and America remain the only
> country wherein it survives. . . .
> America must join the trend toward Fascism as a matter of world
> momentum. . . .[21]

In another issue of his paper Pelley expressed the same point of
view:

> It is not a question as to whether or not the United States *wants*
> to go in for Fascism, the question will be, if she doesn't go in for
> Fascism, she must openly espouse and shed her blood for Bol-
> shevism. . . .
> It is something to prepare for, *the certainty of Fascism in the
> United States, if for no other reason than world inertia!*
> We are moving toward Fascism in Seven League Boots! [22]

Pelley's attitude toward detractors who dub him "Fascist" has been the indignant, ambiguous "call me Fascist if you like."

> So when Christian preachers write the Chief of the Silver Shirts as to how far he endorses or approximates Fascism, his answer is blunt—
> He doesn't give the kippered tail of a *gveltefische* what sort of wordy smokescreen the despoilers of America apply to their opponents! This nation, forthwith, must be purged of its scoundrels.
> If the scoundrels say that men who love their homes and traditions, who want to see their country grow and prosper, cannot oppose them without having the tag of some foreign governmental system slapped upon their efforts——all of it is twaddle in the necessity for the effort.
> The Reds and the Jews—can call the Christian Silver Shirts Fascists, Nazis, Esquimau, or Hottentots—or plain angry Americans battling for their firesides.[23]

In other issues of his magazine Pelley has stated:

> The man who can make himself heard above the angered roar of that vast drove of sterling Americans in that hour and who has the Plan and the spine to take hold of an utterly bankrupted, looted, and stricken concern that is the United States as a nation, will be the Boss and fulfill his destined place in history—call his regime Fascism, Naziism, Constitutional Protectorate, Organization for the Relief of One-Armed Bill Posters. . . .[24]
> Whoever says I am scheming to alter the American form of government—to Fascism, Naziism, or any other form of "ism" is a Strategizing Prevaricator working secretly for Communism or Communistic Jews.[25]

Pelley's altercations over the epithet "Fascist" appears to be a tempest in a teapot. More important are his methods for liberating America. On a number of occasions he has frankly acknowledged the necessity for violence. His references to this necessity began shortly after Hitler came to power in 1933:

> America may undergo a brief bath of violence. . . . But it will be the same cleansing bath that awakened Italy, that awakened Hungary, that awakened Spain, that awakened Germany. It will awaken thousands of Americans to a realization of the menace.[26]

For several years thereafter Pelley kept quiet on the matter of violence. After the Presidential election of 1936, however, he became quite loquacious:

> Let us understand thoroughly that if a second civil war comes to this country, it will not be a war to overthrow the American government, but to overthrow the Jew-Communist usurpers who have seized the American government and bethought themselves to make it a branch office of Moscow. . . .[27]

> Bolshevism has eventually lost in every country where it has been attempted. It will eventually lose out in the United States, but frankly I should add, *not before the undisciplined American has run riot in mob spirit and slaughtered Jews wholesale in history's greatest pogrom.*[28]

In the spring of 1938, Pelley's magazine reprinted part of an anti-New Deal editorial that had appeared in the *Deutsche Allsmeine* (a newspaper published in Germany), and voiced the "hope that the American house will soon be put in order." Pelley then commented:

> . . . the editor [of the German newspaper] added this final dry remark, which carries significance to those versed in the fundamentals of the political and economic situation of the United States: *"What means are employed is not our affair."* And we take the liberty—and pleasure—of supplying the emphasis.[29]

In June of the same year Pelley stressed the country's need for a dictator:

> Now, if ever, the Sons of Jacob must take a last desperate gamble and find out if they can actually seize the government of the country before the vigilante storm breaks and a major part of the 7,000,000 Yiddishers who have managed to get into this country over the past ten years are slated for deportation—or worse. . . .[30]
>
> Sooner or later, when the country is quivering and absolutely supine, a strong leader must arise who shovels out the burglars by strong-arm expedients.
>
> If such a leader does not arise, if he does not succeed in putting the Jewish Reds in their places, the nation . . . is to be known as the United States of Soviet America.
>
> To oppose such a colossal sabotage, to make such shoveling effective, to reestablish orderly government and industrial prosperity, civic aphorisms are but silly. Someone must *do* the job and talk the ethics of it afterward.
>
> The Jewish Red beclouds the issue—purposely—by screaming that this is Fascism.[31]

William Zachery, "Field Marshal" of the Silver Shirts, has been as unequivocal in his advocacy of violence as his chief. Addressing a group in Chicago, he said:

> We will stop Communism by force. It cannot be voted out. . . .
>
> Ballots are not now stopping Communism in Spain. And ballots will not stop Communism in America. I want all of you to go out and get your silver shirts as quickly as possible. I want all of you to go out and get guns, and I want each of you to get plenty of ammunition. . . .
>
> So I warn you again to get your shirts quickly, and arm yourselves with guns and ammunition.

Not only has Pelley accepted the necessity of violence, but, hewing close to the historical pattern of Hitlerism, he has asserted that the big industrialists must finance American Fascism:

> The thing resolves itself down to this hardheaded equation: *What* leadership is going to do the same thing for these United States that has been realized by the industrialists of Germany, and how is that leadership going to capture and hold the sponsorship attention of the only caste in the American scene that can raise it to power at the Functioning Top: the sizable industrial elements that still possess the affluence to make such leadership effective.[32]

According to Pelley, American Fascism would reward the industrialists for their support as its German prototype did:

> "There is no such thing as any C.I.O. in the German steel industry. All that voracious Red nonsense has been squelched to stay squelched." [33]

He then referred to himself as "the likeliest candidate for a similar induction of affairs in the United States." In another issue of his magazine, Pelley described the Hitler-like fate awaiting his political enemies.

> More than all else, a Silvershirt Regime—call it Fascist, Nazi, Populist, or Mugwump—will make rigorously certain that alien despoilers are forthwith defranchised, their leaders lodged in Federal penitentiaries, and the scum of their evil reasoning scoured from screen and press.[34]

Silver Shirt leaders are not the only anti-semites who foresee incipient Fascist violence in the United States. James True has stated:

> Urge your congressional representatives to oppose all anti-gun and registration legislation. Remember that the Constitution gives all United States citizens the right to bear arms, and unless all signs fail we shall need that right.[35]

After police had prevented Edmondson from addressing a meeting of the American Nationalist Party at Englewood, New Jersey, he wrote the following description of the crowd's reaction:

> But the Vigilante Spirit which will save America was there. Milling around, muttering angrily, crowds of individual Americans from two states needed but a spark to explode in anti-alien patriotic wrath. Law and order prevailed but tension was taut! [36]

Father Coughlin has suggested the possible need of "the Franco way" and has enjoined his followers to "meet force with force as a last resort." [37] The leaders of groups making up the Christian Front echo Coughlin's words. Joseph McWilliams has stated that he would not stand for a situation "like the one in Spain before the Civil War. If we can find no other way, we may have to do it as Father Coughlin suggested—under a Franco." [38] Some of Coughlin's organizers seem to relish the prospect of violence. George Van Nosdall, for instance, told a Christian Front meeting, "Boys, we are going to work. I am ready to line the God-damned Jews right up against the wall." [39] At another meeting of the Front he shouted: "When we get through with the Jews in America they will think the treatment they received in Germany was nothing . . . Judaistic gore will soon flow in the streets of New York City." [40] Edmond Westfall even instructed a Christian Front audience: "When you are in a crowd yell 'Kill the Jew.' " [41]

The German-American Bund not only predicts bloodshed in America but urges its adherents to be ready to fight for Fascism. In a lecture to the *Ordnungs Dienst* of the Astoria, New York Bund local Herman Schwartzmann declared:

> I tell you that exactly what happened in Germany some years ago is now happening in this country. The Jews are grabbing control of everything they can lay their sticky hands on. This is exactly what took place in Germany. Finally the people rose up in resentment. This will happen here—it is inevitable. When that day comes, and it probably is not far off, we must be prepared to fight for the right kind of government. We must win the masses, the good people to our side.
>
> There will likely be bloodshed and fighting. We shall have to do our part. [42]

Such statements have been frequent according to a *Chicago Times* reporter who was for a time a Bund member: "Again and again at drill meetings and lecture sessions members are told they must be ready for 'any emergency'. They must study and learn the duties of a *Fuehrer*, since all members of the presently composed compact group of O.D.'s expect to be *Fuehrers* in their own right "when the trouble comes".[43] Fritz Kuhn himself told a United Press correspondent that "we are waiting for the communists to start something. It will come sooner than you think. Then we will step in and stop them." [44]

In summary, only the Silver Shirts are openly working towards the establishment of Fascism in America. Occasionally other groups comment approvingly on Fascist methods and principles. On the whole, however, the implicit, ultimate goal of the anti-semitic movement does not appear to be Fascism—as yet.

TYPES OF PSYCHOLOGICAL APPEALS

Successful propaganda is based on the astute handling of emotions of aggressiveness, guilt, weakness, and affection.[45] Before the effectiveness of anti-semitic propaganda can be determined, it is necessary to analyze the appeals made to these four emotions.

PROPAGANDA TECHNIQUES

The psychological problem involved in appealing to aggressiveness is that of releasing inhibitions placed on assertive impulses; the propaganda must present the enemy as so menacing and insolent that hating him wholeheartedly appears justifiable. The following subtitles and excerpts from anti-semitic literature are examples of how aggressiveness is provoked:

Minnesota Close to Red Abyss as Murder Terrorizes Voters.

Insolent Poetry Shows Jew Plot; Jews Gloat over Their Protocolian Schemes in Denmark.

Dictator for America Looms; Reds Concentrating Energies behind Pro-Jewish Despot.

A death list of the enemies of Jewish Bolshevism exists in the United States.

Over seven million Ashkenazic Jews have been inducted into this country in the past ten years.

The Jewish population in the United States is growing. . . . There is, therefore, every evidence to indicate . . . that the High Control of World Jewry has designated the United States in particular . . . as the next area to be brought into complete Jewish Bolshevik control.

Communism has been given the right of way by the administration. . . . Deportation of thousands of aliens, many of them criminals, has been prevented to increase the power of radical labor.

The C.I.O. has about completed the rebuilding of the old University Club here for its headquarters. . . . One who carefully inspected the job said that the partitions were lined with thick steel and furnished with bullet-proof glass one and one-half inches thick.

A Jewish Antichrist . . . presupposes an international system of Jewish government. There can be little doubt that such a system, based upon the Jewish Money Power, has already been created—and is ready to step out into the open and assume control of affairs as soon as the time is ripe.

By presenting an enemy as unscrupulous, defiant of sexual mores, and fiendishly cunning in plotting, anti-semitic propaganda may divert any emotional stress of guilt suffered by its readers.

"Lie and Live" is the accepted slogan of the Yiddishers.

The churches of America were recently compelled to boycott the flood of "indecent movies" . . . Jews dominate this industry.

Undoubtedly through political trading (with the New Deal administration of Arkansas) Commonwealth College, a training school for communist agitators, has been allowed to flourish at Mena, Arkansas, for a number of years . . . free love and promiscuity were practiced at the college, where an unspeakable condition existed.

Have not our readers noted that whenever there are any dope and white slave traffic rings uncovered, we always find the Jews the directing master minds behind the scenes?

Press report from Riverside, California: An astounding interracial community of sixty-five boys and girls from twelve to twenty years old, believed to be a Communist camp, was raided today by Sheriff

Carl F. Rayburn. The camp, assertedly for "underprivileged" children, was in charge of four negro men and a Russian Jewess, with another white woman living intimately with the negroes.

. . . a small group of men, all of them Jews, are deliberately and systematically forcing immoral songs, vicious movies, filthy musical comedies and indecent dancing upon the country, spending hundreds of thousands of dollars in the effort and reaping as their reward millions of dollars in profits.

The enemy, diabolical in its violation of the mores, is depicted craftily in *Liberation*. Discussing the widespread publicity given to the recent federal anti-syphilis campaign and to the Illinois law requiring Wassermann tests of all applicants for marriage licenses, the magazine concluded:

Judging from other Jewish New Deal governmental agencies set up, we know that the various administrative boards would be packed with Jews, all of which leads to the logical conclusion that this entire scheme is one leading up to the wholesale inoculation of Gentiles with vaccine syphilitic germs.[46]

Effective propaganda must counteract the individual's feeling of weakness. A simple method is to emphasize victories in order to make adherents feel part of a victorious army instead of a single weak individual. There is tonic for the ego in such statements:

Heavy Meetings in Washington State; Christian Party Work makes Big Headway.

Washington Goes into Action. Christian Party Covering State.

In all parts of the United States, the children of God are starting on the march, to the tune of "Onward Christian Soldiers."

Anti-semitic feeling runs higher in this nation than it has ever run. . . .

When immediate victories are few, anti-semitic propaganda asserts that ultimate victory is assured or that irresistible forces are working for ultimate victory:

Both the Bible and the Great Pyramid foretell that the United States is to be rescued from the hands of the alien.

. . . in obedience to Divine Prophecy bring the Christ Democracy into effect.

A clairvoyant child in Tennessee, who knows nothing of the Silver Shirts, has been insistent to her parents since 1934, that "Mr. Pelley follows Roosevelt!" and has given extraordinary apt details concerning a Red dictator who lasts a matter of days, in between the two men.

Conversely, the illusion of strength may be heightened by verbally reducing the enemy to a state of weakness, making him appear frightened and confused:

B'nai B'rith Making Desperate Effort to Combat Pelley Men
The Jews have been hysterically expressing their fear that Pelley
would obtain "ample financial backing" for the Silver Legion's program.
Is it not becoming increasingly clear that the Jews are in full retreat on all fronts?

Successful propaganda plays upon the emotion of affection by building up the concept of "The Leader". The method most frequently used
is that of publicizing "The Leader" as completely unselfish—as a man
who has abandoned personal gain and comfort to work for the salva-
tion of his country. Qualms of modesty seem rare as evidenced by the
fact that many leaders of anti-semitic groups do not hesitate to laud
their own virtues. Edmondson, for instance, writes:

. . . my position, namely that of a $50,000-a-year executive who
has given up his regular business to unselfishly devote all his time,
money, and ability to a crusade whose aim is the liberation of America from an alien politico-economic-publicity subversion. . . .
My documentary record of a desperate two-year selfless attempt to
peacefully enlighten. . . . I will say to you that I consider any
sacrifice justified to redeem Washington and Lincoln's Representative
Government. . . .[47]

James True tells a similar story:

After the new deal got under way, the undersigned refused to join
in the propaganda ballyhoo. Because he insisted on writing facts and
pointing out economic fallacies, newspapers and business magazines
refused to publish his articles for the first time in his life. Then, because he was convinced that the truth was indispensable to business
interests, he began publication of the reports.
He was assured of adequate financial support for two years; but it
did not materialize. About that time, although the writer did the
work of several men, the venture was precarious and was continued
as a patriotic duty. Then the writer sold his property at a great
sacrifice, and invested the return in the publication and the subsequent meagre living of his family.[48]

Pelley is more laconic in presenting himself as worthy of admiration.
He states that "Pelley can't be intimidated, he can't be bought . . ."[49]
Another psychological problem confronting anti-semitic propagandists arises from the fact that, indulging in unrestrained expressions of
hatred for the Jews and revolutionaries, they occasionally make demands counter to the mores. In deference to their supporters' collective
conscience, the propagandists must provide moral justifications for
their hates and demands. The justification most often used is self-
defense against the "Red-Jew menace". The Silver Shirts have adroitly
embodied it in their demand that the Jews be "wholly disfranchised

and if necessary expropriated, that they may no longer work in our midst mischievously." Edmondson has used the same type of appeal:

> In consideration of the foregoing for the "Safety of the State," why shouldn't New York's Gentile majority, defending itself against the Jewish Anti-American subversions herein recited, disfranchise Jewish voters, put them in the class of wards of the nation and segregate Jews as in the case of our Indians?

Father Coughlin has appreciated the problem of conscience. He handled it with great skill when he told his radio audience:

> Nevertheless the Christian way is the peaceful way until—until—until all argument having failed, all civil authority having failed, there is left no other way but the way of defending ourselves against the invaders of our spiritual and national rights, the Franco way. And when your rights have been challenged, when all civil authority has succumbed before the invaders, then and only then may Christians meet force with force.

Pelley has frequently run into the problem of conscience in connection with his advocacy of an American Fascism. The appeal of self-defense again is his solution:

> The cunning despoilers from overseas bethought them to commit the Greatest Crime in History. If men of principle rise up to halt them they are entirely within their rights. The Moral Law comes before academic blither. . . .

> The Silver Shirts of America have a peculiar job to do. . . . But they refuse to be beguiled, and will not enter into academic brawls, as to whether names applied to them stack up with one-time American conditions. The United States is either going to be a happy, wholesome, prosperous nation for the people of Christian aspirations to live in, or it is crashing down presently beneath the heel of Jewish Bolshevism.

> It never seems to dawn on the squeamishness of civic purists that the United States of America stands on the brink of losing its government, anyhow.
> . . . the fact is lost sight of, that most of our liberties have been quashed and killed already.

In short, the "Red-Jew menace" is presented as so immediate and overwhelming that certain mores and inhibitions of conscience must be abandoned at once or the country will perish.

Anti-semitic leaders employ another method for buttressing their followers' conscience: they rally the ghosts of the great as supporters of anti-semitism. For instance, Pelley reprinted from the *Deutscher Weckruf und Beobachter* a list of fifty famous persons who, it was alleged, were Jew-baiters in their day.[50] The list included Cicero, Mohammed, Voltaire, Samuel Adams, Benjamin Franklin, Thomas Carlyle, Napoleon, Bismarck, and General Grant.

The most ingenious "conscience-bolsterer" is the resort to the supernatural—to a force that has already predestined victory for the anti-semitic movement. An issue of *Liberation* maintained that "both the Bible and the Great Pyramid foretell that the United States is to be rescued from the hands of the alien". Another issue states confidently that the Silver Shirts will "in obedience to Divine Prophecy bring the Christian Democracy into effect." Nothing could be more in accord with conscience than carrying out the will of the Almighty as expressed in prophecy.

Yet another question presents itself to the analyst of anti-semitic propaganda, viz., what are the most widely used "pro-self" and "anti-other" symbols? A "pro-self" symbol is the badge that members of any group adopt in order to differentiate themselves from the rest of the world. It is the name given to "our side." Such symbols are *American, Mason* and *Republican*. An "anti-other" symbol is the detractive designation given to all members of the enemy group. The question may be answered in three parts. First, the anti-other symbols vastly outnumber the pro-self symbols. Secondly, all anti-semitic groups have accepted two particular "anti-other" symbols. Thirdly, no "pro-self" symbol has been developed or has been accepted as the correct designation for the anti-semitic movement as a whole or for its philosophy.

An examination of any piece of anti-semitic literature will reveal that the "anti-other" symbols outnumber the "pro-self" symbols in a ratio of at least ten to one. The literature consists almost entirely of statements excoriating an approaching menace and rarely specifies how best to combat it; hence, the preponderant need for "anti-other" symbols that describe this menace. The two accepted anti-other symbols are *Jew (Jewish)* and *Communist (Communistic, Communism)*. They are seldom used together in the form of *Communistic-Jew*, for they are considered synonymous. Some groups may use one symbol more frequently than the other; they may emphasize either the anti-revolutionary aspect, or the anti-semitic. On the whole, however, the symbol *Jew* and its derivatives appear more frequently. Additional "anti-other" symbols that are sometimes used include *Bolshevik, (ism), Red Jew, Red, liberal, alien Jewish, racial minority, Jewish-Bolshevist. Jewish minority, radical, alien, anti-Aryan.*

That no common "pro-self" symbol has developed is not surprising, for anti-semitic groups have been unsuccessful in their efforts to form a common front and their goal as well as the means to their goal are, as yet, obscure. Only the Silver Shirts have employed persistently and preponderantly a "pro-self" symbol—*Gentile*. Among the most overworked pro-symbols are *Christian, patriot, American, Christian American, Christian patriotism, American (ism), non-Jew*. The first three symbols, used singly or in some combination, run second to *Gentile* in frequency. An examination of the names of the 121 anti-semitic organizations listed in the preceding chapter offers an effective way of determining the "pro-self" symbols and their numerical frequencies. The important results are given in the following table:

Table 11

PRO-SELF SYMBOLS AND THEIR FREQUENCY IN THE NAMES
OF ANTI-SEMITIC GROUPS

America (n)	43	Fascist	2
Anti-Communist	5	Gentile	7
Aryan	4	Labor (Workers)	4
Christian	16	National (ist)	11
Constitution (al)	2	National Socialist	2
Defenders (or Protectors)	11	Patriots	7
Democracy (crats)	2	Vigilantes	2

The above table significantly indicates that anti-semitic groups operate especially under national symbols. They consider themselves Americans, patriots, and nationalists; these three symbols total 61. Twenty-seven groups are Christian, Aryan, or Gentile. (Incidentally, Pelley favors *Gentile* rather than a national symbol because Jews are acknowledged as Americans.)

Moreover, 13 consider themselves defenders, protectors, or vigilantes guarding the nation from some menace. Foreign-sounding labels are avoided. The terms *Fascist* and *National Socialist* occur only twice.

An omnipotent compound pro-self symbol would be the "American Christian Defenders" (actually the name of one of the groups).

Before drawing final conclusions on the effectiveness of anti-semitic propaganda, three diverse aspects should be considered: attitudes toward Catholics, Negroes, and Japanese imperialism. Although the groups constituting the anti-semitic movement have some members who were formerly Klansmen, only one group—Winrod's Defenders of the Christian Faith—occasionally expresses hostility towards Catholics. All groups, however, appear to be passively anti-Negro. Winrod's anti-Catholicism, that of the Fundamentalist, is mild compared to his vigorous anti-semitism, as the following indicates:

> The rapidly developing cooperation of Catholics and Jews in gaining control of the American government was illustrated when Al Smith and Jim Farley (Catholics) united their efforts recently in supporting Governor Lehman (Jew) for reelection in New York. . . . All religious groups are organized *except* Protestant evangelical Christians— they have an inferiority complex.
> It seems strangely paradoxical that the Roman Catholic Church should be leading the fight against the filthy Jewish motion picture industry. Rome has never been particularly famous for moral reform efforts. Prohibition has no greater foe than the Roman church.
> Mr. Pius, of Vatican City, can simply never resist throwing slurs at Protestants. Speaking recently before the Catholic Press Exposition . . . he denounced Protestantism and referred to Catholicism as "the only guardian of true and genuine Christianity." In the same breath he voiced approval of Mussolini's Ethiopian massacre.
> The final destruction of the Greek Orthodox and Roman Catholic Churches in the end-time of this age is anticipated in Revelation 17:16.

Ironically, Winrod disseminates the same anti-semitic ideology as Father Coughlin, the Catholic priest. For a time, the Silver Shirts appeared to have excluded Catholics from membership. Chief Pelley, however, has specifically denied any anti-Catholicism and has boasted of a large Catholic following.[51] That his statements have some validity is suggested by material that appeared in his magazine.[52] One pertinent article, for example, recounts a speech given before a French Jewish society and notes that the speaker not only depicted the Catholic Church as the one obstacle to world domination by the Jews but emphasized the necessity for its speedy destruction.

Anti-semitic groups tacitly assume that their followers are "respectable people" who are anti-Negro. Usually, the anti-Negro attitude manifests itself in connection with certain anti-semitic propaganda, the object of which is to show, as further proof of infamy, that Jews and revolutionaries have been friendly to the Negro. James True has reported:

> . . . a recent new deal conference, attended by large groups of negro editors and publishers. The negroes attended several peaceful meetings, received their instructions, were wined and dined by new deal officials, and left town with all expenses paid with taxpayers' money.[53]

At another time, True expressed his disgust at Mrs. Roosevelt's entertaining Negroes in the White House. Pelley has stated that Negro "Communist" C.I.O. organizers in the South have been anxious to overthrow "white supremacy."[54]

Harry Jung is the author of a pamphlet entitled *Communism and the Negro* (published by the Defenders of the Christian Faith). In it, he held that the Communists had already made great inroads among the Negroes and that their eventual purpose was to use them as the "shock troops of the revolution."

Anti-semitic groups have made many friendly references to Japan in connection with the undeclared Sino-Japanese war. Japan's assertion that she is fighting Communism seems to be enough to put these groups on her side. Edmondson has asserted that "Moscow Jewish Communism is behind China." In opposing the boycott on Japanese goods on the ground that "Japan is fighting Communism," James True has bemoaned the "diabolical unfairness of our press in handling news of the Sino-Japanese conflict," using this allegation as proof that American press is Jew-controlled. Pelley has on several occasions approvingly referred to Japan, but has usually referred to the Chinese as "Reds." On one occasion he asked:

> Where have you seen in the Jew-kept press that when the Chinese Red aviators bombed the American Dollar Liner, *President Hoover,* that it was a Japanese warship that came to her rescue and saved the passengers not killed?

Since there are no generally accepted criteria for judging the effectiveness of propaganda, certain hypotheses may be laid down.[55] Skillful propaganda must take into consideration matters of both tactics and strategy. Detailed, short-term procedures are tactics; general, long-term orientations are strategies. Tactical skillfulness is shown in both distinctiveness and adaptiveness. Distinctiveness involves the selection of demands and a set of symbols differentiating the movement from its rivals. Adaptiveness involves choosing both established practices and symbols appropriate to the end in view. The particular practices employed must be acceptable to the particular section of the public to be reached. The symbols must be part of the average American's vocabulary and must play on his loves and hates. The principles of distinctiveness and adaptiveness may sometimes conflict. A too distinctive set of symbols might be so foreign to the attitudes of the average American that he would reject it; a too adaptable (or common) set would not stand out from its rivals. Consequently, a successful application of these conflicting principles must arrive at a golden mean.

According to the hypothesized criterion of distinctiveness, anti-semitic groups have shown a great degree of individuality. The host of words that anti-semitic groups employ as "pro-self" and "anti-other" symbols have already been listed on preceding pages. In addition to these words, the *Ordnungs Dienst* of the German-American Bund and, for a time, some Silver Shirt units, have used uniforms as symbols. Nevertheless the failure to adopt a clear, long-term program not only has prevented anti-semitic groups from achieving greater distinctiveness but has caused some of them to teeter on anonymity.

According to the hypothesized criterion of adaptiveness, the symbols and forms of propaganda selected by the anti-semitic groups have been fairly appropriate. Most groups have used symbols embodying traditional American nationalism and have publicized themselves as protecting America from scheming international plotters and as saving the American tradition from subversion by alien Jews. The one group whose sincerity in these directions appeared unconvincing is the Bund. Its affairs have too frequently emphasized Germany. Its symbols have not conformed with the American idiom. As a result, the Bund was early dubbed "alien" and has succeeded in attracting as members recent German immigrants only. More skillful propaganda would have put less emphasis on the swastika flag, the Hitler salute, the marching storm troops. These key symbols of the Bund are alien to the American tradition.

Anti-semitic propaganda has shown great adaptiveness and ingenuity in the way its appeals keep abreast with the changing focus of public attention. All current events are construed so that they appear as further proof of the Jewish-revolutionary conspiracy. For instance, the anti-syphilis campaign recently conducted by the United States Public Health Service was interpreted as a Jewish plot to infect the Gentile population with syphilis. And the eviction riots in the earlier stages of the depression and the rise of the Committee for Industrial Organization in 1936 and 1937 have been cited as positive indications of Jew-inspired revolt.

Adaptiveness has also been shown by the use of many channels of propaganda discussed in the first section of this chapter. Both Winrod and Pelley have utilized channels they had already established prior to espousing anti-semitism. Winrod adapted his magazine for Fundamentalists and his bible conferences, and Pelley adapted his magazine for spiritualists.

Despite the degree of skill shown in adaptation, anti-semitic propaganda has had one glaring technical weakness. The appeal has been to the general public, to an undifferentiated audience. Skillful propaganda singles out particular groups, appeals to them on the basis of their particular grievances, and tries to show that these grievances will be remedied by adherence to a cause.

Strategical skill may be judged according to the principles of combination and precaution. Combination involves two groupings that differ slightly with each other in principles and the successful effort of one to unite with the other or at least to cooperate with it. Accordingly, anti-semitic organizations would have been wise to cooperate with organizations that were merely anti-revolutionary. Cooperating with such organizations on the basis of common opposition to revolutionary ideology and tactful efforts to spread the idea that most revolutionaries are Jews might have been quite astute. Winrod's address before the Peabody Kansas American Legion Post and Hunter's addresses before Chapters of the Daughters of the American Revolution are examples of the use of this technique. Nevertheless, it has not been fully exploited. The principle of precaution means that a proponent's propaganda must be of such a nature that it will not bring about an invincible combination of opponents. The anti-semitic movement as a whole has observed this principle, for it has not made the mistake of also being anti-Catholic. It might have fallen into this trap quite easily; in the past, anti-semitism and anti-Catholicism have been combined. Lack of precaution would, of course, have resulted in a union of America's two great religious minorities—the Jews and the Catholics. That this mistake has been avoided is indicated by the presence of Father Coughlin and his vast Catholic following in the anti-semitic movement.

In summary, anti-semitic groups have been only moderately skillful in their propaganda. They have selected fairly distinctive and idiomatic symbols and they have adapted their ideas fairly well to established practices. Their chief tactical blunder has been the unspecialized nature of their appeal. And as for strategical considerations of combination and precaution, they have been observed, though not so fully as they might have been.

CHAPTER XV

Conclusions

CERTAIN conclusions dealing with leadership, membership, and funds of the anti-semitic movement can now be ventured.

LEADERSHIP

The leaders of the eleven groups examined most closely are for the most part middle-aged or old men. The exact ages of eight leaders are available: Gerald Winrod 43, Father Coughlin 50, William Pelley 56, James True 60, Edward Hunter 66, Robert Edmondson 69, Colonel Hadley 69, and Colonel Sanctuary 71.[1] As for G. Wilhelm Kunze, Harry Jung and Royal Scot Gulden, the first appears to be even younger than Winrod and the other two are certainly not less than fifty. Only three of the eleven leaders have a college education—Hadley, Sanctuary, and Coughlin. Seven possess one skill or more naturally fitting them for leadership of their organizations. True and Edmondson were formerly journalists; Pelley, a writer of novels, short stories, and scenarios; and Winrod, a writer of religious tracts. Jung and Hunter, through their experience in labor espionage, developed skill in secretly gathering information. Coughlin and Winrod became orators through preaching.

Only Hadley and Sanctuary are independently wealthy. Coughlin and Edmondson have sources of income apart from the finances of their organizations. Seven leaders depend upon their organizations for their bread and butter. Gulden is the only one about whom there is some uncertainty. He does not appear to have been wealthy, and yet his small organization could hardly yield much of a salary. Somewhat significant are Pelley's and Edmondson's assertions that they were $50,000-a-year men at one time. Whether or not their assertions are accurate or even true, both have certainly suffered serious deprivations in recent years. The sharp reduction of their incomes has doubtlessly been an important factor in the shaping of their prejudices.

The fact that seven leaders have made their living from their organizations brings up the question of sincerity. General jealousy among leaders, unwillingness to fuse their organizations into one that might be effective, Hunter's and Pelley's competing efforts to solicit money from German diplomats and consuls, Jung's payment of 40 per cent commission for all contributions collected and his employment of an ex-convict as a field representative—these and many other facts suggest that at least some of the leaders are insincere. The term "insincere" can certainly be applied to a leader who not only exploits his organization for personal gain but also does not believe in its anti-semitic propaganda. An hypothetical instance may make the definition clear. An unemployed person with experience in public relations notices that the businessmen of his city are greatly aroused over Communism. Though he does not believe that any Communist menace exists, he organizes the businessmen into a society to "fight Communism." By doing this he obtains a job and an income. Since Hadley and Sanctuary are independently wealthy, they cannot be described as interested in anti-semitism as a means of income. That Hunter has continued his anti-semitism even though it has alienated some of his wealthy supporters has demonstrated his sincerity; had he been as insincere as our hypothetical gentleman, he would have backtracked on his anti-semitism, promised to refrain from it in the future, and thereby continued to receive the support of his wealthy backers. Jung's sincerity in the role of a leader of an anti-semitic group (though perhaps not as a labor spy) is demonstrated by the way he was duped by Alfredo Caputo, an international crook. Caputo had spun a yarn about the world "Jewish-Communist" menace.[2] If Jung had not been impressed, he would not have paid Caputo's expenses in Chicago or his fare back to Europe. All things considered, though many anti-semitic leaders are insincere and are aware that their organizations are petty rackets, there are some who are thoroughly sincere fanatics.

Many leaders and their immediate lieutenants appear to be emotionally unstable. Pelley and his subordinates seem to have this trait.[3] Jung has attracted several persons with criminal records.[4] Hunter has been married three or four times.[5] James True, the most unstable of all, has a sadistic proneness.[6]

Who has the characteristics necessary for a united front leadership? Such a leader would of course, have to be skilled in oratory, writing, and organizing. The age factor immediately eliminates Sanctuary, Edmondson, Hadley, and Hunter; their average is about 70. Of the men in their fifties, True has shown the least ability as an organizer or speaker. Moreover, he has never achieved a large circulation for his *Industrial Control Reports.* Jung also has demonstrated no great ability as an organizer or speaker. He is essentially a salesman of "secret" information. Gulden could not even keep alive his "grub-sized" Order of '76. Consequently, only Kunze, Pelley, and Winrod are left. Kunze may be eliminated because he appeals to too narrow an audience. As the Bund consists chiefly of German-born members, Kunze cannot hope to attract a large American following. Pelley and Winrod are the outstanding contenders for leadership of any unified anti-semitic movement. Both are fairly good organizers, effective speakers (Winrod is probably a shade better), and prolific writers. Winrod contributes frequently to his publication *Defender* and constantly pens new pamphlets and tracts. Pelley has virtually written all the issues of *Liberation* and yet has found time for an occasional book. From the standpoint of propagandistic style, Pelley is the best writer in the anti-semitic movement. He uses the vernacular effectively; he refers to the Jews as "Heebs," the "Yiddishers," and the "Sons of Jacob." Though his humor is crude, it makes his articles much more entertaining reading than the corsetted writings of many of his co-workers. In the matter of age, Winrod has the advantage; he is 42. Pelley is 53. Winrod's youth may explain his greater energy. He tirelessly travels about the country to speak at Bible conferences and, between his trips, he sandwiches in radio talks and articles. Winrod's chief weakness is the limitation of his potential following. His appeal is greatest among small-town and rural Fundamentalists; to a more sophisticated urban audience his Evangelism has little appeal. Pelley's appeal is less limited. While his spiritualism would alienate many people, he is able to keep it in the background; Winrod cannot escape his Fundamentalism. However, Winrod is more realistic. In 1936 Pelley ran for President on a Christian Party ticket in the state of Washington and obtained a thousand or so votes; Winrod, less ambitious, ran in the 1938 Republican Senatorial primary in Kansas, polling a much greater vote; during his campaign he discreetly refrained from anti-semitic utterances.[7] Similarly, while Pelley has managed to secure some aid from the wealthy, Winrod has been comparatively, much more successful. Winrod's primary campaign, for instance, showed all signs of being generously financed. In short, both men are politically ambitious, but Winrod has his two feet on the ground.

Two outstanding anti-semites—Father Coughlin and Major-General Van Horn Moseley—were purposely not considered as possibilities for the national *fuhrerschaft* of a united anti-semitic movement, though both men possess many of the essentials for such a position. Coughlin is shrewd, unscrupulous, and ambitious—by all odds the most brilliant orator and the ablest leader in the anti-semitic movement. Without real ability he could never have raised himself from a humble parish priest to a nationally-known personality. He could easily have become the national leader of the anti-semitic movement but for one fact: the United States is a predominantly Protestant country. The anti-semitic movement was almost entirely Protestant until Coughlin brought his Catholic following into it. To suggest that Protestant organizations are likely to subordinate themselves to the leadership of a Catholic priest is to speak without knowledge of American psychology. The irony becomes manifest. Coughlin's propaganda generates suspicion against the Jews, a religious minority. The average Protestant is suspicious of the Catholics, another religious minority. As a result, the Protestant majority's suspicion of the Catholic minority bars Coughlin from leadership of a movement directed against the Jewish minority. If couched in the vernacular, the sentiment of the emphatic Protestant anti-semites would be, "We don't want a damn Catholic leading our movement against the damn Jews."

Major-General Moseley, the other possible candidate for national leadership, was retired from the United States Army in 1938. In November of that year he made his first public address against the New Deal, revolutionaries, and Jews. His attacks continued in the subsequent months. Leaders of important anti-semitic organizations promptly sensed his possibilities as the head of a united movement. Usually the best that could be hoped for from a prominent person was under-cover sympathy. Here was Moseley, a major-general, willing to come out openly for the cause. The idea of a leader with military experience appealed particularly to those who advocated "strong arm methods" and the "Franco way." Admittedly, Moseley had—and has—many of the requirements for an ideal anti-semitic leader. But a man old enough to be retired from the Army is too old for the task of bringing 121 separate organizations into a united front. The task requires more energy and more years of active life than Moseley has ahead of him. The ideal leader must be a young Protestant with Coughlin's shrewdness and oratorical skill and with a military title. No such leader has yet appeared on the horizon.

MEMBERSHIP

What types of persons belong to anti-semitic organizations? This question will be first examined from the standpoint of national extraction. Down to Father Coughlin's entry into the anti-semitic movement in late 1938, the members of most anti-semitic groups were, by and large, people of early American stock. Available membership lists studied in the preceding chapters indicate that the names were nearly all of Anglo-Saxon origin; names of Latin or Slavic origin were rare.

CONCLUSIONS

Persons of recent immigrant stock—first and second generation Americans—were almost never found in these organizations. The Bund, of course, was the one exception, its members almost invariably having been born in Germany. Significantly, an organization consisting of foreign-born and a group of organizations consisting of old American stock both disseminated the same propaganda, and in many instances actively cooperated. Since Coughlin entered the anti-semitic movement, bringing with him a large Irish following of recent immigrants, the situation has, of course, changed.

Classifying the social status of the members of anti-semitic groups is difficult. Most organizations are neither exclusive clubs catering to the wealthy nor proletarian groups appealing to the lowest income citizenry. Several factors, however, substantiate the description "middle-class." All the organizations are bitterly anti-union. The leaders of two organizations—Harry Jung of the American Vigilant Intelligence Federation and Edward Hunter of the Industrial Defense Association—are former labor spies and still carry on small-scale espionage. Had anti-semitic organizations desired working class members they would have concealed their anti-labor bias. The organizations have, however, attracted numerous professional men. The Silver Shirts, the American Vigilant Intelligence Federation, and the Industrial Defense Association contain physicians, lawyers, clergymen, and engineers. The field representative of the Federation has addressed Rotary and Kiwanis Clubs—two middle class groups—and has tried to recruit members there. The correspondence of the Silver Shirts frequently refers to 32d degree Masons and Scottish Rite Shriners, again middle-class persons. Two observers familiar with the Industrial Defense Association have referred to the fact that its members have included "people of standing." These references to middle-class people become more significant in view of the rarity of such references to manual or factory workers. Then too, Jung, True, and Hunter have represented their literature as indispensable to every businessman in the intelligent conduct of his affairs.

It should, of course, be remembered that such organizations as Paul Reveres, the Industrial Defense Association, and James True Associates have a higher proportion of wealthy members than do the Defenders of the Christian Faith, the Christian Front, Silver Shirts, etc.

Questions on the membership's religion, geographical distribution, education, and affiliations with patriotic and military organizations cannot be conclusively answered, for no complete information on any of these matters is available.

Until late 1938 the anti-semitic movement was unquestioanbly

Protestant. The validity of the characterization is attested by the following facts: most members of the Defenders of the Christian Faith have been Fundamentalists and its leader, Winrod, has been outspokenly anti-Catholic; the Silver Shirts have numbered many former Klansmen among their members; no leader of an anti-semitic group was Catholic; and almost all members were of old American stock. In the autumn of 1938, however, Father Coughlin and his vast Catholic following entered the ranks of the anti-semitic movement. Since the exact or even approximate number of these Catholic recruits as well as of the old Protestant participants is unknown, the religious group that has a proportionately greater number of adherents in the anti-semitic movement cannot be determined.

Although all regions of the United States contain anti-semitic groups two have the greatest concentration—the Pacific Coast and metropolitan New York.[8] The Pacific Coast is the home of numerous active locals of the German-American Bund and the stronghold of the Silver Shirts. California, a coastal state, contains one of the three largest groups of subscribers to Winrod's *Defender*. Furthermore, the percent of the 121 anti-semitic groups that have headquarters on the Pacific Coast exceeds by far the percent of the national population in that region—16.8 percent to 6.7 percent. The sections of the Pacific Coast that have the largest number of such groups are Southern California and the state of Washington. Metropolitan New York houses headquarters of 26 groups. The Bund has 17 of its 71 locals in that area; they include the largest and the most active, and hold the best attended meetings. The region is also the citadel of Father Coughlin's Christian Front.

Of the nine anti-semitic groups specially treated in the preceding chapters the German-American Bund, the Christian Front, the Silver Shirts, the Defenders of the Christian Faith, and the Edmondson Economic Service—the five most important—and the James True Associates have a nationwide sphere of operations. The three others have much smaller spheres: the American Vigilant Intelligence Federation confines itself to the region within a few hundred miles of Chicago; the American Christian Defenders to metropolitan New York; and the Industrial Defense Association to Boston and New England. Two defunct groups, The Paul Reveres and the Order of '76, had spheres identical with those of the Federation and the American Christian Defenders respectively. The Bund, the Christian Front, the Silver Shirts, the Federation, and the Industrial Defense Association—all for the most part draw upon urban centers for their membership. The only large group that has an almost completely small-town and rural membership is the Defenders of the Christian Faith. The Silver Shirt group has also made efforts to recruit members in the rural sections of the state of Washington, and the Federation in the small towns of Michigan and Northwestern Ohio.

The middle-class character of the anti-semitic movement suggests that its followers have enjoyed at least average educational opportunities. Nevertheless the educational level of both the Silver Shirts and the Defenders of the Christian Faith appears to be lower than that of other anti-semitic groups: the Defenders are almost all staunch believers in Biblical and Great Pyramidal prophecies; many Silver Shirts are spiritualists as well as believers in the Great Pyramidal prophecy.

The anti-revolutionary nature of both anti-semitic organizations and military (or patriotic organizations) leads to the belief that the membership of both are somewhat the same. Supporting this belief is certain evidence: Army officers have belonged to the Industrial Defense Association, the Order of '76, and the Paul Reveres; many members of the Daughters of the American Revolution to the Industrial Defense Association; and some sailors and marines to the San Diego local of the Silver Shirts.

In summary, the memberships of the anti-semitic organizations are, by and large, urban middle-class people who have had at least an average education. Some of these members are also affiliated with military (or patriotic) groups. While no one region of the country possesses a majority of the anti-semitic organizations, the Pacific Coast and metropolitan New York have the largest number.

FUNDS

The three major sources of funds are sale of literature, dues payments, and contributions. Sale of literature, the most common source, is tapped by all organizations specially treated in the foregoing chapters. Dues payments, though a somewhat less important source, yield revenue for the Bund, the Silver Shirts, the American Vigilant Intelligence Federation, the Order of '76, and The Paul Reveres. As the third major source—the solicited contribution—requires extended examination, the minor sources will be briefly enumerated. Advertisements in their publications bring income to the Bund and the Defenders of the Christian Faith; lecture fees to the American Christian Defenders, Industrial Defense Association, Edmondson Economic Service, and the Defenders of the Christian Faith; and social events and a subsidy from Germany to the Bund. Collections taken at meetings have helped support the Bund, the Defenders of the Christian Faith, and The Paul Reveres. The Federation has charged admission fees to its meetings. Some leaders—Hadley, Edmondson, and True—have used their own money in launching their organizations.

For the sake of expedient discussion, contributions will be arbitrarily divided into two categories: "small," up to fifty dollars; "large," fifty dollars or more. Five groups have solicited small contributions—the Silver Shirts, the Industrial Defense Association, the Defenders of the Christian Faith, the Christian Front, and Edmondson Economic Service. Evidence has indicated that eight groups have received large contributions, obviously given by the well-to-do or wealthy. These groups are the Bund, the Defenders of the Christian Faith, the Christian Front, the Edmondson Economic Service, the American Vigilant Intelligence Federation, the Industrial Defense Association, the Silver Shirts, and the American Christian Defenders. Of the three that are not known to have received such financial backing, two have passed out of existence: the Order of '76 and The Paul Reveres. The third, The James True Associates, has led a precarious existence; for nearly a year after the 1936 election, it published nothing. The Silver Shirts apparently carried on for five years without known support from the wealthy; in those years they probably did not receive such support for they were frequently in debt and several times nearly went out of business. That an anti-semitic group must have support from the wealthy if it is to have a secure existence is obvious. A would-be founder of a new anti-semitic group cannot expect his group to be a financial success on the pennies, nickels, and dimes tossed in the collection basket; he needs one or more financial "angels" able and willing to contribute from 25 to 50 percent of the annual organizational budget.

The fact that a large percentage of the income of some groups does come from the wealthy should occasion no surprise. Since anti-revolutionary, anti-semitic groups assert that they are fighting those who would expropriate the wealthy, they have a potent argument in their solicitations. Nevertheless the sums contributed by the wealthy are frequently exaggerated. Wealthy persons are usually unwilling to espouse any group that is openly anti-semitic.

FUTURE OF THE ANTI-SEMITIC MOVEMENT

Do the American anti-semitic organizations constitute a national radical revolutionary movement? What does the future in the United

CONCLUSIONS

States probably hold for these groups? In order to answer the first question, a definition offered in the first chapter should be repeated: a national radical revolutionary movement stands for the achievement of fundamental changes in the social practice by drastic methods. Certainly the American organizations as a whole do not conform with this definition. In the chapter on propaganda, the study inquired whether the organizations had Fascism as their goal and whether they believed in violence as a means for attaining their goal, be it Fascism or not. These two questions embodied the two criteria of a national radical revolutionary movement—a fundamental change and drastic methods. The Silver Shirts have constituted the only organization fully meeting these criteria. Pelley, chief of the Silver Shirts, has scorned "Jew-communist democracy" and advocated "strong-arm expedients" and dictatorship. For a brief time his San Diego unit practiced military maneuvers in anticipation of violence. Other groups have met the criteria in part. The Bund has urged its members to be ready to fight for the "right kind of government." Father Coughlin has sanctioned the "Franco way." The Federal Bureau of Investigation arrested 17 Christian Front followers for plotting insurrection against the United States Government. Though he has expressed his views somewhat less baldly, Edmondson has referred approvingly to "the Vigilante Spirit which will save America" and stated that "Civil War and Fascistic Dictatorship may be inevitable." James True has told several interviewers that a pogrom is the only solution to America's difficulties. Since the 1936 election the number of references to violence has been rapidly increasing. Nevertheless the propaganda of most anti-semitic organizations has not called for either the use of violence or for a change in the present form of government. It has confined itself to raising the bogey of a "Jewish-communist conspiracy" and to demanding that this conspiracy be suppressed. Consequently, at present, the anti-semitic movement as a whole cannot be called a national radical revolutionary movement.

Will the anti-semitic organiations grow stronger in the future? Will they become a national radical revolutionary movement? Although the future of any movement cannot be predicted with certainty, the conditions under which a given movement is very likely to develop may be listed. A good method of determining the conditions under which anti-revolutionary, anti-semitic ideology flourishes would be possible through a careful examination of the specific economic and political circumstances of all the countries in which this ideology has appeared. Unfortunately, the standard histories of anti-semitism do not furnish this information. The following list of conditions, is, of necessity, based upon a general knowledge of the conditions fostering this ideology:

Periods of economic depression.
War, threats of war, or any other event that results in an intensification of nationalism.
Growth of a strong revolutionary movement or widespread publicity of what is alleged to be a revolutionary movement.
Rise of an anti-semitic political party to power in a foreign country.
Prosperity and international prestige of those countries that have adopted anti-semitism as part of national policy.
Large Jewish immigration.
Appointment or election of Jews to prominent political offices.

The first condition, periods of economic depression, requires little explanation. When people are suffering from economic deprivation, the grip of the old ideology weakens. Beliefs formerly accepted without question begin to be doubted. Anti-semitic ideology is well adapted to such periods because it can attribute the ills of society to the scheming "Communistic Jew."

Any intensification of nationalism—whether from war, threat of war, or other causes—results in the demand that everyone conform to the standard national pattern and in the suspicion of all minority groups. Jews—the perpetual alien minority—as well as adherents of any liberal or revolutionary ideology do not find an aroused nationalism a congenial atmosphere. Complete solidarity in the name of the nation will be demanded, differences will not be tolerated, and drastic methods will be used to crush any dissenting group. Such conditions would not, of course, exist in the event of a war with Germany, a country officially sponsoring the anti-semitic ideology. At the end of the war, however, the Jews and revolutionaries would make excellent whipping boys for the returning veterans. National humiliation, resulting from defeat in war or even in diplomacy, would also intensify nationalism and start a hunt for scapegoats.

The growth of a strong revolutionary movement would stimulate the growth of anti-revolutionary, anti-semitic organizations. This was true in Russia, in Poland, in Hungary, and in Germany. A genuine revolutionary movement, however, may not be necessary. Widespread publicity focused on what is alleged to be a revolutionary movement may achieve the same result. During the 1936 Presidential campaign, the mildly reformist New Deal was vigorously and widely attacked as revolutionary, and, as a result, many new anti-semitic organizations were born.

CONCLUSIONS

The Nazis' rise to power in Germany had the immediate effect of starting anti-semitic groups in the United States. The more widely it is accepted throughout the world, the more readily Fascist ideology circulates in the United States. Moreover, the growth in prosperity and in international prestige of the Fascist countries will enhance the attractiveness of their ideology and will increase its acceptability in the United States. Germany military successes in Europe have already enabled American disseminators of this ideology to say, "See what a Jew-purged country can do."

The other two conditions—Jewish immigration to the United States and the appointment or the election of Jews to prominent political offices—are less important factors, but nonetheless significant. Anti-semitic propaganda asserts that "Communistic Jews" are dominating the country, that they occupy key positions; accordingly, it gives a vast amount of publicity to the fact that some Jews hold offices in the "Communist" New Deal administration. The greater the number of Jews in political positions, the more convincing will the anti-semitic propaganda appear—the more probably will Jews be used as scapegoats for what ever difficulties the country encounters. Should the number of Jewish refugees entering the United States increase, the propaganda will herald this immigration as the beginning of a new "Communist-Jewish" assault on the United States. To be sure, Pelley is already making such charges.

These, then, are the seven conditions fundamental to the growth of the anti-semitic movement. The intensity or lack of intensity of these conditions will determine whether the anti-semitic organizations in the United States will grow stronger or weaker.

One further fact must be noted in any effort to conjecture the future of the American anti-semitic movement. About a dozen new anti-semitic organizations have been formed each year since 1933. This steady growth suggests that anti-semitism has taken root in the United States and will, even under the most unfavorable conditions, remain as a minor ideology for some time. The anti-semitic movement in the United States can no longer be treated as if it were a transient phenomenon.

In summary, the 121 anti-semitic organizations that have appeared in the United States in recent years are products of the depression, the repercussion of Hitler's rise to power, the slight growth of revolutionary sentiment, and the belief that the New Deal is "Communistic." These organizations are far less formidable than they seem to be; many of them consist merely of a fanatic and a letterhead. Their members are drawn primarily from the middle-class. Though some individual wealthy persons have contributed to these organizations, the economic elite as a group has ignored their existence. The sources of funds most commonly used are dues and the sale of publications. The skill in propaganda is only moderate. The organizations as a whole do not fall within the definition of a national radical revolutionary movement, although individual organizations do.

BIBLIOGRAPHY

BOOKS

American Jewish Yearbook. Philadelphia: the Jewish Publication Society of America
Brown Network, The. New York: Knight, 1935
Catlin, G. E. C. *The Science and Method of Politics.* New York: Knopf, 1927
Coudenhove-Kalergi, Henrich. *Anti-Semitism Throughout the Ages.* London: Hutchinson, 1935
Drennan, James. *B. U. F., Oswald Mosley and British Fascism.* London: John Murray, 1934
Dutt, R. Palme. *Fascism and Social Revolution.* New York: International, 1934
Editors of *Fortune. Jews in America.* New York: Random House, 1936
Finer, Herman. *Mussolini's Italy.* London: Gollancz, 1935
Gessner, Robert. *Some of My Best Friends are Jews.* New York: Farrar and Rinehart, Inc., 1936
Gunther, John. *Inside Europe.* New York: Harpers, 1937
Hapgood, Norman. (ed.) *Professional Patriots.* New York: Boni, 1927
Heiden, Konrad. *A History of National Socialism.* New York: Knopf, 1935
Hoover, Calvin B. *Germany Enters the Third Reich.* New York: Macmillan, 1933
Jaszi, Oscar. "The Ideologic Foundations of the Danubian Dictatorships" in *Propaganda and Dictatorships.* Edited by Harwood L. Childs. Princeton, New Jersey: Princeton University Press, 1936
Kernan, Reverend William C. *The Ghost of Royal Oak.* New York: Free Speech Forum, 1940
Lasswell, Harold D. *World Politics and Personal Insecurity.* New York: Whittlesey House, McGraw-Hill, 1934
——————. *Politics: Who Gets What, When, How.* New York: Whittlesey House, McGraw-Hill, 1936
Levinger, Rabbi Lee J. *Anti-Semitism, Yesterday and Tommorrow.* New York: Macmillan, 1936
——————. *A History of the Jews in the United States.* Cincinnati: Union of American Hebrew Congregations, 1935
Loucks, E. H. *The Ku Klux Klan in Pennsylvania, a Study of Nativism.* New York: Telegraph Press, 1936
Mecklin, J. M. *The Ku Klux Klan, a Study of the American Mind.* New York: Harcourt, Brace, 1924
Merriam, Charles E. *Political Power.* New York: Whittlesey House, McGraw-Hill, 1934
Mosca, Gaetano. *The Ruling Class.* New York: McGraw-Hill, 1938
Mosley, Sir Oswald. *Fascism in Britain.* London: British Union of Fascists, 1938
Mowrer, Edgar Ansel. *Germany Puts the Clock Back.* New York: Morrow, 1933
Salvemini, Gaetano. *The Fascist Dictatorship.* New York: Holt, 1927
Schuman, Frederick L. *Germany Since 1918.* New York: Holt, 1937
——————. *The Nazi Dictatorship.* New York: Knopf, 1935
Seldes, George. *Sawdust Caesar.* New York: Harpers, 1935
Spivak, John L. *Shrine of the Silver Dollar.* New York: Modern Age, 1940
Swing, Raymond Gram. *Forerunners of American Fascism.* New York: Julian Messner, 1935

ORGANIZED ANTI-SEMITISM IN AMERICA

Valentin, Hugo. *Anti-Semitism, Historically and Critically Examined.* New York. Viking, 1936
Werth, Alexander. *Which Way France?* New York: Harpers, 1937
Wirth, Louis. *The Ghetto.* Chicago: University of Chicago Press, 1928

PUBLIC DOCUMENTS

U. S. Congress, House. *Investigation of Nazi and Other Propaganda.* House Report 153, 74th Congress, 1st Session. Washington: Government Printing office, 1935. See also the *Hearings* of the committee upon which this report is based. (McCormack Committee)
U. S. Congress, House. *Investigation of Un-American Activities.* 1938—Ten volumes. (Dies Committee)

ARTICLES

Dinneen, Joseph F. "An American Fuehrer Organizes an Army," *American Magazine,* August, 1937
"The Friends of New Germany". *Today,* March 31, 1934
"Jews in America". *Fortune,* February, 1936
Pelley, William Dudley. "My Seven Minutes in Eternity", *American Magazine,* March, 1929
Smertenko, John. "Hitlerism Comes to America", *Harpers,* November, 1933
Periodicals Published by Anti-Semitic Groups Defender. Wichita, Kansas. Monthly
Deutscher Wockruf and Beobachter. New York. Weekly
Edmondson Economic Service. Bulletin. New York. Weekly
Industrial Control Reports. Washington, D. C. Weekly
Items of Interest. Chicago. Monthly
The Revealer. Wichita, Kansas. Bi-monthly
Social Justice. Royal Oak, Michigan. Weekly
The Vigilante. Chicago. Monthly

PAMPHLETS PUBLISHED BY ANTI-SEMITIC GROUPS

Edmondson, Robert E. *Anti-Semitic Causes of Today.* New York: Edmondson Economic Service, 1937
——————. *The Jewish System Indicted.* New York: Edmondson Economic Service, 1937
——————. *Women of America! Rescue the Republic.* New York: Edmondson Economic Service, 1935
Hunter, Edward L. *Does the CIO Seek to Promote Red Revolution?* Boston: Industrial Defense Association, 1937
——————. *Jewish Jazz: Tin Pan Alley.* Boston: Industrial Defense Association
——————. *Legislation for Hatred.* Boston: Industrial Defense Association, 1935
——————. *The Grave Diggers of Russia.* Boston: Industrial Defense Association, 1933
Jung, Harry A. *Questions and Answers.* Chicago: American Vigilant Intelligence Federation, 1934. (Mimeographed)
—————— and Sanctuary E. N. *The Man Behind the Men Behind the President.* Chicago: American Vigilant Intelligence Federation, 1936
Nilus, Serge. *The Protocols of the Elders of Zion.* Chicago: Right Cause Publishing Co., 1934
Potter, Irvin L. *Are Jews God's Chosen?* Boston: 1935
——————. *The Cause of Anti-Jewism in the United States.* Boston: 1933
——————. *The Evidence of Jewish Financial Control.* Boston: 1935
——————. *The Psychological Cause of Anti-Jewism.* Boston: 1935
——————. *The Secret of the Jew's Financial Success.* Boston: 1935

BIBLIOGRAPHY

Potter, Irvin L. *Truths Gentiles Should Know.* Boston: 1935
Sanctuary, Eugene N. *Blind Leaders.* New York: World Alliance Against Jewish
    Aggressiveness, 1935
————. *Communism, Its Heart and Goal.* New York: Sunday School
    Times, 1936
————. *Is the New Deal Communism?* New York: World Alliance
    Against Jewish Aggressiveness
————. *Litvinoff, Foreign Commissar of the USSR.* Philadelphia:
    Deutscher Weckruf und Beobachter
————. *Roosevelt Warming the Serpent.* New York: World Alliance
    Against Jewish Aggressiveness, 1934
————. *Tainted Contacts.* New York: World Alliance Against Jewish
    Aggressiveness
Schrader, Fredrick F. *The New Germany Under Hitler.* Philadelphia: Deutscher
    Weckruf und Beobachter
Sincere, Earnest *Facing the Facts.* Elgin, Illinois: Brandt, 1933
————. *The Plan in Action.* Elgin, Illinois: Brandt, 1933
Squire of Krum Elbow, The. *Our Neighbor and World Unrest.* Newport, Rhode
    Island: Newport Historical Association
————. *Toward Armageddon.* Charleston, South Carolina: Militant
    Christian Association, 1936
Winrod, Gerald B. *Anti-Christ and the Tribe of Dan.* Wichita: Defender Pub-
    lishers, 1936
————. *Communism and the Roosevelt Brain Trust.* Wichita: Defender
    Publishers, 1936
————. *Subversive Movements.* Wichita: Defender Publishers, 1937
————. *The Curse of Modern Deism.* Wichita: Defender Publishers, 1936.
————. *The Hidden Hand; the Protocols and the Coming Superman.*
    Wichita: Defender Publishers, 1935
————. *The Jewish Assault on Christianity.* Wichita: Defender Publishers,
    1935
————. *The NRA in Prophecy and a Discussion of Beast Worship.*
    Wichita: Defender Publishers, 1933
————. *The Truth about the Protocols.* Wichita: Defender Publishers,
    1935
————. *The United States and Russia in Prophecy and the Red Horse of
    the Apocalypse.* Wichita: Defender Publishers, 1933
————. *Three Modern Evils—Modernism, Aetheism, and Bolshevism.*
    Wichita: Defender Publishers, 1932
————. *World Trends Toward Anti-Christ.* Wichita: Defender Publishers,
    1934

MOST WIDELY READ BOOKS OF THE ANTI-SEMITIC GROUPS

Gaebelein, Dr. Arno C. *The Conflict of the Ages.* New York: Our Hope, 1933
Hitler, Adolf. *My Battle.* New York: Houghton Mifflin, 1933
Pelley, William Dudley. *No More Hunger.* Asheville, North Carolina: Pelley
    Publishers, 1936
Sanctuary, Eugene N. *Are These Things So?* New York: World Alliance Against
    Jewish Aggressiveness, 1934

ORGANIZED ANTI-SEMITISM IN AMERICA

Notes for Chapter I

[1] For more elaborate statements of this type of political analysis see H. D. Lasswell, *World Politics and Personal Insecurity,* (New York: Whittlesey House, McGraw-Hill, 1935); Charles E. Merriam, *Political Power,* (New York: Whittlesey House, McGraw-Hill, 1934); G. E. C. Catlin, *The Science and Method of Politics,* (New York: A. A. Knopf, 1927); Gaetano Mosca, *The Ruling Class,* (New York: McGraw-Hill, 1938); H. D. Lasswell, *Politics—Who Gets What, When, How,* (New York: Whittlesey House, McGraw-Hill, 1936).

[2] Violence and the distribution of goods and services are, of course, other methods by which an élite retains power.

[3] Obviously an ideology can be anti-revolutionary without being anti-semitic. Such prominent American groups as the Daughters of the American Revolution and the American Legion are very active in distributing anti-revolutionary propaganda that is not anti-semitic.

[4] Of course, in this anti-revolutionary, anti-semitic ideology the Jew is often presented in other roles than as a revolutionary, but our purpose at present is simply to explain the association between anti-semitism and the anti-revolutionary ideology.

[5] For the history of anti-semitism see Hugo Valentin, *Anti-Semitism, Historically and Critically Examined* (New York: Viking, 1936); Henrich Coudenhove-Kalergi, *Anti-Semitism throughout the Ages* (London: Hutchinson, 1935). For a briefer treatment see Rabbi Lee J. Levinger, *Anti-Semitism, Yesterday and Tomorrow* (New York: Macmillan, 1936), Part I.

[6] Valentin, *Anti-Semitism,* p. 87.

[7] See footnote one, chapter XIV, for a discussion of this work.

[8] Valentin, *Anti-Semitism,* p. 100.

[9] For a good brief account of developments in Hungary at this period see Oscar Jaszi, "Ideologic Foundations of the Danubian Dictatorships," in *Propaganda and Dictatorships,* ed. by Harwood L. Childs, (Princeton, New Jersey: Princeton University Press, 1936), pp. 90-97.

[10] For studies of the rise of National Socialism, in contrast to descriptions of the Nazi regime as it exists at present, see: Konrad Heiden, *A History of National Socialism,* (New York: Knopf, 1935); Fredrick L. Schuman, *The Nazi Dictatorship,* (New York: Knopf, 1935); Edgar Ansel Mowrer, *Germany Puts the Clock Back,* (New York: Morrow, 1933); Calvin B. Hoover, *Germany Enters the Third Reich,* (New York: Macmillan, 1933); R. Palme Dutt, *Fascism and Social Revolution,* (New York: International, 1934); Fredrick L. Schuman, *Germany Since 1918,* (New York: Holt, 1937).

[11] For a further discussion of this matter see Valentin, *Anti-Semitism,* pp. 60-63.

[12] Schuman, *The Nazi Dictatorship,* p. 97.

[13] *Ibid.,* p. 87.

[14] The fact that in 1938 Italy took certain anti-semitic measures—the expulsion of all Jews who have entered the country since 1919 and limiting the number of Jewish teachers and students in schools—does not affect the validity of this analysis. The rise of the Nazis in Germany has given a tremendous impetus to anti-semitism everywhere; it has made the world Jew-conscious. In the early days of Italian Fascism the Jews actually were not an eligible target. The increased Jew-consciousness of the world has magnified the importance of the same number of Italian Jews to the point where they are now an eligible target. Thus, Mussolini takes measures against the Jews to allow the discontent under his regime to be discharged in a channel harmless to his regime, i.e., against the Jews. Further, anti-semitic measures were an easy way for Mussolini to demonstrate his solidarity with Germany and the reality of the Rome-Berlin axis.

[15] For detailed descriptions of the rise of Fascism in Italy see: Gaetano Salvemini, *The Fascist Dictatorship,* (New York: Holt, 1927); H. W. Schneider, *Making the Fascist State,* (New York: Oxford University Press, 1928); Herman Finer,

CHAPTER FOOTNOTES

Mussolini's Italy, (London: Gollancz, 1935); R. Palme Dutt, *Fascism and Social Revolution*, (New York: International, 1934); George Seldes, *Sawdust Caesar*, (New York: Harpers, 1935).

[16] For a survey of the British Union of Fascists see John Gunther, *Inside Europe*, (31st ed.; New York: Harpers, 1937), pp. 263-266. For an exposition by a member of the B. U. F. see James Drennan, *B. U. F., Oswald Mosley and British Fascism*, (London: John Murray, 1934). Mosley explains his ideas in his own volume, *Fascism in Britain*, (London: British Union of Fascists, 1933).

[17] For discussions of these groups see John Gunther, *Inside Europe*, (New York: Harpers, 1937), Chapter 11. Also Alexander Werth, *Which Way France?* (New York: Harpers, 1937).

Notes for Chapter II

[1] See end of this chapter for data concerning revolutionary parties in the United States.

[2] For a more extended discussion, see Levinger, Lee J., *Anti-Semitism, Yesterday and Tomorrow*, New York, Macmillan Co., 1936, pp. 127-133.

[3] For a discussion of the Ku Klux Klan, see Mecklin, J. M., *The Ku Klux Klan, a Study of the American Mind*, New York, Harcourt, Brace & Co., 1924; Loucks, E. H., *The Ku Klux Klan in Pennsylvania, a Study in Nativism*, New York, Telegraph Press, 1936.

[4] *American Jewish Yearbook*, Philadelphia, Jewish Publication Society of America, Vol. XLII.

[5] Levinger, Lee J., *A History of the Jews in the United States* (Second revised edition), Cincinnati, Union of American Hebrew Congregations, 1935, p. 375.

[6] *Ibid.*, p. 377.

[7] *Ibid.*

[8] *American Jewish Yearbook*, XXXIX:744.

[9] *Ibid.*

[10] Levinger, *op. cit.*, p. 265.

[11] *Ibid.*, p. 264. The percent of Jews in the total American population in subsequent years is given in the *American Jewish Yearbook*, XXXIX:747, as follows: 1897—1.31%; 1907—2.00%; 1917—3.27%; 1927—3.58%.

[12] *American Jewish Yearbook*, XXXIX:761.

[13] Levinger, *op. cit.*, p. 265.

[14] *Ibid.*, pp. 262, 265. *American Jewish Yearbook*, XXXIX:766-767, gives the detailed figures on Jewish immigration since 1899 as follows: 1899-1907, 829,244; 1908-1914, 656,397; 1915-1920, 79,921; 1921, 119,036; 1922-1924, 153,232; 1925-1930, 67,686; 1931-1936, 26,042.

[15] According to the *American Jewish Yearbook*, XXIX:767, the figures on Jewish immigration for these years are: 1931—5,692; 1932—2,755; 1933—2,372; 1934—4,134; 1935—4,837; 1936—6,252.

[16] Levinger, *op. cit.*, pp. 520-522, 550.

[17] Postal, Bernard, *B'nai B'rith Magazine*, "Jews in National Political Convention", XLVI (1933): 268,305.

[18] *American Jewish Yearbook*, XXIX:737.

[19] The best detailed refutation to the argument that the Jews control the economic life of the nation is found in *Jews in America* (by the Editors of *Fortune*) New York, Random House, 1936. The volume originally appeared in article form in *Fortune*, Feb. 1936. The facts on pages 17-19 are based upon this source.

[20] See Chapter I.

Notes for Chapter III

[1] Both committees were officially designated as the "Special Committee on un-American Activities". Rep. John W. McCormack was chairman of the first, Rep. Martin Dies, of the second. In this study the printed records of the hearings before

the committees will be termed "McCormack Hearings" and "Dies Hearings". The final report of the McCormack Committee was published Feb. 15, 1935, under the heading *Investigation of Nazi and Other Propaganda*, House Report 153, 74th Congress, first session.

² *Kampfendes Deutschtum* (1937 edition), yearbook of the German-American Bund.

³ *Ibid.;* see also *McCormack Hearings*, DC-4, p. 72.

⁴ *McCormack Hearings*, DC-4, p. 73.

⁵ *Ibid.;* see also p. 72.

⁶ XY information. "XY" is a designation for an organization, part of whose work is the collection of information on anti-democratic activities. Since the effectiveness of this work is enhanced by its being carried on with a minimum of publicity, the name of the organization and further footnote references to it will not be given.

⁷ *McCormack Hearings*, DC-4, p. 74.

⁸ *McCormack Hearings*, NY-12, p. 44.

⁹ A word should be said about the Friends of the Hitler Movement, an organization mentioned in articles appearing in *Today* of Mar. 31, 1934 and the *Jewish Daily Bulletin* of Mar. 22, 1933. Apparently these two periodicals learned of the organization through the first issue of the New York Nazi paper, the *Deutscher Beobachter*, in Jan. 1933, wherein it was stated that the Friends of the Hitler Movement would be formed for American citizens who wanted to affiliate with some pro-Nazi group. No subsequent record of the Movement can be found and evidently it was never organized. Its purposes, however, were carried out by the Friends of Germany and the Friends of the New Germany.

¹⁰ *McCormack Hearings*, DC, p. 152.

¹¹ According to a witness before a Congressional Committee—Mr. Kruppa, who had formerly been very active in the Friends of New Germany and close to Spanknoebel—Spanknoebel was kidnapped from the United States by German secret service men. They forced him at pistol-point to board the *Europa* and kept him secreted until the boat reached Germany. See *McCormack Hearings*, NY-12, pp. 13-15.

¹² *McCormack Hearings*, DC-4, pp. 178, 216-218; see also DC-6, p. 346.

¹³ *Ibid.*, DC-4, pp. 91, 150; DC-6, pp. 296-297.

¹⁴ *Ibid.*, DC-4, pp. 218-219.

¹⁵ *Nazis Among Themselves*, p. 29. A pamphlet published by the Action Committee of the German Progressive Societies of Chicago, an anti-Nazi group.

¹⁶ *Kampfendes Deutschtum* (1937 ed.)

¹⁷ *Deutscher Weckruf und Beobachter*, Dec. 30, 1935.

¹⁸ *Dies Hearings*, VI, p. 3,712; *Deutscher Weckruf und Beobachter*, Dec. 30, 1935; *cf.* Anonymous, *The Brown Network*, New York, Knight, 1935, p. 258.

¹⁹ *Dies Hearings* VI, p. 3,786.

²⁰ *Ibid.*, VIII, p. 5,200.

²¹ *Chicago Daily Times*, Sept. 9, 1937; see also *New York Times*, June 24, 1938.

²² *New York Times*, June 24, 1938; confirmed by the *Chicago Daily Times*, Sept. 1937.

²³ *Deutscher Weckruf und Beobachter*, Dec. 30, 1935.

²⁴ *Today*, Mar. 31, 1934.

²⁵ 1936 Constitution of German-American Bund, Art. VI, Sec. 1.

²⁶ *Ibid.*, Art. XIII, Sec. 2.

²⁷ *Ibid.*, Art. XVI, Sec. 6.

²⁸ *McCormack Hearings*, DC-4, p. 107.

²⁹ *Ibid.*, DC-4, p. 69.

³⁰ *Ibid.*, NY-12, p. 45; see also footnote 11.

³¹ *Ibid.*, NY-12, p. 27.

³² *Ibid.*, NY-12, p. 33.

³³ *Ibid.*, DC-4, p. 152.

[34] *Ibid.,* NY-7, pp. 68-69.
[35] *Ibid.,* DC-4, p. 119.
[36] *Dies Hearings,* IX, p. 5,512.
[37] *McCormack Hearings,* DC-4, p. 181.
[38] *Chicago Daily Times,* Sept. 19, 1937.
[39] *Ibid.*
[40] *Dies Hearings,* IX, p. 5,498.
[41] *Ibid.,* VIII, p. 5,183.
[42] *Ibid.,* p. 5,187.
[43] *Ibid.,* p. 5,184.
[44] *Ibid.,* p. 5,187.
[45] *McCormack Hearings,* DC-4, p. 226.
[46] *Chicago Daily Times,* Sept. 9, 1937.
[47] *Dies Hearings,* I, p. 21.
[48] *McCormack Hearings,* NY-7, p. 55.
[49] *Kampfendes Deutschtum* (1937 ed.).
[50] *Dies Hearings,* X, p. 6,071.
[51] *Ibid.,* pp. 6,094-6,095.
[52] *Ibid.,* VI, p. 3,883.
[53] *Investigation of Nazi and Other Propaganda,* p. 7; see footnote 1.
[54] *McCormack Hearings,* NY-12, p. 7.
[55] *Chicago Daily Times,* Sept. 23, 1937.
[56] *Chicago Daily Times,* Sept. 21, 1937.
[57] *McCormack Hearings,* DC-6, p. 318.
[58] *Ibid.,* p. 6.
[59] *Ibid.,* NY-7, p. 127.
[60] *Dies Hearings,* II, p. 1,083.
[61] *Brooklyn Daily Eagle,* Apr. 8, 1938.
[62] *Dies Hearings,* IX, p. 5,497.
[63] *Dies Hearings,* VI, p. 3,773.
[64] There is no evidence to prove that the Bund definitely gets money from the *Deutsch Konsum Verband,* or DKV as it is commonly called. The DKV, the counter-boycott group formed against the Jewish boycott of German goods, charges dues of fifty cents a month to all German-American merchants who want to be listed in its directory. Although these two groups cooperate, the DKV is not a part of the Bund or subordinate to it.

Notes for Chapter IV

[1] *Who is Pelley?,* a Silver Shirt leaflet.
[2] Pelley, William Dudley, *American Magazine,* "Seven Minutes in Eternity", Mar. 1929. At the time Pelley wrote this article, he was not the head of a political organization and, consequently, could afford to describe himself more frankly than he has been willing to do since.
[3] *Who's Who in America,* 1924-25.
[4] Pelley chose Asheville because he learned clairvoyantly of the coming of a great cataclysm in which only this city would be saved.
[5] *McCormack Hearings,* Washington, D. C., June 7, 1934, p. 247. For the financing of these business ventures, see *Dies Hearings,* VI, pp. 4,186-4,191.
[6] *Investigation of Nazi and Other Propaganda,* House Report 153, p. 11, 74th Cong., 1st sess.
[7] *The Salt Lake City Telegram* of Nov. 3, 1933, reported that the same Mrs. Marie Ogden, describing herself as the reincarnation of the Virgin Mary, had led a sect called the Truth Seekers to a colony established at Dry Valley, Utah. The July 5, 1936, issue of the same paper said that Mrs. Ogden had kept the corpse of a sectarian in her house over a year while trying to revive it.
[8] *McCormack Executive Hearings,* Asheville, May 2, 1934, pp. 64-65.

[9] A reference to the Great Pyramid of Gizeh. Pelley and his spiritualist followers, in common with many other sects, believe that if the hieroglyphics that cover the corridors of the pyramid are correctly interpreted they will foretell all events in world history down to Judgment Day.

[10] *McCormack Executive Hearings*, Asheville, May 2, 1934, pp. 65, 68.

[11] *Dies Hearings*, VI, p. 4,217.

[12] See Chapter XI.

[13] *Dies Hearings*, VI, p. 4,209.

[14] *McCormack Hearings*, Washington, D. C., June 7, 1934, pp. 281-283.

[15] *The Punxsutawney Spirit*, Oct. 11, 1933.

[16] *Pelley's Weekly*, Mar. 18, 1936.

[17] *Liberation*, Jan. 28, 1938.

[18] *Pelley's Weekly*, Feb. 12, 1936.

[19] *McCormack Hearings*, Washington, D. C., June 7, 1934, p. 272.

[20] *Ibid.*, p. 255.

[21] See chapters VI and VII.

[22] See footnote 7.

[23] *Dies Hearings*, VI, p. 4225.

Notes for Chapter V

[1] Swing, Raymond Gram, *Forerunners of American Fascism*, New York, Julian Messner, 1935, pp. 37-38.

[2] *Ibid.*, p. 42.

[3] Spivak, John L., *Shrine of the Silver Dollar*, New York, Modern Age Books, 1940, p. 15.

[4] *Ibid.*, p. 15*ff.*, gives a careful examination of the ownership of this enterprise.

[5] For another example of a Coughlin misquotation, see *Father Coughlin: His "Facts" and Arguments*, New York, (General Jewish Council and its Affiliates), 1939, see pp. 8-10.

[6] Spivak, *op. cit.*, p. 153.

[7] On this phase of the Front. *cf* Kernan, Rev. William C., *The Ghost of Royal Oak*, Free Speech Forum, 1940, pp. 128-132.

[8] *Christian Social Action*, "Christian American Jew-Baiting," Sept., 1939.

[9] *Ibid.*

[10] *Ibid.*

[11] Smith, Alson J., in the *Christian Century*, "The Christian Terror," Aug. 23, 1939.

[12] A month after the Federal Bureau of Investigation arrested the 17 plotters, all but 27 officers had left the Front.

[13] Bromley, Dorothy Dunbar, *Portrait of a Christian Fronter*, (a leaflet), Toledo Committee of the Unitarian Fellowship for Social Justice.

[14] Pope Pius XI stated the church's stand again anti-semitism, on Sept. 25, 1928, and again on Dec. 5, 1938. The Pope's full statements are reproduced in *Father Coughlin: His "Facts" and Arguments*, New York, General Jewish Council (and its affiliates), 1939, pp. 52-53. Late Cardinal Mundelein made this statement at the start of Coughlin's anti-semitic campaign. These facts must be borne in mind because Coughlin invariably tries to distort any criticism of his activities as an attack on the Catholic Church.

[15] *Spivak, op. cit.*, pp. 160-163.

[16] For a more extended discussion, see Spivak, *op. cit.*, Chapter VIII, "The Mystery of the Deficits."

Notes for Chapter VI

[1] Winrod, Gerald B., *Redeeming the Years the Locust Hath Gathered*, Wichita. (Kans.) Defender Publishers, 1932, p. 31.

[2] Wichita *Independent*, Mar. 4, 1938.

[3] See chapter entitled "Propaganda."

[4] Noted earlier in connection with the Silver Shirt membership.

CHAPTER FOOTNOTES

Notes for Chapter VII

[1] Data from Edmondson's bulletin of March 1, 1935.
[2] See Chapter VIII.

Notes for Chapter VIII

[1] Committee on Education and Labor, U. S. Senate, *Violations of Free Speech and Assembly and Interference with Rights of Labor* (La Follette Committee Report), I, p. 322.
[2] According to William Tracy, Secretary-Treasurer of the United Brick and Clay Workers of America.
[3] Hapgood, Norman, *Professional Patriots,* New York, Boni and Liveright, 1927, p. 164.
[4] United Brick and Clay Workers of America.
[5] According to William Tracy, Secretary-Treasurer of the United Brick and Clay Workers.
[6] William Tracy thinks it possible that Jung gave several locals their initial impetus.
[7] Hapgood, *op. cit.,* p. 163.
[8] *Ibid.*
[9] *National Republic,* May, 1930, p. 46.
[10] Memorandum of the Chicago Better Business Bureau, June 12, 1931.
[11] *McCormack Executive Hearings,* Chicago, pp. 140-145.
[12] *McCormack Executive Hearings,* Chicago, pp. 144-145.
[13] *Ibid.,* pp. 140-141.
[14] Fredric C. Walcott, U. S. Senator from Connecticut, 1929-1935.
[15] Probably refers to Chase S. Osborn, the former Republican governor. In the July 1934 *Defender* an article headed "Michigan Governor Explains Roosevelt's Jewish Ancestry" quotes Mr. Osborn as the authority on this matter of genealogy.
[16] *McCormack Executive Hearings,* Chicago, p. 135.
[17] *Ibid.,* p. 135.
[18] *Ibid.,* pp. 135-136.

Notes for Chapter IX

[1] *Hearings of the Massachusetts Legislative Investigating Committee on Un-American Activities* (unpublished), Oct. 25, 1937.
[2] *Ibid.*
[3] *Ibid.*
[4] *Dies Hearings,* III, p. 2,376.
[5] *Hearings of the Massachusetts Legislative Investigation Committee on Un-American Activities* (unpublished), Oct. 25, 1937.
[6] Many of the individuals mentioned in Table 6 are affiliated with groups of the types listed.
[7] See Chapter IV.

Notes for Chapter X

[1] *Chicago American,* June 29, 1934.
[2] *Who's Who in Chicago,* 1931 ed.
[3] Interview with the author.
[3a] Letter dated Feb. 1, 1934.
[4] Major John L. Griffith; interview with the author.
[5] Interview with the author.
[6] *National Defense,* vol. 2, no. 7, p. 3.
[7] *McCormack Executive Hearings,* Chicago, p. 22.
[8] *National Defense,* vol. 7, No. 2, p. 3.
[9] *Ibid.*
[10] According to Major John L. Griffith; interview with the author.

[11] According to Mr. Dilling; interview with the author.
[12] *Ibid.*
[13] Interview with the author.
[14] See Chapter IX.

Notes for Chapter XI

[1] One of the publications to which True contributed occasionally was *Printers Ink.*
[2] No evidence shows that this organization exists outside Mr. True's imagination.
[3] For similar interviews with True see Niles, Porter, *New Masses,* "Pogrom in September," Aug. 18, 1936; Hale, Michael, *New Masses,* "Fifteen Leading Jews Marked for Death," Aug. 25, 1936.
[4] See Chapter VII.
[5] William Dudley Pelley, chief of the Silver Shirts, believes that True's members are in the upper-income groups, for in the Feb. 7, 1938 issue of *Liberation* he uses the expression, "It starts the James Trues of the country writing for the People-Who-Count."
[6] See Chapter VII.
[7] Spivak, *loc. cit.*
[8] *Ibid.*

Notes for Chapter XII

[1] *Dies Hearings,* VI, pp. 3,815-3,519.
[2] *Chicago Times,* Sept. 20, 1937.
[3] *Ibid.,* Sept. 12, 1937.
[4] *Liberation,* May 14, 1938.
[5] *Pelley's Weekly,* June 1, 1936.
[6] *Hearings of the Massachusetts Legislative Investigating Committee on Un-American Activities* (unpublished), Oct. 25, 1937.
[7] *McCormack Hearings,* D. C., p. 105.
[8] Interview with the Reverend L. M. Birkhead, National Director of the Friends of Democracy.
[9] See Chapter VII.
[10] Interview with the Rev. L. M. Birkhead.
[11] *Defender,* Mar. 1937.
[12] June 28, 1937.
[13] *Liberation,* Feb. 14, 1938.
[14] *Industrial Control Report,* Jan. 15, 1938.
[15] See Chapter VII.

Notes for Chapter XIV

[1] For accurate accounts of the history of this forgery, see Segel, Benjamin Wolf, *The Protocols of the Elders of Zion, the Greatest Lie in History,* New York, Bloch, 1934; Valentin, Hugo, *Anti-Semitism,* pp. 165-183; Levinger, Lee J., *Anti-Semitism, Yesterday and Tomorrow,* New York, Macmillan Co. 1936, pp. 187-203; Bernstein, H., *The Truth About "The Protocols of Zion",* Covici Friede, 1935. For the background of anti-semitism in the United States, see Chapter II.
[2] Hadley, Edward Marshall, *T.N.T.,* Chicago, Tower Press, 1929, pp. 66.
[3] *Defender,* April 1934.
[4] Newsletter of Edmondson Economic Service, Oct. 5, 1935.
[5] Hadley, *op. cit.,* p. 39.
[6] Sincere, Earnest, *The Plan in Action,* Elgin, Brandt Publishing Co., 1933, p. 20.
[7] *Liberation,* June 14, 1938.
[8] Hadley, Edward Marshall, *The Rape of the Republic,* p. 17.
[9] *Liberation,* June 28, 1938.
[10] *Industrial Control Report,* Feb. 5, 1938.
[11] *Revealer,* Nov. 15, 1934.
[12] *Liberation,* May 15, 1938.
[13] *Social Justice,* Feb. 13, 1939.

CHAPTER FOOTNOTES

[14] *Liberation*, Nov. 11, 1937.
[15] *Ibid.*, Mar. 21, 1938.
[16] *Deutscher Weckruf und Beobachter*, Feb. 18, 1937.
[17] Newsletter of Edmondson Economic Service, Oct. 1, 1937.
[18] *Pelley's Weekly*, Nov. 18, 1936.
[19] *Social Justice*, Aug. 1, 1938.
[20] Newsletter of the Edmondson Economic Service, Jan. 13, 1938.
[21] *Pelley's Weekly*, Nov. 18, 1936.
[22] *New Liberation*, Jan. 1937.
[23] *Liberation*, June 21, 1938.
[24] *Ibid.*, Nov. 21, 1937.
[25] *Ibid.*, Nov. 7, 1937.
[26] *Ibid.*, Dec. 30, 1933.
[27] *Pelley's Weekly*, Nov. 18, 1936.
[28] *Liberation*, Mar. 1937.
[29] *Ibid.*, May 21, 1938.
[30] *Ibid.*, June 14, 1938.
[31] *Ibid.*, June 21, 1938.
[32] *Ibid.*, Mar. 21, 1938.
[33] *Ibid.*
[34] *Ibid.*, June 21, 1938.
[35] *Industrial Control Report*, Oct. 9, 1937.
[36] Leaflet, May 10, 1938.
[37] See Chapter V.
[38] Innisfail Park, New York City, Aug. 23, 1939.
[39] Smith, Alson J., *Christian Century*, "The Christian Terror," Aug. 23, 1939.
[40] Quoted in Spivak, John L. *The Shrine of the Silver Dollar*, p. 137.
[41] Smith, *loc. cit.*
[42] *Chicago Daily Times*, Sept. 9, 1937.
[43] *Ibid.*
[44] *Ibid.* For other occasions on which the Bund has expressed its belief in violence, see *Dies Hearings*, II, pp. 1112, 1205-1206.
[45] For an exposition of this type of propaganda analysis, see Lasswell, H. D., *Politics, Who Gets What, When, How*, New York, Whittlesey House, 1936, pp. 39-41.
[46] *Liberation*, Jan. 28, 1938.
[47] Newsletter of Edmondson Economic Service, Apr. 22, 1936.
[48] *Industrial Control Report*, Nov. 14, 1936.
[49] *Liberation*, May 21, 1938.
[50] *Pelley's Weekly*, Mar. 18, 1936.
[51] *Ibid.*
[52] *Liberation*, Jan. 28, 1938.
[53] *Industrial Control Report*, Feb. 5, 1938.
[54] *Liberation*, Feb. 14, 1938.
[55] For a more detailed statement of these hypotheses and an evaluation of them in terms of the propaganda of the American Communist Party in the years 1930-1935, see Lasswell, H. D., and Blumenstock, Dorothy, *World Revolutionary Propaganda; a Chicago Study*, New York, Alfred A. Knopf, 1939.

Notes for Chapter XV

[1] All ages are as of 1941.
[2] See Chapter VIII.
[3] See Chapter IV.
[4] See Chapter VIII.
[5] See Chapter IX.
[6] See Chapter XI.
[7] See Chapter VI.
[8] See Chapter XIII.